Austin, San Antonio &
the Texas Hill Country

Dining along the Riverwalk in San Antonio

A COMPLETE GUIDE

FIRST EDITION

AUSTIN, SAN ANTONIO & THE TEXAS HILL COUNTRY

Amy K.
Brown

The Countryman Press
Woodstock, Vermont

First Edition

ISBN 978-1-58157-040-3

Cover and interior photos by the author
Book design Bodenweber Design
Page composition by Melinda Belter
Maps by Mapping Specialists, Ltd., Madison, WI, © The Countryman Press

Published by The Countryman Press, P.O. Box 748, Woodstock, Vermont 05091

Distributed by W. W. Norton & Company, Inc., 500 Fifth Ave., New York, NY 10110

Printed in the United States of America

10 9 8 7 6 5 4 3 2 1

GREAT DESTINATIONS TRAVEL GUIDEBOOK SERIES

Recommended by *National Geographic Traveler* and *Travel + Leisure* magazines.

[A] CRISP AND CRITICAL APPROACH, FOR TRAVELERS WHO WANT TO LIVE LIKE LOCALS.
— *USA Today*

Great Destinations™ guidebooks are known for their comprehensive, critical coverage of regions of extraordinary cultural interest and natural beauty. The authors in this series are professional travel writers who have lived for many years in the regions they describe. Each title in this series is continuously updated with each printing to ensure accurate and timely information. All the books contain more than one hundred photographs and maps.

Current titles available:

THE ADIRONDACK BOOK

AUSTIN, SAN ANTONIO & THE TEXAS HILL COUNTRY

THE BERKSHIRE BOOK

BIG SUR, MONTEREY BAY & GOLD COAST WINE COUNTRY

THE CHARLESTON, SAVANNAH & COASTAL ISLANDS BOOK

THE CHESAPEAKE BAY BOOK

THE COAST OF MAINE BOOK

COLORADO'S CLASSIC MOUNTAIN TOWNS: GREAT DESTINATIONS

THE FINGER LAKES BOOK

THE HAMPTONS BOOK

THE HUDSON VALLEY BOOK

THE NANTUCKET BOOK

THE NAPA & SONOMA BOOK

PALM BEACH, MIAMI & THE FLORIDA KEYS

PLAYA DEL CARMEN, TULUM & THE RIVIERA MAYA: GREAT DESTINATIONS MEXICO

THE SANTA FE & TAOS BOOK

THE SARASOTA, SANIBEL ISLAND & NAPLES BOOK

THE SEATTLE & VANCOUVER BOOK: INCLUDES THE OLYMPIC PENINSULA, VICTORIA & MORE

THE SHENANDOAH VALLEY BOOK

TOURING EAST COAST WINE COUNTRY

If you are traveling to, moving to, residing in, or just interested in any (or all!) of these enchanting regions, a Great Destinations guidebook is a superior companion. Honest and painstakingly critical, full of information only a local can provide, Great Destinations guidebooks give you all the practical knowledge you need to enjoy the best of each region. Why not own them all?

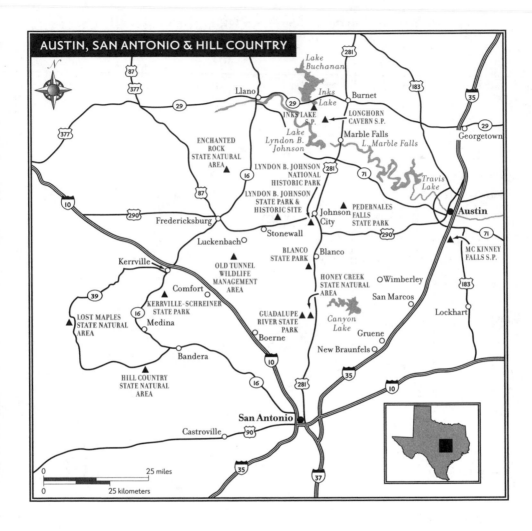

AUSTIN, SAN ANTONIO & HILL COUNTRY

N

87
377
377
10
290
Fredericksburg
Kerrville
39
16
Comfort
KERRVILLE-SCHREINER
STATE PARK
Medina
LOST MAPLES
STATE NATURAL
AREA
Bandera
HILL COUNTRY
STATE NATURAL
AREA
Castroville
90

29
Llano
29
16
87
ENCHANTED
ROCK
STATE NATURAL
AREA
LYNDON B. JOHNSON
NATIONAL
HISTORIC PARK
LYNDON B. JOHNSON
STATE PARK &
HISTORIC SITE
Stonewall
Luckenbach
OLD TUNNEL
WILDLIFE
MANAGEMENT
AREA
GUADALUPE
RIVER STATE
PARK
Boerne
16
10
16
281
San Antonio
35
37

Lake
Buchanan
281
Inks
Lake
INKS LAKE
S.P.
Lake
Lyndon B.
Johnson
281
Burnet
LONGHORN
CAVERN S.P.
Marble Falls
L. Marble Falls
71
Johnson
City
PEDERNALES
FALLS
STATE PARK
BLANCO
STATE PARK
Blanco
HONEY CREEK
STATE NATURAL
AREA
Canyon
Lake
New Braunfels
Wimberley
San Marcos
Gruene

183
35
Georgetown
29
Travis
Lake
Austin
71
MC KINNEY
FALLS S.P.
183
Lockhart

0   25 miles
0   25 kilometers

Contents

ACKNOWLEDGMENTS AND INTRODUCTION

Everything really is bigger in Texas.

The people in Central Texas have huge hearts, plenty of patience, and a friendliness that seems super-sized.

As I traveled the region researching this book, Texans graciously answered numerous questions, refilled countless cups of coffee, and served up some of the biggest slices of pie I've ever seen. They shared generously the names of their favorites—from burgers to honky-tonks, enchiladas to swimming holes.

While the list was long, a guidebook can only be so big. This book is big enough to include all the basics and many of the extras, but as you make your way between the featured establishments, feel free to stray from the path I've laid out. Change your plans, pull into a farm stand, stop at a bakery, have a beer, and by all means ask a Texan for directions, suggestions, and recommendations. Let 'em lay some hospitality on you.

Extra-large thanks to all the good folks living in Austin, San Antonio, the surrounding communities, and the towns of the Hill Country. I gratefully appreciate your courtesy, knowledge, and kindness. Since most of you did not know I was writing a guidebook, the sincerity of your gestures was truly heartwarming.

Enormous thanks to the folks at Countryman—Kim Grant, Kermit Hummel, and Jennifer Thompson—for the opportunity to write about a region I love.

Deepest gratitude to my beautiful children, who make life such a wonderful journey, and to my husband, Ed, with whom I will always choose to travel.

Thank you.
Amy K. Brown
www.amykbrown.com

The Way This Book Works

This book is divided into two introductory chapters followed by four main chapters—on Austin, San Antonio, the Hill Country, and Nearby and In Between—each with suggestions of lodging, dining, and things to do and see, arranged by neighborhood. The first, introductory chapter describes the region's shared landscape and common history, and it is followed by a short chapter on regional transportation. The unique histories of Austin and San Antonio and the towns of the Hill Country and Nearby and In Between are addressed in the introductions to their respective chapters. Considering the scale of Texas, the cities, towns, and parks covered in this book are relatively close to one another, so as you read bear in mind that many destinations make easy stopovers or day trips.

All the information in this book was verified at the time of its writing. However, things change, and it is always prudent to call ahead. Web site addresses have been provided for the establishments that have them, and I would strongly encourage their use, as you will find details, menus, updates, photos, and sometimes discounts online.

Instead of listing specific prices for the establishments featured in the Food and Lodging sections, I have indicated a range. For lodging, the range indicates the cost of a double-occupancy room, and prices may rise and fall with the seasons. For Dining, the price range indicates the cost of an entrée; it does not include the cost of appetizers, desserts, drinks, tax, or tip.

Lodging Price Code

Inexpensive	Up to $100
Moderate	$100 to $150
Expensive	$150 to $250
Very Expensive	Over $250

Dining Price Code

Inexpensive	Up to $12
Moderate	$12 to $25
Expensive	$25 to $40
Very Expensive	$40 or more

Please assume that all establishments accept cash or credit cards, unless otherwise noted. Most of the establishments in this book will not accept personal checks.

AUSTIN, SAN ANTONIO, AND THE HILL COUNTRY

Deep in the Heart of Texas

The subject of legends and lore, Texas has a reputation that has always preceded it. And as an icon of strength and swagger, Texas plays an essential part in the story of America. Filled with opportunistic cattle rustlers and hunky cowboys thundering off into the endless crimson sunset, the Texas of myth and movies is larger than life, hotter than hell, and rougher than a ride at the rodeo.

Deep in the heart of Central Texas is a region that will challenge all your assumptions with its distinct mix of friendly casualness, edgy creativity, discerning taste, and a strong inclination toward celebration. Each city and town offers its own incomparable mix of culture, food, music, and heritage, and plenty of festivals—from cultural to culinary, kites to *kolaches*—which give visitors numerous opportunities to experience life in Central Texas as an honorary Texan-for-a-day.

With roots stretching back to the 17th century, San Antonio (see chapter 4) is now home to over a million people. Its pedestrian-friendly downtown, the celebrated Alamo, historic Mission Trail, and bustling Riverwalk cluster together to give the city an intimate feeling that belies its size. A strong sense of cultural history pervades all, with San Antonio's Native American origins, Spanish influences, and Mexican overtones zealously expressed in art, food, architecture, and festivals.

While San Antonio embodies something quintessentially Texan, people are fond of observing that Austin (see chapter 3) inhabits a category all its own. Austinites are an educated, energetic, and decidedly unconventional bunch, and while they tend to be less conservative than the rest of the state, their live-and-let-live attitude very much mirrors the overall spirit of Texas. Nightlife in Austin abounds, thanks to its internationally recognized live music scene, though acres of parks, bike trails, and gardens make recreational activities almost as popular.

The Hill Country (see chapter 5), easily accessible from either Austin or San Antonio, is the place to be if you really want to slow down and smell the bluebonnets. To drive the lazy, winding, rural roads past wineries and lavender fields, around limestone outcroppings, and through shady state parks is to experience carefree wanderlust at its most enjoyable. The region's rustic towns are brimming with gourmet restaurants, antiques and knick-knack shops, and bed and breakfasts and make pleasant stopovers or destinations unto

Hill Country byway

themselves. Nearby and In Between (see chapter 6), several towns along I-35 make wonderful day trips for the thrill of area amusement parks or tubing along cool spring-fed Texas rivers.

The folks in Central Texas are passionate about living here, and their infectious enthusiasm begins with the land that they love, a land rich in both resources and beauty that has been fought over for centuries.

NATURAL WONDERS

Though now divided into two major cities, many towns, and numerous communities, Central Texas shares a common natural history that has been ages in the making.

Based on fossils of fish and aquatic plants, and other clues dating from the Cretaceous period (65–144 million years ago), we know that the Central Texas region was once submerged under a shallow lake. At some point, possibly 10–20 million years ago, movement along the Balcones Fault uplifted a massive hunk of limestone now known as the Edwards Plateau. The southeastern edge of this uplift was exposed to the elements, and its newer, softer rock eroded to form the dramatic cliffs and rocky outcroppings characterizing the present-day Balcones Escarpment, the ridge separating the undulating Hill Country to the west from the level Texas Coastal Plain to the southeast.

The movement in the earth's crust also created the Edwards Aquifer. A karst aquifer, the Edwards was formed over time as limestone and bedrock dissolved, creating holes

through which water enters from the surface and an underground honeycomb network of pockets and caverns through which it percolates. The sinkholes, disappearing streams, and cave entrances of the Hill Country are all telltale signs of karst regions. When it rains, water rushes over the Cretaceous limestone streambeds of this "contributing zone" and into the aquifer, topping off its massive holdings. As the Edwards is also an artesian aquifer, the water within is held under hydrostatic pressure, producing the region's many springs, such as Barton Springs in Austin, Comal Springs in New Braunfels, and Aquarena Springs in San Marcos. While the aquifer contains enough water for use well into the future, if its levels drop, so too does the flow of its springs, threatening the vegetation and many endangered species that rely upon them. Central Texans are aware of their own complete dependency on the Edwards Aquifer, a circumstance made increasingly complicated by rapid growth and growing demands for water.

For the nature enthusiast, the biodiversity of flora and fauna living in or migrating through Austin, San Antonio, and the Hill Country can be fascinating. For instance, millions upon millions of Mexican free-tailed bats roost in the nooks, crannies, and caves of Central Texas; the region is home to one of the largest maternity roosts for bats in the world. The bats give birth in area caves, take turns feeding and minding their young, and scour the countryside for insects, devouring tens of thousands of pounds' worth each night between May and October. While their presence has not always been met with much enthusiasm or tolerance, in time and with education folks around here grew to enjoy them, and public sentiment has morphed from fear to appreciation. With half a million bats, the Congress Avenue Bridge in Austin is home to the largest urban bat population in the world, and watching them take flight each night is a popular entertainment.

Sharing the great Texas sky with the bats is the state's huge variety of birds. An astonishing three-fourths of all American birds are represented throughout the diverse avian habitats of Texas. Some birds are residents and others migratory, passing through Central Texas on the 300-mile-wide "Central Flyway," one of the great routes for migration between Canada and Central and South America. Of the thousands of birds to make the trip, the golden-cheeked warbler is the only one to nest exclusively in Texas and, due to loss of habitat, is the most critically endangered of all warblers.

Also traveling the Central Flyway is the monarch butterfly, Texas's state insect. Monarchs are unusual among butterflies in that they migrate instead of hibernate; those that make the trip through Texas tend to originate in the upper Midwest, funneling through the Central Flyway on their way to Mexico. During this migration, in October, Central Texas enjoys the spectacle of millions of orange and black monarchs gliding along on favorable winds or resting and refueling at area gardens.

Central Texas has a wealth of parks and trails, making the region a natural spot for ecotourism. One of the best ways to commune with nature is to visit a state park, and there are many to choose from. From the bald pink dome of Enchanted Rock to the limestone canyons of Lost Maples, the state parks showcase the diversity of the regional landscape and the variety of wildlife it supports. Gray fox, armadillo, coyote, opossum, raccoon, bobcat, rock squirrel, roadrunner, white-tailed deer, and javelina are all common, and the patient observer can sometimes catch a glimpse of rarer species, such the Cagle's map turtle, the San Marcos salamander, or the Guadalupe bass.

THE PEOPLES OF TEXAS

The unique terrain of Central Texas, with its clear springs, sheltering caves, and abundant wildlife, has made the region naturally attractive to humans for well over 11,000 years. Looking to the relatively recent past, Tonkawa and Lipan Apache Indians are thought to have lived here from the 14th century, with the Comanche and Kiowa arriving in the 18th century. While many of the other peoples living concurrently in neighboring regions had already begun to live in villages, the groups living in this region were fairly nomadic, following food sources throughout the seasons and varying weather conditions. Although there is still much to learn, the archaeological record of the region is extraordinary, certainly one of the longest continuous records of hunters and gatherers in North America. Prior to the arrival of Europeans, approximately 45,000 Native Americans lived in the region, organized in groups, each with its own language, identity, and customs. However, the elements that attracted the first peoples would, of course, attract others, and people kept coming.

Tejanos

From the 1600s through the 1800s, pioneers from Mexico journeyed north and began settling into the Texas frontier, creating towns, building roads and ranches, and governing themselves. Throughout the 1700s they put down roots, establishing the settlements that would become El Paso, Galveston, Laredo, San Antonio, Victoria, and the large ranches of Central and South Texas. Those industrious pioneer ranchers, in particular, were so successful that they were able to contribute 2,000 head of longhorn cattle to the Revolutionary War effort, driving a herd from Texas to New Orleans in 1776.

As the land under them shifted from Spanish, French, Mexican, Texan, then American governance (see sidebar, "Six Flags over Texas"), these people of Mexican, Spanish, or indigenous descent continued to live independently. Generations passed, citizenship changed, and cultural influences came and went; these early settlers created their own unique culture, calling themselves *Tejanos* as early as the 1830s. Distinguished Tejanos Gregorio Esparza and Toribio Losoya both died in 1836 defending the Alamo, the mission that had been their birthplace, and José Antonio Navarro and José Francisco Ruiz were the only native Texans to sign the Texas Declaration of Independence that same year.

Spanish

Though the Spanish explorer Alonso Álvarez de Pineda mapped the Texas coastline in 1519, the first Europeans to really get their boots dirty with Texas soil were Álvar Núñez Cabeza de Vaca and several companions, who found themselves shipwrecked on the Gulf Coast in 1528. Once ashore, Cabeza de Vaca and his men spent years living with Native Americans before heading to Mexico City and, eventually, back to Spain. The journey of these men, while extraordinary, might have been entirely forgotten had Cabeza de Vaca not prepared a report of his adventures and delivered it to the Spanish court in the late 1530s, thus providing the first written record of the land and peoples of Texas.

After colonizing Mexico the Spanish made inroads north, bringing with them the horse, which the Apache quickly mastered and rode to regional domination. The Comanche followed suit, and together the mounted Native Americans proved such a threat that the Spanish were hard-pressed to set foot in the region for another two hundred years. In the 1700s Franciscans passed through on their way to East Texas to convert Native Americans into Roman Catholics and Spanish citizens. There the threat of the French and French-allied Native Americans near the Louisiana border forced them to backtrack to Central Texas, where they established the mission San Antonio de Valero, later known as the Alamo.

Native Americans

The arrival of Europeans was clearly the pivotal historic moment for Native Americans in Texas, as elsewhere. When the Franciscans arrived in the 1700s proposing mission life, the reaction of the Native Americans varied immensely. Some wanted nothing to do with the newcomers, while some smaller groups saw the missions as a refuge from harassment and hostilities at the hands of larger groups. In the 1800s settlers came to Texas by the wagon-full, bringing with them the notion of land claiming. Native Americans asked for, and were promised, ownership of the land they considered theirs, yet years of fighting, alliances, treaties, surprise attacks, and broken promises failed to yield documentation. While land ownership remained elusive, tensions boiled.

President Sam Houston of the Republic of Texas brokered treaties with the Tonkawas, the Lipan Apaches, the Comanches, Kichais, Tawakonis, Wacos, and Taovayas throughout 1837 and 1838, creating a tenuous peace. In the 1850s, after Texas joined the United States of America, these many treaties and agreements were broken, and many Native Americans were forced to leave Texas or relocate to reservations. The disastrous Red River War in 1874 was the final straw, and in June 1875 the mighty Comanche surrendered at Fort Sill. In short, the 1800s were catastrophic for Native Americans in Texas, leaving their populations decimated by disease, violence, starvation, or genocide. These days, their descendants host the Austin Powwow and American Indian Heritage Festival, the largest annual Native American gathering in Texas, a huge celebration of Native American heritage and a commemoration of their shared history.

Texas History Online

The history of Texas is fascinating in its depth and breadth. A cultural crossroads for centuries, the state is crisscrossed by the footprints of many. Some have just passed through, while others hung their hat for a while; they have come and gone on horseback, in wagons, on trains, and even in space shuttles. Texas's roots are deep and spread wide. In addition to the recommended readings at the end of this book (chapter 7, "Suggested References"), a wealth of information exists online for anyone wanting to learn more.

Center for American History (www.cah.utexas.edu): a useful site for locating sources of information regarding the various ethnic groups in Texas

Texas Almanac (www.texasalmanac.com): timelines, photos, and historical essays clearly presented

Texas Archeological Research Lab at the University of Texas at Austin (www.texasbeyondhistory.net): interactive Web site offering archaeological facts and information

The Texas State Historical Association (www.tsha.utexas.edu): exhaustive online handbook of Texas history

Texas Historical Commission (www.thc.state.tx.us): comprehensive site including information on historic courthouses, cemeteries, and archaeological sites

Texas Parks and Wildlife (www.tpwd.state.tx.us): information and photographs regarding the natural and cultural history of Texas

Anglos

Anglos, a convenient term for people of various European backgrounds arriving primarily from the United States, came to Texas following the promise of plentiful, inexpensive land at precisely the time that Spain was having difficulty convincing its own citizens that this isolated, unknown, and generally hostile environment was a good investment. As long as these incoming Anglos agreed to become both Catholic and Spanish, they were guaranteed large land grants, and many, sincere or not in their desire to convert, took the bait. When Mexico gained independence from Spain in 1821, it extended the deal, giving *empresarios*, those willing to help organize and oversee large groups of immigrants, land grants to begin

Lucky, TX

Always self-reliant, Texans have also been blessed with tremendous good luck. Rebounding from defeats suffered in the Civil War, Texans returned to find a population explosion of wild longhorn cattle. Rounded up by cowboys and taken to market along the Chisholm Trail in legendary cattle drives between 1867 and 1884, they provided a steady source of income for a state in dire need. Agriculture too flourished. Then, in 1901, one of the state's greatest natural resources was tapped at Spindletop, near Beaumont. After drilling for hours, amid much skepticism, exhausted workers struck "black gold," and a 150-foot geyser of the oil that would finance much of Texas's future came rocketing out of the ground.

Longhorn cattle

Six Flags over Texas

The flags of six countries have flown over Texas, making it one of the most sought-after and fought-over pieces of land in North America. Spain was the first, claiming Texas as its own from 1519 to 1685 as an extension of its holdings in Mexico, but it never created much of an actual presence in its far-flung acquisition.

In 1685 the French, emboldened by their success in Louisiana, planted their flag on Texas soil just across the eastern border, but mishaps and misfortune caused them to abandon their claim in 1690, at which time the Spanish regained control, which they kept until 1821.

During their rule the Spanish focused on expanding their empire and establishing a solid foothold in North America. In Texas, PRESIDIOS (forts) were built to protect and defend, and MISIONES (missions) were established in the hopes that self-sustaining communities of Spanish Catholic citizens might arise.

When Mexico won independence from Spain in 1821, Texas became the land of opportunity for both Hispanic pioneers from the south and Anglos from the north, all considering themselves citizens of Mexico. Out on the frontier people were used to being their own masters, however, and when General Santa Anna dismissed the Mexican Constitution, effectively declaring himself king, they revolted.

Battles at Gonzales and the Alamo in San Antonio tested the resolve of the revolutionaries, but the definitive battle at San Jacinto on April 21, 1836, secured their independence, giving rise to the fourth flag, that of the Republic of Texas.

The republic had its ups and downs during its almost 10 years of existence from 1836 to 1845, but its rugged individualism, gritty determination, and boundless energy, not to mention lots and lots of land, made it a very attractive addition to the United States, which it joined on December 29, 1845.

Sixteen years later, the Civil War tore the fledging nation apart, and Texas, though advised by Governor Sam Houston to remain neutral or reestablish a republic, sided with the Southerners, and the flag of the Confederacy flew over Texas from 1861 to 1865. While Texans valiantly fought, and won, the last battle of the Civil War, it was, unfortunately, after the Confederacy had already surrendered, and Texas suffered the rebels' fate. The flag of the United States of America has hung over Texas, the 28th state, since 1865.

Still, for many Texans, the flag that suits Texas best is its state flag, that of the tumultuous but short-lived former republic—the simple, straightforward, iconic Lone Star Flag, a proud reminder that though Texas may have been ruled by many, it has been controlled by none.

their settlements. During this time, immigrants came for many reasons. Some, Stephen F. Austin for one, made the trip with the promise of land ownership, while others came on the lam, taking advantage of the fact that the United States and Mexico had not yet established an extradition agreement. Slave-owners brought slaves, incensing the Mexican government, which not only had forbidden the African slave trade, but whose president, Vicente Ramón Guerrero, had emancipated all slaves on September 15, 1829, in commemoration of Mexican independence. Nevertheless, slaves were bought and sold in Texas until 1840, with Mexico turning a blind eye in the hopes that the cotton production so dependent on slave labor might prove profitable.

Being so far removed from the long reach of government, over time the new Texans started to organize, think, and act for themselves. In 1830, after much tension and fearing rebellion, the Mexican government passed the Law of April 6th, effectively making unorganized immigration from the United States to Texas illegal. Europeans, however, kept coming, and in 1831 Johann Friedrich Ernst, his wife, and their children were the first German family to arrive in Texas, settling near present-day Austin. Ernst was so impressed with his new surroundings that he wrote glowing letters back to Germany detailing his new home. Word spread, and by 1850 people of German descent totaled 5 percent of the state's total population, settling mostly in New Braunfels or fanning out into the Hill Country.

Texans soon began to chafe under Mexican leadership, growing restless for self-determination. In 1833 Antonio López de Santa Anna Pérez de Lebrón, the legendary Santa Anna, was installed as the president of Mexico. A lifelong military man, Santa Anna, though elected as a liberal, once in power established himself as a dictator. After crushing opponents in Mexico, he headed north to San Antonio to confront the growing rebellion in Texas, attacking the Alamo in the early morning hours of March 6, 1836. His victory there—a dramatic example of winning the battle but losing the war—only galvanized Texans' support for independence. Months later, Mexico was defeated at the battle of San Jacinto, and the Republic of Texas was born. When Texas passed from a republic to a state, tiny Austin was thrust into the limelight—a brand-new city for a brand-new Texas.

Transportation

To and from the Region

Interstate 35 links Austin and San Antonio. Sometimes called the NAFTA Highway, I-35 originates at the Mexican border and bisects the United States on its way to Duluth on Lake Superior. Consequently, the six-lane route is constantly jammed with 18-wheelers, livestock trailers, delivery trucks, and overloaded pickups headed north and south. When traffic is flowing, I-35 is perfectly functional, but when it's not, be prepared to sit and wait ... and wait and wait. In and around both Austin and San Antonio, it is always wise to budget some extra time into your itinerary for inevitable congestion. Conversely, traffic in the Hill Country flows at a leisurely pace; generally speaking, you can breeze undeterred over the windy, rural roads between towns.

Hauptstrasse, or Main Street, in Boerne

Inside Austin and San Antonio the paths of interstate highways, U.S. highways, and state highways often merge. In San Antonio, for example, I-10 is also US 87 or US 90 at various points; US 281 north of town suddenly becomes I-37 south of town. Some state highways have names in addition to their numbers. Loop 360 in Austin is known as Capital of Texas Highway. Loop 1, also in Austin, is commonly referred to by its nickname, "MoPac."

The Hill Country is traversed by plenty of small highways known as farm–to-market (FM) or ranch-to-market (RM) roads, which were built to be reliable trade routes between agricultural Texas and nearby cities or market centers. Constructed in the 1940s, these secondary roads are well maintained by the Texas Department of Transportation. County roads (CR), maintained by individual counties, are also secondary roads, though their size and conditions vary.

GETTING TO CENTRAL TEXAS

By Air

Air travelers coming to the region might consider flying into either Austin or San Antonio. Depending on your destination and time of travel, prices can vary widely; being flexible in your travel plans can sometimes yield big savings.

Austin-Bergstrom International Airport
512-530-2242
www.ci.austin.tx.us/austinairport
3600 Presidential Blvd., Austin, TX 78719

The airport is located in southeast Austin, just east of the intersection of TX 71 and US 183, approximately 8 miles from downtown.

TAXI
American Yellow Checker Cab (512-452-9999; www.yellowcabaustin.com) Price: approximately $25.

AIRPORT SHUTTLE
Super Shuttle (512-258-3826 or 1-800-258-3826; www.supershuttle.com) Price: $12.

BUS
Capital Metro Bus (512-474-1200; www.capmetro.org) The *Airport Flyer* travels between the airport and two centrally located downtown stops, Sixth St. & Brazos and 18th St. & Congress Ave. Price: 50 cents.

San Antonio International Airport
1-866-289-9673
www.sanantonio.gov/aviation
9800 Airport Blvd., San Antonio, TX 78216

The airport is located near the intersection of Loop 410 and US 281, approximately 8 miles from downtown San Antonio.

TAXI
San Antonio Taxis (210-444-2222) or **Yellow Checker Cab** (210-650-8600) Price: approximately $20–$25.

AIRPORT SHUTTLE
SATRANS (210-281-9900 or 1-800-868-7707; www.saairportshuttle.com) Price: One-way $14, round-trip $24.

BUS
VIA Metropolitan Transit (210-362-2020; www.viainfo.net) Price: $1.

While train or bus travel to the region and between its cities and towns is possible, it is not very efficient.

By Train

Amtrak (1-800-872-7245; www.amtrak.com)
Austin: 250 N. Lamar Blvd., Austin, TX 78703
San Marcos: 338 S. Guadalupe St., San Marcos, TX 78666
San Antonio: 224 Hoefgen St., San Antonio, TX 78205

By Bus

Greyhound (www.greyhound.com)
Austin: 512-458-4463; 916 E. Koenig Lane, Austin, TX 78751
San Antonio: 210-270-5824; 500 N. St. Mary's St., San Antonio, TX 78205

Got Wheels?

Most visitors to the region rent a car, and most major rental companies have kiosks in each airport. While it is possible to get around most of Austin or San Antonio using public transportation, a car is essential for touring the Hill Country. The percentage of uninsured motorists in Texas is high, and while lawmakers are attempting to curb the problem, a fender bender, regardless of fault, may end up costing you a pretty penny. Be sure to check your insurance policy before you drive.

Reservations are strongly recommended.

Advantage (1-800-777-5500; www.arac.com)
Alamo/National (1-800-462-5266; www.alamo.com)
Avis (1-800-331-1212; www.avis.com)
Budget (1-800-527-0700; www.budget.com)
Dollar (1-800-800-3665; www.dollar.com)
Enterprise (1-800-261-7331; www.enterprise.com)
Hertz (1-800-654-3131; www.hertz.com)
Thrifty (1-800-847-4389; www.thrifty.com)

Street musician on South Congress Avenue

Austin

Rising Star

The seat and center of Travis County, Austin is smaller than San Antonio and just a fraction of the size of Dallas or Houston but nevertheless the capital of Texas. The city is, and has always been, quick with opinions, purposeful in action, and unlikely to follow anyone else's lead. An intellectual powerhouse, Austin has a nationwide reputation for brains and creativity, encouraged and supported by the University of Texas, whose campus occupies a large swath of the city. Sunshine, hike-and-bike trails, parks, and rooftop bars satisfy the city's penchant for all things outdoors. At open-air concerts or just lounging under the shady oaks, Austin is a city that likes to hang out, having perfected the art of doing so. And here in the "Live Music Capital of the World," you can see performances every day and dozens of music festivals throughout the year.

EARLY DAYS

Situated at the eastern edge of the Edwards Plateau, where the land of prairies and lakes is thrust suddenly into the dips and curves of the Hill Country, Austin is blessed with natural resources and beauty. In 1839, the then thinly settled area anchored by the tiny village of Waterloo was chosen for the capital of the Republic of Texas and was promptly named after its most famous Anglo-American, Stephen F. Austin, who was revered long before being immortalized along with the other fallen heroes of the Alamo. Standing on the edge of the western frontier, in full view of Mexicans and Native Americans, both of whom had their eye on the property, Austin seemed unsafe, its future uncertain. Some, including Sam Houston, were skeptical of the choice. But the republic's president, Mirabeau B. Lamar, who had become smitten with the location on a buffalo hunt, gave the go-ahead for the purchase of 7,735 acres along the Colorado River. Surveyors, planners, and workers immediately set about building a city, with the hope of having it finished by the next scheduled meeting of the Texas Congress, just months away in November 1839. A grid of 14 blocks was laid out on a 640-acre plot starting at the river, bounded on two sides by Shoal and Waller Creeks; Congress Avenue bisected the grid on its way northward to the hill on which a temporary one-story wooden capitol was built. Austin was incorporated on December 27, 1939, Congress successfully convened as planned, and the city welcomed diplomats from England, France, and its neighbor to the north, the United States.

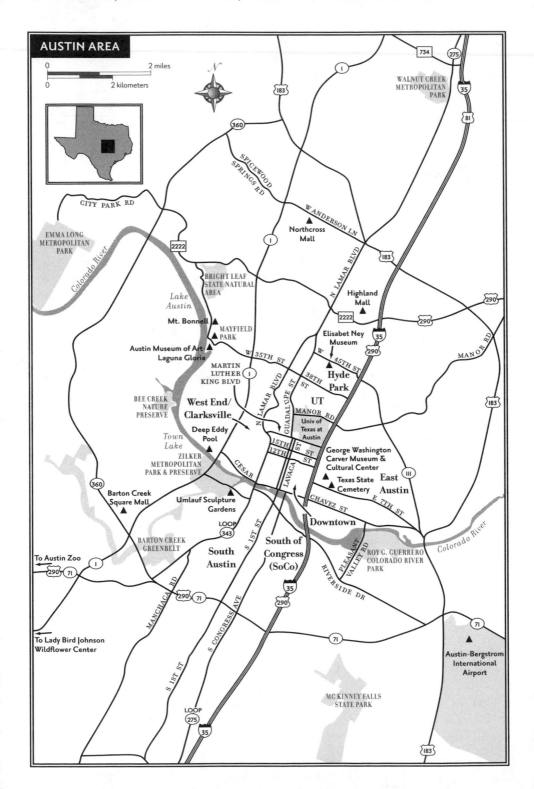

AUSTIN AREA

0   2 miles
0   2 kilometers

N

CITY PARK RD

EMMA LONG
METROPOLITAN
PARK

Colorado River

2222

*Lake
Austin*

BRIGHT LEAF
STATE NATURAL
AREA

Mt. Bonnell ▲

▲ MAYFIELD
PARK

Austin Museum of Art-
Laguna Gloria

MARTIN
LUTHER
KING BLVD

BEE CREEK
NATURE
PRESERVE

**West End/
Clarksville**

*Town
Lake*

Deep Eddy
Pool

ZILKER
METROPOLITAN
PARK & PRESERVE

360

Barton Creek
Square Mall

Umlauf Sculpture
Gardens

BARTON CREEK
GREENBELT

LOOP
343

To Austin Zoo ←

290 71

**South
Austin**

To Lady Bird Johnson
Wildflower Center ←

290 71

MANCHACA RD

S 1ST ST

S CONGRESS AVE

**South of
Congress
(SoCo)**

35

290

LOOP
275

35

SPICEWOOD
SPRINGS RD

360

183

1

W ANDERSON LN

▲ Northcross
Mall

183

N LAMAR BLVD

Highland
Mall ▲

2222

Elisabet Ney
Museum

W 35TH ST

W 45TH ST

38TH
ST

**Hyde
Park**

UT

MANOR
RD

Univ of
Texas at
Austin

15TH ST

12TH ST

LAVACA

CESAR

George Washington
Carver Museum &
Cultural Center

▲ Texas State
Cemetery

CHAVEZ ST

Downtown

**East
Austin**

E 7TH ST

111

RIVERSIDE DR

PLEASANT VALLEY RD

ROY G. GUERRERO
COLORADO RIVER
PARK

Colorado River

71

MC KINNEY FALLS
STATE PARK

71

▲ Austin-Bergstrom
International
Airport

734

275

35

81

1

183

290

290

183

N LAMAR BLVD

GUADALUPE ST

35

W 35TH ST

1

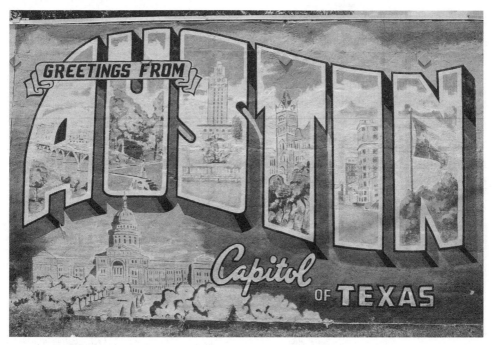

Mural in South Austin

Austin's status as capital didn't sit well with everyone. In 1842 Sam Houston, who had succeeded President Lamar, demanded that the national archives and state-related records be brought to Houston. Folks in Austin took the news personally, feeling that moving the papers would mean moving the fledgling capital, and staunchly refused. Houston acquiesced, allowing Austin to keep the documents, but moved the government all the same, first to Houston and later to Washington-on-the Brazos. Houston quickly grew to regret his hasty compromise; he wanted the papers, and he sent armed men to Austin to get them. In what would become known as the Archive War, the men were met by enraged citizens, and in the end the papers remained in Austin, while the government remained in Houston. It wasn't until the 1845 annexation of Texas by the United States that Austin was established, officially, as capital of Texas—with one caveat. The designation was temporary; a vote would be held in 20 years to let the people decide once and for all.

Taking its role as capital to heart, by 1853 Austin had completed a permanent capitol building and, by 1856, a Governor's Mansion. The city was growing, but it was still essentially an outpost on the edge of the frontier, with only unreliable roads for trading. Austin lobbied hard for railroads, but the Civil War halted all new construction as resources were diverted to the war effort. While the city was initially against secession, skyrocketing food shortages, inflation, and casualties shifted its sentiments. At end of the war in 1865, Union troops occupied a bedraggled Austin.

On December 25, 1871, Austin, still suffering the effects of the war and Reconstruction, was gratefully connected to the greater and newly unified country as the Houston and Texas Central Railway passed through the city. The city's economy took this shot in the arm, and

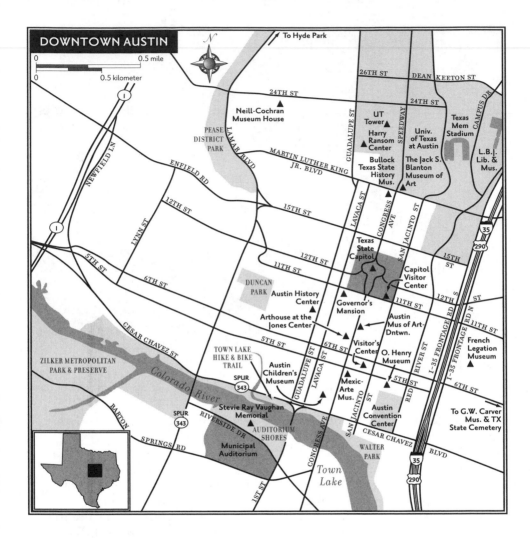

Austin almost immediately became a bustling hub of materials, products, and, most important, immigrants. By 1870, years after the Civil War and the Emancipation Proclamation, 36 percent of Austin's population was African American. These newcomers quickly went to work settling various Austin neighborhoods, opening churches and businesses, and sending their children to local schools. By 1875 there were 757 residents from Germany, 215 from Ireland, 138 from Sweden, and 297 from Mexico—the first from that nation—with each group contributing to the economy of the young and growing city. Public life was getting crowded and chaotic; gas street lamps were installed in 1874, a streetcar line was established in 1875, and a bridge spanned the Colorado River the following year.

In 1872 Austin triumphed at the polls and was declared, once and for all, the Texas capital. In 1881 Austin prevailed again in a statewide ballot, this time for the site of the University of Texas, which started educating students two years later. Also in 1881, the city organized a public school system, and the Tillotson Collegiate and Normal Institute began offering instruction to African American students. Four years later St. Edward's Academy was chartered as St. Edward's College. In 1888, the city finished construction of the huge granite capitol, still so prevalent in its skyline, anchoring Austin at the symbolic center of Texas.

In 1905, despite its statewide importance, Austin had only one paved street, deplorable sanitary conditions, and very few public services. All this changed with the 1928 city plan, the first plan drawn up since the town's beginnings in 1839, and the passage of a $4.25 million bond issue. The money was used to finance a library, a hospital, an airport, roads, and sewers and to further the city's primary goal of boosting its image as the go-to city for education and culture in Texas. A recreation department was put into place; soon after, the city had made huge strides in beautification, giving itself parks, pools, and recreation programs. These public improvements asserted the ideals that define Austin today, a city with progressive ideas and proactive planning.

THE 20TH CENTURY

The Great Depression of the 1930s did not spare Austin, but by all accounts it was the skills of Mayor Robert Thomas Miller and Congressman Lyndon Baines Johnson that kept the city afloat. The population exploded, increasing 66 percent in the 1930s, and with this growth came increasing demands on services. The University of Texas saw enrollment practically double and quickly began construction to expand the campus. The devastating flood of 1935 prompted plans to dam the Colorado River; the Tom Miller Dam, finished in 1940, gave the city Lake Austin, while the Mansfield Dam, completed the following year, created Lake Travis. Dams farther north created the Highland Lakes, used for recreation, water supply, and power. The dawn of World War II brought Del Valle Air Base, later called Bergstrom Air Force Base, and later still retrofitted to become the Austin-Bergstrom Airport.

The Frost Bank Building in downtown Austin

The 20th century brought radical social changes to Austin. Mirroring other cities throughout the country, Austin was mired in the politics and interpersonal dynamics of segregation. While African Americans had previously lived throughout the city, the city plan of 1928 recommended a "Negro district" be established in the city's East Side. By the 1940s this ghettoizing allowed the city to systematically restrict African Americans' access to schools, parks, transportation, and other municipal services, despite the fact that blacks had established numerous businesses, dozens of churches, and two colleges in the city and had participated in civic life since the city's inception. As the city grew, the African American population remained relatively stable in numbers but dropped dramatically in percentage.

At the same time, the number of Hispanic residents jumped from 1.5 percent of the population to 11 percent. Though laws permitted discrimination against African Americans, the discrimination experienced by Mexican Americans, while pervasive, was not as systematic or organized. Over the years, local African American leaders and their supporters worked tirelessly to desegregate schools and other institutions, and in 1956 the University of Texas admitted black students, the first large southern university to do so. The nationwide demonstrations and sit-ins of the 1960s brought about the Civil Rights Act of 1964, which provided some measure of legal protection from discrimination. Ironically, while two African Americans sat on Austin's city council in 1880, African Americans did not serve again until 1968, an advance soon repeated by Hispanic citizens.

Austin is still a young city. Coming of age in the mid-20th century, it has seen its growth hastened by wars, railroads, and social movements. In the 1950s Austin began positioning itself for a future in technology, as several research laboratories and think tanks sprang up and prospered, benefiting from their proximity to the university. By the 1970s rapid growth in the city was met by a politically active population who formed civic groups to preserve the city's history, neighborhoods, and environment and to protect the rights of its citizens. Austin remains the state's undisputed educational and cultural center, with enough parks, lakes, recreation, and cultural events to keep everyone happy. As the popularity of the loosely organized movement "Keep Austin Weird" (www.keepaustinweird.com) demonstrates, the city loves its free-thinkers, artists, and musicians. If, as John Steinbeck wrote, "Texas is a state of mind," then Austin, an unencumbered free spirit of a city, is surely its perfect capital.

NEIGHBORHOODS

Downtown
Overseen by the Capitol, downtown is organized around Congress Avenue, which divides cross streets into east and west. Much of the city's nightlife is located either on Sixth Street, bounded by Congress to the west and Red River Street to the east, or the Warehouse District, on Fourth and Fifth Streets between Congress and Guadalupe.

South Austin and South of Congress (SoCo)
While crossing over the Congress Avenue Bridge used to feel like crossing into a different world, a recent rejuvenation of the area has tempered its edge. Large-scale commercial and residential developments are now springing up in this artsy enclave. Filled with inexpensive eateries, music venues, and funky art and resale shops, South Austin embodies some of the best of Austin.

West End/Clarksville
The area west of Lamar Boulevard between Enfield Road to the north and West Fifth Street to the south, West End and Clarksville is a deceptively modest-looking neighborhood conveniently located beside downtown. The area is atmospheric, with large trees, art galleries, several upscale restaurants, and sidewalks for strolling.

Statue with a Lone Star atop the Texas Capitol

UT and Hyde Park

To the north of the Capitol, the sprawling 350-acre University of Texas campus is bounded by Guadalupe Street (also known as "The Drag") to the west, I-35 to the east, and Martin Luther King Jr. Boulevard to the south. Located just a mile north of the University of Texas, Hyde Park is bounded by Guadalupe Street to the west, Duval Street to the east, 45th Street to the north, and 38th Street to the south. Developed as Austin's first suburb, the neighborhood features homes from the 1930s and '40s interspersed with commercial centers, folksy restaurants, and coffee shops. Students, professors, and young families call Hyde Park home, and the area feels lived in, with bikes in the yards and swings on the porches.

East Austin

Comprising the neighborhoods east of I-35, East Austin retains its historic roots. A diverse neighborhood, it is also home to significant cultural institutions such as the George Washington Carver Museum and Cultural Center and the Texas State Cemetery. While recent economic development has begun to change the face of East Austin, its infectious community spirit is still most evident in its numerous mom-and-pop eateries.

TRANSPORTATION

Getting Around Austin

Austin is not a large city, so driving into, out of, or around it is not a particularly difficult task. However, the major routes that approximate the boundaries of the city are known by several names, making navigation a challenge.

I-35 runs along the eastern part of Austin, dividing East Austin from the rest of the city. Following the western border is Loop 1, also known as the MoPac Expressway, or MoPac, for the Missouri-Pacific Railroad, which runs parallel to it in many places. Farther west is Loop 360, often referred to as Capital of Texas Highway.

US 183 originates in East Austin as Ed Bluestein Boulevard, becoming Anderson Lane, Research Boulevard, and finally Bell Boulevard as it snakes it way along the northern edge of the city. At the southern reaches of the city, TX 71 is also known as US 290 and Ben White Boulevard.

Downtown Austin is more straightforward for both drivers and pedestrians. Spread out in a grid, with generously sized blocks, downtown is easily taken in on foot, but to get to sights in South Austin and beyond, consider riding one of the city's buses.

Austin's Capital Metro (512-474-1200 or 1-800-474-1201; www.capmetro.org) runs an extensive network of efficient city buses, and two are designed specifically for visitors.

On weekdays the 'Dillo circulates through the city along five different routes (Blue, Red, Gold, Silver, and Orange) past virtually all sights and attractions in Austin and extending to several free park-and-ride lots. 'Dillo buses run every 5–10 minutes Monday through Friday, but hours of operation vary, so check schedules. Price: Free. Yes, that's right, free.

On weekends bus route 470 ("Tour the Town") provides service between the university and Zilker Park, stopping at the Capitol, museums, and attractions along the way. Fare: 50 cents per ride, or $1 for a day pass.

All buses traveling the routes listed above are handicapped accessible.

LODGING

Hotel chains dominate the lodging choices in Austin, and many of them cater primarily to business travelers and politicians, charging additional hefty fees for parking, use of fitness facilities, and Internet service; be sure to inquire about such details when making your reservation, and keep in mind that parking on the streets in Austin is free on the weekends. Austin has several historic hotels, boutique hotels, and B&Bs located throughout the city that offer character and individuality, not to mention free WiFi and parking. They are also quick to hand out snacks, drinks, business discounts, DVDs, flowers, and restaurant advice without batting an eyelash or charging you an extra penny. If you appreciate this sort of personal attention, consider patronizing one of these very worthy alternatives.

When choosing an area of town, keep in mind that the neighborhoods surrounding Sixth Street tend to stay up late for the nightlife on which the city has grown its reputation. If you are staying downtown, consider asking for a room as high up as possible. They don't call Austin the Live Music Capital of the World for nothing; if you are used to city sounds, the noise level may not bother you, but if you require silence to sleep, you might consider a hotel in a quieter neighborhood several blocks removed or one of the B&Bs, which have strictly enforced quiet hours.

Generally, guests with limited mobility may find the larger chain hotels to be the best fit, although several B&Bs and boutique hotels have a room or two that meet ADA requirements. If a certain property catches your eye, by all means call and inquire, as special arrangements can sometimes be made. Chain hotels farther from the center of town, in areas such as North Austin, tend to be solid family-friendly values.

The codes here reflect the hotel's advertised rate; keep in mind that rates tend to rise during holidays, festivals, and special events. A two-day minimum stay is usually required on weekends, three days during holidays, festivals, and special events.

Lodging Price Code

Inexpensive	Up to $100
Moderate	$100 to $150
Expensive	$150 to $250
Very Expensive	Over $250

DOWNTOWN

Driskill Hotel
512-474-5911 or 1-800-252-9367
www.driskillhotel.com
604 Brazos St., Austin, TX 78701
Price: Very Expensive
Special Features: Free WiFi; handicapped
  access

You really can't get more Austin than the Driskill Hotel. Constructed by cattle baron Jesse Lincoln Driskill in 1886, a time when the rest of the city was built low to the ground, the hotel was the largest, grandest, and most elaborate structure in Austin. In the 1920s it was remodeled and a new art deco wing added, but even these major changes couldn't stave off long-standing financial problems. LBJ's presidency saw journalists camped out in the Driskill for weeks at a time, but in the 1970s the Driskill fell again on hard times and came close to closing. Saved by the efforts of the Heritage Society of Austin, which drummed up support, investment, and interest in the building, today the Driskill is thriving as the centerpiece of downtown, its elegance entirely intact. Dine at the Driskill Grill

The Driskill Hotel in downtown Austin

(see "Dining," below), have a drink at the bar, or a muffin at the 1886 Bakery, while enjoying the stylish atmosphere of the hotel. Remember that the hotel is old through and through, so modest-size rooms and quirky layouts are the norm. All amenities have been modernized; the bathrooms have granite countertops, and the decor is refined with soft linens, sumptuous drapes, and rich accents. While this sort of luxury isn't cheap, experiencing this grand piece of Austin history is worth it.

Four Seasons

512-478-4500 or 512-685-8100
www.fourseasons.com/austin
98 San Jacinto Blvd., Austin, TX 78701
Price: Very Expensive
Special Features: Handicapped access;
    pool; WiFi $10

Perched on a bluff overlooking Town Lake just south of César Chávez Street near the Congress Avenue Bridge, the Four Seasons is wonderfully located, within easy driving distance and, in many cases, walking distance of all major points of interest, including Sixth Street. Directly outside the hotel is a hike-and-bike path where you can join locals for a run. The lovely pool, with lake views, is a great spot for a dip. Inside, rooms are average size; though the ceilings are somewhat low, the generous windows help compensate. Rooms have either a city view or a lake view (extra charge), and each is enjoyable in its own way. Decorated with an eye toward casual elegance, the rooms aren't the least bit fussy and, in fact, are rather ordinary. The hotel is scheduled to undergo a $15 million makeover in 2007. Guests can look forward to more modern decor and plasma televisions once all the updates and upgrades are completed. Downstairs, the Café at the Four Seasons (see "Dining," below) is one of the best places to eat in town, and the bar is a favorite spot for locals to unwind over after-work drinks.

Hilton Austin

512-482-8000 or 1-800-445-8667
www.hilton.com
550 E. Fourth St., Austin, TX 78701
Price: Very Expensive
Special Features: Handicapped access;
    pool; WiFi $9.95

Well situated in the thick of the action downtown, within easy walking distance of the Convention Center and Sixth Street, the Hilton is a decent option. Essentially a business hotel, the Hilton offers spacious, well-lit rooms, large desks and plush office chairs, beds piled high with pillows, a spa downstairs, and a pool on the roof. There is an extra charge for use of the fitness room.

Stephen F. Austin Inter-Continental

512-457-8800 or 1-888-424-6835
www.ichotelsgroup.com
710 Congress Ave., Austin, TX 78701
Price: Expensive to Very Expensive
Special Features: Handicapped access;
    Internet $10.95

The Stephen F. Austin was built in 1924 and consequently does not have the cookie-cutter consistency associated with many of Austin's newer downtown hotels. In general, the standard rooms tend to be small, though tasteful decor keeps them from feeling cramped. The hotel's age also means different floor plans and different levels of service and amenities, so spending the extra $40–$60 to upgrade to deluxe rooms may very well be worth the money; be sure to inquire about specifics. While the Stephen F. Austin may not have the historic provenance of the Driskill, it is lighter, brighter, and just as well situated.

WEST END/CLARKSVILLE

Brava House

512-478-5034
www.bravahouse.com
1108 Blanco St., Austin, TX   78703

Price: Moderate to Expensive
Special Features: Internet; limited handi-
    capped access

Tall ceilings, windows, and doors, hardwood floors, and dark wood moldings are
all hallmarks of this Victorian beauty built
in the 1880s. The two rooms and three
suites in Brava House are well decorated
with antiques that feel casual and comfortable, not formal or fussy. The tiny, serene,
and wheelchair-accessible Van Gogh room
is a great value at $99–$109. The generously sized and dapper Garbo Suite and art
deco Fitzgerald Suite have foldout couches
for extra guests, and the large Monroe Suite
is really more of a mini-apartment with a
full kitchen. A buffet-style breakfast is
served each morning, and the cozy backyard deck is a nice place to sit and enjoy it.
Brava House is located in a quiet West
Austin neighborhood near the intersection
of North Lamar Avenue and 12th Street, just
four blocks north of the Whole Foods
Market on Lamar.

UT/HYDE PARK

Austin Folk House Bed and Breakfast
512-472-6700 or 1-866-472-6700
www.austinfolkhouse.com
506 W. 22nd St., Austin, TX 78705
Price: Moderate to Expensive
Special Features: Free Internet
Additional Location: The Star of Texas Inn
    (same phone; www.staroftexasinn.com;
    611 W. 22nd St.). Located just one block
    away, this inn is comparable in look,
    feel, and price.

The Austin Folk House, presumably named
for its wonderfully eclectic collection of
folk art, happens also to be very folksy.
Friendly, comfortable, and relaxed, the
Folk House exudes that unmistakable
Austin vibe. Each room is different, but all
have warm color schemes, with crimsons,

golds, and greens dominating, and are simply decorated with personal touches such as
handmade comforters, canopy beds, and
rustic armoires. Breakfast, which includes
such items as raspberry pancakes, *migas*,
and quiche, is served in the informal dining room, where coffee tastes better when
served in a mug from their mismatched
collection.

Carrington's Bluff
512-479-0638 or 1-888-290-6090
www.carringtonsbluff.com
1900 David St., Austin, TX 78705
Price: Moderate to Expensive
Special Features: Free WiFi

Carrington's Bluff sits perched on an acre
of shady Texas soil deep in the heart of
Austin. The B&B consists of two separate
buildings—the Main House, built in 1877,
and the Writer's Cottage, built in 1920,
located across the street. The five rooms in
the Main House are graced with high ceilings and hardwood floors. With jewel-
toned rugs, dark wood beds, a few carefully
chosen antique side tables or bureaus, and
a chair for reading, the rooms are uncluttered yet functional and relaxing. In the
Writer's Cottage there are three cozy, car-
peted guest rooms, a shared living room
and dining room, and a shared kitchen
whose refrigerator is stocked with Texas-
made Blue Bell ice cream. Phoebe, the
innkeeper, makes sure the homemade
cookies, granola, and breakfasts are always
delicious.

1110 Carriage House Inn
512-472-2333 or 1-866-472-2333
www.carriagehouseinn.org
1110 W. 22½ St., Austin, TX 78705
Price: Moderate to Expensive
Special Features: Free WiFi

Located near the University of Texas, this
inn has considerate owners who have truly

The Star of Texas Inn, near the University of Texas at Austin

thought of everything. Allergy and asthma sufferers, along with folks who just like good clean air, will be thrilled to discover that this is a smoke-free, pet-free establishment that uses nonperfumed detergents, refrains from air fresheners, and will supply a HEPA air filter for your room upon request. Each room has gleaming hardwood floors, large wood beds, and pretty lace curtains to catch the sunlight. The bathroom sizes and configurations vary according to room; some have tubs and some have showers, so be sure to inquire if you need one or the other. Breakfast is always homemade, using organic ingredients when available and taking into concern the dietary restrictions of its guests. The lovely organic gardens, featuring a koi pond and seating under a gazebo, are a great place to unwind. There is one vice that will tempt you your entire stay: The owners' handmade chocolate truffles, a very sweet and thoughtful gesture, await each guest in the room when they arrive.

The funky Austin Motel on South Congress Avenue

Woodburn House Bed and Breakfast
512-458-4335 or 1-888-690-9763
www.woodburnhouse.com
4401 Avenue D, Austin, TX 78751
Price: Inexpensive to Moderate
Special Features: Free WiFi

The three-story Woodburn House, built in 1909, features 11-foot ceilings, original rich brown woodwork, and graceful double wraparound porches. Two of the house's four rooms have queen-size beds, and the other two have king-size beds; all are topped with soft sheets, plenty of pillows, and cozy down comforters. Thick towels and pleasant bath products are a nice touch, as are the homemade baked goods for breakfast. All guests have access to the vast porches—once included in the "Ten Best Porches to Sit on This Summer" by *USA Today*—which are perfect for reading or just watching the goings-on in the neighborhood. The house is in the historic Hyde Park neighborhood, a short 2-mile drive from downtown and a pleasant stroll to restaurants in Duval Square.

Star of Texas Inn
(see Austin Folk House, above)

Austin Motel

512-441-1157
www.austinmotel.com
1220 S. Congress Ave., Austin, TX 78704
Price: Inexpensive
Special Features: Limited handicapped
    access; pool; restaurant

The idiosyncratic Austin Motel is the first
to admit that they are "so close in, yet
so far out." The oldest part of this independently owned motel dates to 1938; the
kidney-shaped pool was constructed in
the 1950s, and the two-story addition in
1968. There are spacious suites, cozy singles, and poolside rooms. Each is unique,
with distinctive themes swinging wildly
from waterfall, seashore, or flower photo
murals to big polka dots and kitschy brass
mirrors, to fluffy floral coverlets covered
with pandas. Some of the bathrooms sport
vintage color combinations such as coral
and aqua. The rooms have various bed configurations, making this a popular choice
for small groups in town for the big music
and arts festivals. The Austin Motel is an
older establishment and very well-priced—
just bear in mind that one person's well-
worn might be another's worn-out. In a
terrific location on the north end of South
Congress near downtown, the Austin Motel
and its restaurant, El Sol y la Luna (see
"Dining," below), are well-established
values in SoCo.

Hotel San José

512-444-7322 or 1-800-574-8887
www.sanjosehotel.com
1316 S. Congress Ave., Austin, TX 78704
Price: Moderate to Very Expensive
Special Features: Bar; free WiFi; limited
    handicapped access; pool

Originally opened in 1939, the Hotel San
José has since been remodeled in a style
that harks back to its roots as an "ultra-

A spotless room inside the Hotel San José

modern motor court" but might now be
best described as hacienda-meets-bento-
box, colorful and relaxing, compact and
efficient, with an understated simplicity
that is utterly serene. The European-style
hotel has only 40 rooms, ranging from the
small and Spartan "shared bath" rooms to
the generously sized Courtyard Suite with a
balcony view. The minuscule pool, lovely
gardens, laid-back bar, and adjacent coffee
shop amplify the air of yesteryear. With the
intimacy of a B&B and the amenities of a
small hotel, the Hotel San José has created
a sophisticated oasis of calm on South
Congress.

EAST AUSTIN

Mi Yard

www.miyardbedandbreakfast.com
2307 Riverside Farms Rd., Austin, TX 78741
Price: Inexpensive
Special Features: Free WiFi

Run by longtime Austinites who also own a
club on Sixth Street, Mi Yard is in keeping
with the city's free spirit. Not your traditional B&B, Mi Yard is painted a cheerful
lemon-lime on the outside, and this tropical theme carries through to the rooms
decorated with bright comforters and

coordinating window treatments. There is a fully stocked kitchen, where guests are able to prepare their own breakfasts of fruit, toast, bagels, or breakfast burritos at their leisure. While there is no pressure to wake up early for a scheduled breakfast, the trade-off is that you have to wash your own dishes. The fire pit, hot tub, and decks are nice for relaxing, and Ed, the thoughtful owner, lets guests have plenty of privacy. Its quiet, out-of-the-way East Austin location, just minutes from both downtown and the airport, makes Mi Yard a nice alternative.

North Austin

Staybridge Suites Austin–Northwest
512-349-0888 or 1-800-931-4667
www.staybridge.com
10201 Stonelake Blvd., Austin, TX 78759
Price: Expensive
Special Features: Free WiFi; handicapped
    access; pool

This clean and well-maintained hotel is just 10 minutes north of downtown, near the slightly upscale Arboretum Mall and also the intersection of US 183, MoPac (Loop 1), and Capital of Texas Highway (360), three good routes for easy mobility in and out of the city. There are several room plans to choose from, and all include kitchens, DVD/VCR players (DVDs available at the front desk), and complimentary breakfast. The smaller suites are 350 square feet, and the two-bedroom suites (each bedroom with a private bath) 750 square feet—a very nice amount of space for families or friends traveling together. Each evening, the hotel hosts a reception with snacks or finger foods. It's kid friendly, with a small pool and basketball court, as well as pet friendly, with a dog-walking area outdoors. The Staybridge is a great option for visitors who like the hubbub of the city by day and the quiet of suburbs by night.

Habitat Suites
512-467-6000 or 1-800-535-4663
www.habitatsuites.com
500 E. Highland Mall Blvd., Austin, TX
    78752
Price: Moderate to Expensive
Special Features: Internet; limited handi-
    capped access; pool

Habitat Suites' eco-friendly innovations, from low-flow shower heads to a new 108-panel solar photovoltaic system, helped them win the "Keep Austin Beautiful" Industry Leadership Award in 2005. With no marketing budget and an odd location amid a tangle of highways across from the Highland Park Mall, Habitat Suites could easily be overlooked. While the rooms would benefit from updated carpets and perhaps more inspired decor, guests, especially business travelers and families, seem quite content with the one- and two-bedroom suites complete with living rooms and kitchens, so much so that 85 percent are repeat customers. The ionized-water swimming pool, vegan or macrobiotic hot breakfast, friendly front desk staff, native plant landscaping, and even the toilet paper (recycled), all make Habitat Suites a thoughtful alternative to mainstream chain hotels.

Outer Austin

Lake Austin Spa and Resort
512-372-7300 or 1-800-847-5637
www.lakeaustinspa.com
1705 S. Quinlan Park Rd., Austin, TX 78732
Price: Very Expensive
Special Features: Handicapped access;
    pool; spa

If you enjoy spas and resorts, consider the Lake Austin Spa and Resort. While *Travel and Leisure* placed it on its list of the top ten spas worldwide and *Condé Nast Traveler* bumped it to the top five, as did Zagat, Lake

Austin Spa's biggest compliments have come from its guests, who leave relaxed and rejuvenated. With views of the lake at every turn and expansive use of native Austin limestone and huge cedar beams, this mid-size resort with 40 guest cottages has that earthy, laid-back, rustic feel that typifies the area; the overall effect is both cozy and chic. A popular place for couples, the Lake Austin Spa has a more feminine weekend-of-pampering vibe, easily enjoyed by some men, though the lack of testostero. be noticeable to others. Prices inclu three gourmet meals a day, access to a ness classes, including yoga, pilates, hi ing, and fun salsa aerobics. A bevy of activities and classes from cooking to stargazing to watercolor is also on offer. All spa services are à la carte. Of course, the price of this level of luxury is steep, but the Lake Austin Spa is a good value when compared to similar facilities nationwide.

CULTURE

Historic Places

The Austin History Center is a good place to research the history of the city, and a visit to the Bob Bullock Museum will help you put the facts in the larger context of Texas history.

Texas State Capitol

512-463-0063
www.tspb.state.tx.us
Congress Ave., between 11th and 14th Sts., Austin 78701.
Open: Mon.–Fri. 7 AM–10 PM, Sat.–Sun. 9–8
Admission: Free
Special Features: Free guided tours Mon.–Fri. 8:30–4:30, Sat. 9:30–3:30, Sun. noon–3:30

The Texas Capitol sits on a high point in the city, with the University of Texas to the north and Congress Avenue descending gently southward from it to the Colorado River. The massive Renaissance revival–style building, built to replace its predecessor, which had been destroyed by fire, was completed in 1888 at a cost of over $3.5 million—not paid for in cash, but with the enormous parcel of land in the Texas Panhandle that became the legendary XIT Ranch. The largest capitol building in the nation, save for the National Capitol in Washington, D.C, the Texas State Capitol is big, bold, and—right down to the engraving of "Texas Capitol" on the *inside* of the 7-pound bronze hinges of the massive entrance doors—very Texas.

The Capitol's exterior walls are made of distinctive pink-hued granite known as "sunset red," quarried at Granite Mountain in nearby Marble Falls. The building is topped with a gleaming aluminum Goddess of Liberty, clutching a Lone Star in her hand. The original zinc figure was removed in 1985, painted white, and put on permanent display at the Bob Bullock Museum (see "Museums," below); her star rests at the Capitol Visitors Center. In 1995, the building underwent an extraordinarily expensive $98 million renovation and now sparkles inside and out, with original details restored. In the lobby, Elisabet Ney's sculptures of Texas leaders Stephen Austin, Sam Houston, and Miriam "Ma" Ferguson,

st woman governor and the country's second, are all on display, as are portraits
notables and folk heroes such as Davy Crockett. Inside, centered in the impressive
a, a Lone Star of the Texas Republic looks down on a terrazzo floor mosaic of the
of the six countries whose flags have flown over the state. The serene, parklike
nds, surrounded by the bustling city, are perfect for strolling, and the large shade
es and benches provide relief in the heat. The many monuments dotting the 22-acre

The Capitol

grounds tell the stories of Texas and include statues of an armed Alamo defender, Texas Rangers and cowboys, pioneer women, children, and a volunteer firefighter, war memorials, and even a replica of the Statue of Liberty; they are all detailed in a brochure available at the visitors center.

Capitol Visitors Center

512-305-8400
www.tspb.state.tx.us/CVC
112 E. 11th St., Austin, TX 78701
On the southeast corner of the Capitol grounds
Open: Mon.–Sat. 9–5, Sun. noon–5. Gift shop keeps the same hours but opens
    at 10 AM Sat.

The Capitol Visitors Center is located in the faux-medieval General Land Office Building and is chock-full of information, booklets, pamphlets, videos, and art exhibits. Whether your questions regard history, camping, bus tours, or public restrooms, the folks here have the answer, not just for the Capitol, but for Austin and Central Texas. Interesting exhibits include the O. Henry Room, where you can listen to information about the writer's life and works on old-fashioned telephones, a 1:16 scale model of the Capitol Dome, and a fascinating video that details the creative deal brokered between Texas and a group of Chicago businessmen that financed the construction of the Capitol in exchange for the land that became the XIT Ranch.

The visitors center has a gift shop, and there is also one in the Capitol Extension (Room E1.006, 1400 N. Congress Ave., open Mon.–Fri. 8–4:30, Sat. 10–5, Sun. 10–5) with enough Texas-themed merchandise to satisfy all your personal and gift-giving needs.

Austin History Center

512-974-7400
www.ci.austin.tx.us/library/ahc
Ninth and Guadalupe Sts., P.O. Box 2287, Austin, TX 78768
Open: Mon.–Wed. 10–9, Sat. 10–6, Sun. noon–6
Admission: Free

A division of the Austin Public Library, the Austin History Center is centrally located and certainly worth popping into. Well-presented collections of photos, news clippings, maps, and records trace the history of Austin through exhibits on African American History, the Women's Suffrage Movement, Austinites at Work, and Victorian Architecture.

Lyndon Baines Johnson Museum and Library

512-721-0200
www.lbjlib.utexas.edu
2313 Red River St., Austin, TX 78705
Open: Museum daily 9–5, reading room Mon.–Fri. 9–5
Admission: Free

With the benefit of hindsight and a few intervening decades, it is easy to appreciate Lyndon Johnson's life, times, and presidency, as they were some of the most tumultuous and formative years for the country as a whole. LBJ's terms as vice president and president ompassed the Cuban missile crisis, the civil rights movement, the assassinations of resident John Kennedy, Robert Kennedy, and Martin Luther King Jr., and the Vietnam War. A Texan through and through, LBJ never forgot his childhood in the rural Hill Country, which fueled his passion for the enormous social reforms designed to bring about the "Great Society." A must for history buffs, who might also consider a trip to the LBJ National Historic Park (see Hill Country chapter).

Governor's Mansion

512-463-5516
www.txfgm.org
1010 Colorado St., Austin, TX 78701
Open: Mon.–Thu. 10–noon
Admission: Free

Special Circumstances: Reservations are required and must be made at least 24 hours prior to visit. All visitors will be asked for their name, phone number, birth date, and a valid form of identification. See Web site for details.

The gleaming white, beautifully proportioned Greek-revival Governor's Mansion was built by master builder Abner Cook and completed in 1856. The house proved so big that governors at first had a difficult time furnishing and maintaining it, until Sam Houston, a man who liked to think big, moved in and had it properly appointed. His enormous mahogany four-poster bed still adorns the southeast bedroom. While the mansion and its surrounding gardens are lovely and rich in detail, the guided tours are brisk.

O. Henry Museum

512-472-1903
www.ci.austin.tx.us/parks/ohenry
409 E. Fifth St., Austin, TX 78701
Open: Wed.–Sun. noon–5
Admission: Free

William Sidney Porter was many things in his life. Although to officials in Austin he was a convicted embezzler, to the rest of us he is simply O. Henry or "master of the short story." The museum that bears his name, housed in the charming 1886 Queen Anne–style cottage he lived in for two years at the end of the 1800s, contains a sparse collection of memorabilia from his life. A National Literary Landmark of the City of Austin, the O. Henry Museum offers writing programs and workshops and promotes all manner of wisecracking and witticism at the annual O. Henry Pun-Off (www.punpunpun.com) held in May.

Museums

While music has deep roots in Central Texas, the formal establishment of museums for the visual arts is still relatively recent. The city's two big museums, the Austin Museum of Art and the Jack S. Blanton Museum of Art, are less than 50 years old, but their collections are still growing and their exhibition space is wonderfully intimate. Cultural museums, such as the Bob Bullock Museum, offer a dynamic introduction to the history and personality of the region, while interactive museums, such as the Children's Museum, are just plain fun.

The University of Texas at Austin

Founded in 1883 with only 8 teachers and 220 students, the University of Texas at Austin (UT) has grown into one of the largest universities in the country, with close to 50,000 students, numerous departments, and an enviable reputation that reaches far beyond its 350-acre campus.

UT is located just north of the Capitol, roughly bounded by Martin Luther King Jr. Boulevard to the south, I-35 to the east, and Guadalupe Street ("The Drag") to the west. The campus, a nice place to stroll, is home to the Blanton Museum of Art, the Harry Ransom Humanities Research Center, the LBJ Library and Museum, and the Texas Memorial Museum. The UT Tower overlooks the plaza at Guadalupe and 22nd Streets and offers a bird's-eye view of the city from its observation deck (accessible only by tour). In the fall, Texas Memorial Stadium fills up with football fans every time the University's Longhorns are in town, while the Cactus Café in the Texas Union Building hosts music concerts year-round. (See separate listings below for more information on all of the above.)

The Mustangs, *sculpted by Alexander Phimister Proctor*

Arthouse at the Jones Center
512-453-5312
www.arthousetexas.org
700 Congress Ave., Austin, TX 78701
Open: Tue.–Fri. 11–7, Thu. 11–9, Sat. 10–5, Sun. 1–5
Admission: Free

The Arthouse, the oldest visual arts organization in Texas, was established in 1911. It is currently devoted entirely to contemporary art, providing artists a venue for exhibition and educational opportunities for the public. The Arthouse is renowned for its biannual $30,000 Arthouse Texas Prize, the largest regional visual arts award in the nation, bestowed on a Texas artist whose innovation and talent have enriched the state's art scene. The annual summertime exhibit titled "New American Talent" is one to look for, as is the "5x7 Auction," which features reasonably priced, original postcard-size works.

The Austin Museum of Art
The Austin Museum of Art has two locations, Laguna Gloria and downtown. As was the hope of its benefactor, Clara Driscoll, the museum's mission is to bring a broad range of art experiences to its community. A true community museum, the Austin Museum of Art is as much about educating as it is about exhibits.

Laguna Gloria
512-458-8191
www.amoa.org
3809 W. 35th St., Austin, TX 78703
West of MoPac, south of Camp Mabry
Open: Villa, daily 11–4; grounds, Mon.–Sat. 9–5, Sun. 11–5
Admission: $3 suggested donation

The very talented Clara Driscoll and her husband, Hal Sevier, onetime owner of the *Austin American* newspaper, built Laguna Gloria in 1916 and donated it to the city of Austin in 1943, which established it as a museum in 1961. Situated on a bluff overlooking the Colorado River and the hills opposite, the Driscoll villa is surrounded by terraced gardens created by Clara herself and filled with native foliage. Tropical plants, statues and sculptures, and found objects such as a mission bell, an Italian wishing well, and other bits of whimsy dot the grounds. Contemporary works, such as the sculptures of Nancy Holt, Clyde Connell, and Jesus Morales, have been added more recently. The focus of Laguna Gloria is on its historic building and grounds, coupled with some low-key art shows, leaving the large and attention-grabbing exhibits up to the Austin Museum of Art–Downtown.

Austin Museum of Art–Downtown
512-495-9224
www.amoa.org
823 Congress Ave., Austin, TX 78701
Open: Tue.–Sat. 10–6, Thu. 10–8, Sun. noon–5
Admission: Adults $5, seniors and students $4, under 12 free; Tue. $1; first Saturday of the month pay what you wish

The Austin Museum of Art, referred to as AMOA–Downtown, is located in the heart of the city, several blocks south of the Capitol complex. The museum has a rather modest permanent collection, with some works by big names, such as Chuck Close, Robert Rauschenberg, and Andy Warhol. The real thrill of this museum is that it is small and intimate, and when large exhibits come to town, such as the Quilts of Gee's Bend, you never have to fight the crowds for a close-up. In the spirit of a community museum, the AMOA–Downtown has a wonderful family-friendly interactive art space for making art and exploring art together (free with admission).

The Jack S. Blanton Museum of Art
The University of Texas at Austin
512-471-7324
www.blantonmuseum.org
Congress Ave. and MLK Jr. Blvd., Austin, TX 78712
Open: Tue., Wed, Fri., Sat. 10–5, Thu. 10–8, Sun. 1–5
Admission: Adults $5, seniors $4, children $3; free on Thu.

Praised for both the focus and depth of its collection, the Blanton Museum has over 17,000 works of art. Many of its holdings have not been on display since 2001, when preparations began for the construction of a new and substantially larger museum. As the new exhibition space was being built, the Blanton expanded its holdings, most notably with additions to its 20th-century American and Latin American collections, the latter of which is almost unparalleled in the U.S. and one of a handful worldwide. In the spring of 2006, the Blanton opened the doors to its expansive new digs, and for art lovers the wait was over. The first Friday of the month, the museum is open 6 PM–midnight for live music and drinks ($10).

The Bob Bullock Texas State History Museum
512-936-8746
www.thestoryoftexas.com
1800 N. Congress Ave., Austin, TX 78712
Open: Tue.–Sat. 9–6, Sun. noon–6
Admission to exhibit: Adults $5.50, seniors $4.50, youths $3, children 4 and under free
Admission to exhibit and both theaters: Adults $13.50, seniors $10.50, youths $8.50, children ages 3–4 $6.50

The 35-foot-tall bronze star sculpture out front is your first indication that this museum thinks big. Spearheaded by former Lieutenant Governor Bob Bullock and opened in 2001, the Texas State History Museum has quickly become a must-see destination. Known for its elaborate and educational interactive exhibits, many of which challenge myths and misconceptions, the permanent collection of the museum is organized around the themes of Land, Identity, and Opportunity. Special exhibits have included "It Ain't Braggin' if It's True" which explores, among other things, the gray area between pride and swagger, and "The Faces of Texas," a lovely portrait series taken by Austin photographer Michael O'Brien. The vast sunsets, galloping herds of horses, and NASA space shuttles featured in *Texas: The Big Picture* are well-suited to the enormous screen at the museum's IMAX theater. The Story of Texas Café on the second floor is a convenient spot to enjoy lunch or a

The Bob Bullock Texas State History Museum

snack, either inside or out on the balcony. Open: Mon.–Sat. 10–5, Sun. noon–5; lunch is served from 10–3.

Children's Museum
512-472-2499
www.austinkids.org
201 Colorado St., Austin, TX 78701
Open: Tue. and Thu.–Sat. 10–5, Wed. 10–8, Sun. noon–5
Admission: Adults and children 2 and older $5.50, children 12–23 months $3.50, under 12
    months free; by donation Wed. nights 5–8; free Sun. 4–5

Austin's Children's Museum is a bonanza for children in preschool and elementary school. Children can dress up for a Japanese tea ceremony, process milk in Miss Moo Moo's Dairy Processing Plant, or flip flapjacks and eat at the counter of the Global Diner. In addition to these permanent exhibits, featured exhibits tend to be very interactive and creative, illustrating simple science, math, or music principles. The gift shop is a great place to pick up an educational souvenir that your children will actually enjoy when the trip is over. The museum is located at the eastern end of the Sixth Street/Warehouse District, making it an easy place for families to pop into for a few hours and just let the kids be kids.

Mexic-Arte Museum
512-480-9373
www.mexic-artemuseum.org
419 Congress Ave., Austin, TX 78701
Open: Mon.–Thu. 10–6, Fri.–Sat. 10–5
Admission: Adults $5, seniors and students $4, children $1

What began in 1983 as a 300-square-foot gallery/studio has grown into one of a very few museums in the U.S. dedicated to traditional and contemporary Mexican and Latino art. The Mexic-Arte Museum has two exhibition spaces; the main gallery is reserved for major exhibits, and a smaller gallery houses the museum's Diversity and Emergence series, which highlights new talent. Exhibits can be political or personal, transcultural or transcendent, but they are always thought-provoking and timely. Recent shows have included such wide-ranging topics as "Los Hilos de Oaxaca," an exhibition of textiles and costumes vividly embroidered by different indigenous groups living in the Mexican state of Oaxaca, and a retrospective of the legendary Mexican political cartoonist, muralist, and printer José Clemente Orozco. Exhibits aside, the Mexic-Arte Museum is also a cultural and educational center, hosting the Annual Taste of Mexico in May and sponsoring after-school programs for children. With big plans to expand, this is one museum to watch.

Neil-Cochran Museum
512-478-2665
2310 San Gabriel St., Austin, TX 78705
Open: Wed.–Sun. 2–5
Admission: $2

Built by the same architect responsible for the Governor's Mansion (see above), this Greek-revival mansion dating to 1855 shares the neighborhood with others of its vintage,

Remember East Austin

With so many of Austin's sights concentrated on the west side of I-35, the city's east side doesn't get as many visitors, but that doesn't mean there aren't interesting spots to check out, notably the Carver Museum and Cultural Center. Be sure to leave time to stop in at one of the neighborhood's eateries (see "Dining," below) for a great taste of everyday Austin.

French Legation Museum

512-472-8180

www.frenchlegationmuseum.org

802 San Marcos St., Austin, TX 78702

Open: Tue.–Sun. 1–5

Admission: Adults $4, seniors $3, children $2

Originally built to house the French representative to the Republic of Texas, the French Legation Museum comprises two buildings: the mansion and the kitchen. The mansion is the oldest building in Austin, having survived thanks to the good care of the Robertson family, who owned it from 1848 to 1940 and whose Victorian furnishings still grace the interior, and the Daughters of the Republic of Texas, who restored it in the 1950s. An example of French neoclassical architecture, the house feels very Continental, right down to the French wine cellar. The original kitchen burned down in 1880; the current building is a replica based on evidence from the archaeological record, and antique kitchenware adds authenticity. Docent-led tours bring the property to life. Each July, Bastille Day festivities add an air of celebration.

including the nearby Mansion at Judges' Hill. The home, which is shiny clean and filled with Victorian furnishings, offers a glimpse back in time to a historic Austin opulence.

Elisabet Ney Museum

512-458-2255

www.ci.austin.tx.us/elisabetney

304 E. 44th St., Austin, TX 78751

Open: Wed.–Sat. 10–5, Sun. noon–5

Admission: Free

Elisabet Ney was a 19th-century German-born sculptor who, after moving to Texas in 1872, relocated to Austin in 1892, building herself a neoclassical studio in what was then rural Hyde Park. Ney's studio was a salon of sorts, with those who would become leaders of Texas frequently gathering to discuss ideas, politics, and, of course, art. In 1893, she was asked to sculpt life-size likenesses of Texans Stephen Austin and Sam Houston for the Chicago World's Fair; these sculptures are on display at the state Capitol in Austin and the national Capitol in Washington, D.C. Today, Ney's studio is a museum, owned by the city of Austin, containing a collection of her sculptures and portraits of notable European royalty and American leaders. A plaster model of her favorite sculpture, one of Lady Macbeth, is prominently displayed; its marble counterpart is in the Smithsonian in Washington, D.C.

The Historic Hyde Park Homes Tour (see "Tours," below), held annually on Father's Day weekend, commences at the Ney Museum.

Remember East Austin continued

George Washington Carver Museum and Cultural Center
512-974-4926
www.ci.austin.tx.us/carver
1165 Angelina St., Austin, TX 78702
Open: Mon., Wed., Fri. 9:30–6, Tue. and Thu. 9:30–8, Sat. 1–5
Admission: Free

What began in 1926 as a tiny library—no bigger than a house—serving the neighborhood's mostly African American population has grown into a museum and cultural center celebrating African American heritage, the first of its kind in Texas. The centerpiece of the museum is its exhibit on Juneteenth (see "Festivals," below), which celebrates the announcement of the Emancipation Proclamation of 1862. A thoughtful exhibit featuring the history of 10 African Americans in Central Texas whose lives illustrate perseverance is also interesting. There is also a small interactive area for children, an art gallery, and the Boyd Vance Theater, which hosts music and film events throughout the year.

Just a block further east is the Henry Madison Log Cabin (2300 Rosewood Ave.), built in the 1860s by the man who would become the first African American city councilman in Austin. Though you cannot enter the building itself, a quick drive past will give you a glimpse of pioneer life.

Texas State Cemetery
512-463-0605
www.cemetery.state.tx.us
909 Navasota St., Austin, TX 78702
Between E. Seventh and E. 11th Sts.
Open: Daily 8–5; gallery and visitors center Mon.–Fri. 8–5

This parklike cemetery in the heart of East Austin is the final resting place of many of Texas's leaders and personalities. Governors, authors, Texas Rangers, Confederate generals, and signers of the Texas Declaration of Independence are all buried here. Originally planned in 1851, the cemetery underwent a much-needed restoration, spearheaded by Bob Bullock, who has since been buried there, in the 1990s. The results include a gallery and sleek visitors center with displays and information designed to make the cemetery as educational as it is reverential. Genealogists will appreciate the very thorough online master list of burials.

Texas Memorial Museum
512-471-1604
www.utexas.edu/tmm/exhibits
2400 Trinity St., University of Texas at Austin, 78705
Open: Mon.–Fri. 9–5, Sat. 10–5, Sun. 1–5
Admission: Free

The exhibit hall of the Texas Natural Science Center, the Texas Memorial Museum is dedicated to geology, paleontology, zoology, and anthropology, which translates into an eclectic mix of meteorites and dinosaur skeletons, a stuffed Mexican lizard, and Native American artifacts. The knowledgeable and personable staff enlivens what is otherwise a fairly dry presentation. A good museum for the super-curious. The small gift shop stocks some real gems for gift-giving.

Shopping

Austin has perfected the look of vintage urban chic. Shops are filled to the brim with coffee tables, clothing, housewares, signs, and any number of knickknacks from various eras. With other shops selling books, music, and folk art, as well as museum stores and galleries, Austin is great fun for folks who love the thrill of the hunt. Art Austin, www.artaustin.org, a collaborative effort to promote the visual arts in the city, lists additional art galleries on its Web site.

DOWNTOWN AND WEST AUSTIN

Antone's Record Store (512-322-0660; www.antonesrecordshop.com; 2928 Guadalupe St.) Jazz, folk, bluegrass, tons of Texas music, and lots of great blues.

Book People (512-472-5050; www.bookpeople.com; 603 N. Lamar Blvd.) Austin's much-loved independent bookstore and "an outpost for the literate." Almost daily readings, author visits, and public events make it a great destination for bibliophiles young and old. In addition to all manner of books spread out on two floors, Book People carries quirky Texas-themed gifts, both in their store and online.

By George (512-472-5951; www.bygeorgeaustin.com; 524 N. Lamar Blvd.; additional location: 512-472-2731; 2346 Guadalupe St.) In Austin since 1977, By George is a smart clothing store with distinctive style. Urban, sophisticated, and modern without being faddish, the designer clothing reflects the store's owners' personalities, and the store itself is a work of art.

Folk art from Oaxaca, Mexico

Clarksville Pottery (512-454-9079, 877-907-9079; www.clarksvillepottery.com; 4001 N. Lamar Blvd.) What started in 1976 as a tiny pottery studio in Austin's artsy Clarksville has grown into a large professional gallery next to Central Market featuring ceramics, jewelry, art glass, and wood pieces all handcrafted by artisans from Texas and beyond.

Tesoros Trading Company (512-479-8377; www.tesoros.com; 209 Congress Ave.) Purveyors of colorful folk arts, crafts, furniture, and jewelry from more than 15 countries, Tesoros has a wonderful selection of items from Latin America, including Lucha Libre (Mexican wrestling) collectibles.

Waterloo Records (512-474-2500; www.waterloorecords.com; 600A N. Lamar Blvd.) A perennial favorite, Waterloo Records is a die-hard music lover's music store run by die-hard music lovers, a love affair in which sparks still fly. Though the store itself has evolved from its humble beginnings into something big and modern, its philosophy has not. The staff at Waterloo has encyclopedic knowledge of Texas music and would be thrilled to send you home with some local music you'll just love.

Women and Their Work (512-477-1064; www.womenandtheirwork.org; 1710 Lavaca St.) This intriguing art gallery hosts dozens of events each year featuring the visual art, dance, theater, music, literature, and film of female artists; check Web site or call for current listings. The gift shop is packed with pieces from local artisans.

SOUTH AUSTIN

Stroll South Congress Avenue for antiques, resale, and vintage shops.

Allen's Boots (512-447-1413; www.allensboots.com; 1522 S. Congress Ave.) Allen's carries a huge selection of boots, hats, shirts, and belt buckles for cowboys and cowgirls of all ages. Boots range from the modestly priced utilitarian ropers to the fashion-forward, best-selling Old Gringo Celeste Vintage Style # L171-2, a boot with turquoise-colored stars inlaid in warm brown leather, slightly distressed for comfort, which will set you back $300.

Flipnotics (512-322-9750; www.flipnotics.com; 1601 Barton Springs Rd.) New clothes, vintage clothes, and hipster clothes. Also a coffee shop with live music (see "Coffee," below).

Mi Casa Gallery (512-707-9797; www.micasagallery.com; 1700 S. Congress Ave.) What began as one family's love affair with Latin America has grown into a large collection of international treasures ranging from the $3,500 French armoire to hand-hammered copper items from Santa Clara de Cobre, Mexico.

Quincy's Guitars (512-383-0456; www.quincysguitars.com; 515 S. Congress Ave., Suite 106) Quincy's Guitars is a dream for guitar aficionados. The shop has both the comfort of a living room, with guitar picks on the coffee table, and the reserve of a gallery, with Bourgeois, Collings, Goodall, National Reso-phonic, and Webber guitars on display.

Yard Dog (512-912-1613; www.yarddog.com; 1510 S. Congress Ave.) This South Congress gallery gravitates toward folk, outsider, and contemporary art, pieces created by self-taught artists, and anything else that seems to fit its ethos. The small gallery shows national artists, and its exhibits tend to be dynamic and varied. Yard Dog hosts free backyard parties during SXSW (see "Festivals," below), making it a great place to enjoy some visual art in a city overflowing with music.

EAST AUSTIN

Big Red Sun (512-480-9749; www.bigredsun.com; 1102 E. César Chávez St.) Unique gifts, interesting objects for the home, and plenty of plants.

Flatbed Press (512-477-9328; www.flatbedpress.com; 2830 E. MLK Jr. Blvd.) The Flatbed Press is both a publishing workshop specializing in etchings, lithographs, woodcuts, and mono-prints and an art gallery exhibiting the same, as well as paintings, drawings, and photographs.

Pitchforks and Tablespoons (512-494-1464; www.eastsidecafeaustin.com; 2113 Manor Rd.) This tiny shop located beside the Eastside Café sells gardening tools, seeds, and whimsy.

The Performing Arts

Austin just loves to express itself. From classic, contemporary, and country music to dramatic theatrical productions and dance, the city hosts performances practically every day of the year. Construction of the centrally located state-of-the-art Long Center for the Performing Arts is scheduled to finish in spring 2008, bringing dance, music, and the performing arts together under one roof. Until then, be sure to check the Web sites of the various performing arts organizations for the location of their performances. Although less formal, the city's large number of festivals demonstrates its pervasive creativity.

Austin Lyric Opera

512-472-5992 or 1-800-316-7372
www.austinlyricopera.org
901 Barton Springs Rd., Austin, TX 78704

The Austin Lyric Opera (ALO) was founded in 1986, but this newcomer has been producing outstanding opera ever since. Along with other local performing arts organizations, the ALO has plans to move into a permanent performance space at the Long Center for the Performing Arts once the facility is complete.

Austin Symphony

512-476-6064 or 1-888-462-3787
www.austinsymphony.org
1101 Red River St., Austin, TX 78701

The Austin Symphony is essentially homeless, but that doesn't dampen its enthusiasm or its music. Eagerly anticipating its move in 2008 to the brand-new, as-yet-unfinished Long Center for the Performing Arts, the symphony will spend its condensed 2006–7 season at the Bass Concert Hall on the UT campus, ending the season in February before switching to the Riverbend Center (512-372-9416; 722 Jester Blvd.) for the 2007–8 season. In a more settled year, the Austin Symphony typically plays a classical concert series from September through April. Free concerts, including the Fourth of July extravaganza of patriotic music and fireworks, keep listeners happy throughout the summer. Big holiday events, such as Handel's *Messiah* in December and a children's concert at Halloween, make the symphony a perennial favorite.

Ballet Austin

512-476-2163
www.balletaustin.org
501 W. Third St., Austin, TX 78701

Under the direction of Stephen Mills, Ballet Austin dances works such as Twyla Tharp's *The Golden Section*, a blithe rendition of *The Taming of the Shrew*, and the expected holiday tradition, *The Nutcracker*. The ballet has broken ground on a much-needed new facility, with a grand opening scheduled for May 2007.

Dougherty Arts Center

512-397-1468
www.ci.austin.tx.us
1110 Barton Springs Rd., Austin, TX 78704

A local arts center with charming low-key productions put on by groups such as Second Youth Family Theatre.

Esther's Follies

512-320-0198, tickets 512-320-0553
www.esthersfollies.com
525 E. Sixth St., Austin, TX 78701
Showtime: Thu. 8 PM, Fri.–Sat. 8 and 10 PM
Admission: $20, $25

Satirical comedy performed in campy costumes, outrageous makeup, and wacky hairdos. From magic to impersonations, juggling to political parody, Esther's Follies is hysterical. The fact that there is a window onto Sixth Street on the back wall of the stage, through which pedestrians see performers and vice versa, only helps to blur the line between reality and ridiculousness.

Hideout Coffee House and Theatre

512-443-3688
www.hideouttheatre.com
617 Congress Ave., Austin, TX 78701

Located in the little theater district along Congress Avenue, the Hideout shelters improv classes by day and improv performances by night. The frequent performances of the Heroes of Comedy (www.heroesofcomedy.com) will leave you laughing.

Long Center for the Performing Arts

512-482-0800
www.longcenter.org
P.O. Box 301449, Austin, TX 78703
2008 location: 701 W. Riverside Dr., Austin, TX 78704

The Long Center is currently being built. Once finished in the spring of 2008, it will be home to the Austin Symphony, the Austin Lyric Opera, and Ballet Austin, thus consolidating the performing arts in Austin in a venue that rests center stage on the banks of Town Lake. The project is an adaptive reuse of the oval-shaped Palmer Auditorium, adding the expansive and acoustically advanced Michael and Susan Dell Foundation Hall, the flexible Debra and Kevin Rollins Studio Theatre, and the City Terrace, with what should be stunning views of the downtown cityscape.

Paramount Theatre

512-472-5470
www.austintheatrealliance.org
701 Congress Ave., Austin 78701

The Paramount Theatre has been in the entertainment business since 1915, starting with vaudeville, then talkies, and now Broadway shows and classic films. The regional hit *Greater Tuna*, a live comedy performance depicting small-town life in fictional Tuna, Texas, opened here in 1982 to rave reviews. The Paramount Theatre is partners with the nearby State Theater, known for its classic and contemporary plays, which was heavily damaged by flooding in 2006 and remains closed. Details of its reopening may be available on the shared Web site above.

Salvage Vanguard Theater

512-474-SVT6
www.salvagevanguard.org
902 E. Fifth St., Suite 103, Austin, TX 78702

Under director Jason Neulander, the Salvage Vanguard has cut a path all its own, "defying theatrical tradition" without leaving audiences in the dust. A recent play, *The Intergalactic Nemesis*, combines a journey of time travel, the threat of alien invasion, and battles with evildoers in a high-energy production that is both funny and mind-bending.

University of Texas Performing Arts Center

512-471-1444 or 1-800-687-6010
www.utpac.org
510 E. 23rd St., Austin, TX 78712

The University of Texas Performing Arts Center (UTPAC) is made up of several venues: Bass Concert Hall, McCullough Theatre, and Bates Recital Hall on East Campus across from the LBJ Library, just north of the Memorial Stadium; and, on West Campus, Hogg Auditorium near the intersection of 24th and Guadalupe Streets. UTPAC hosts an impressive lineup of touring talent, performing everything from dance, opera, and comedy, to rock, classical, and world music.

Zachary Scott Theater

512-476-0594
www.zachscott.com
1510 Toomey Rd., Austin, TX 78704

While the Zach can do all genres, the ones it seems to do best are the joyous, bittersweet, touching, and wonderfully exuberant musicals. While the season's offerings change, the recent production of *Crowns: The Joyous Gospel Musical*, based on the book *Crowns: Portraits of Black Women in Church Hats*, is a perfect example. Soul-stirring and nothing short of regal, *Crowns* has been held over several times due to overwhelming attendance and enthusiasm. A homage to Austin, *Keepin' It Weird* is so uproariously funny you'll barely flinch when you find out that the material used was culled from over two hundred interviews of residents and notables, all doing their part to keep life in Austin interesting.

The State Theater

Zilker Hillside Theatre

512-479-9491
www.zilker.org
P.O. Box 685093, Austin, TX 78768

Zilker Theatre Productions performs fun Broadway musicals under the stars in the summertime. The theater is essentially a grassy knoll, so bring your own blanket to sit on.

Cinema

When writer/director Richard Linklater and cinematographer Lee Daniel joined forces to make *Slacker* (1991), they endeared themselves to a generation of twenty-somethings trying to figure out what to do with their lives. Following up with *Dazed and Confused* (1993), Linklater garnered a national following and put Austin on the map as a city of slow and creative hipsters. Daniel's latest project, Margaret Brown's much anticipated *Be Here to Love Me: A Film about Townes Van Zandt*, is rumored to be a gem of a tribute. The Austin Film Festival and Cinematexas Film Festival (see "Festivals," below) both offer yet more films to a city in which going to the movies is still about art.

Alamo Drafthouse

512-476-1320
www.drafthouse.com
409-B Colorado St., Austin, TX 78701

The beauty of this Austin-based movie theater chain is that it strives to fulfill the ultimate movie fantasy of great food delivered to your seat with permission to munch as much as you'd like throughout the movie. There are the usual appetizers—mozzarella sticks, jalapeño poppers, and fried pickles served with ranch dressing. You can order the classic Alamo Burger, an angus burger with lettuce, tomato, onions, American cheese, and chipotle mayo, or the vegetarian Splendor in the Grass pizza with zucchini, mushrooms, olives, tomatoes, garlic, and onions. Savor the Dolce Vita—chocolate ice cream bathed in a shot of espresso—and plan to stay up all night. The Alamo shows first-run movies all the time but also hosts special events like Anime Monday, Baby Day Tuesdays, and, on the last Thursday of the month, that essential flick shown by all great movie houses, *The Rocky Horror Picture Show*. Frequent theme nights pair food with film. Additional locations at 2700 W. Anderson, 512-476-1320; 13729 Research Blvd., 512-219-8135; and 1120 S. Lamar, 512-476-1320.

Austin Film Studios

512-322-0145
www.austinfilm.org
1901 E. 51st St., Austin 78723

What started as a bunch of friends watching movies together in 1985 has grown into a nonprofit organization dedicated to the promotion of films and support of creative filmmaking. This translates into a huge range of films, from foreign to independent to documentaries, and some a combination of all, flickering across the screens of the various Alamo Drafthouse Theaters in the city. A must for film buffs.

Dobie Theatre
512-472-3456
www.landmarktheatre.com
2025 Guadalupe St. (in the Dobie Mall), Austin, TX 78705

The Dobie Theatre is located on "The Drag" near UT and was just another college-town theater when Richard Linklater chose it to premiere his films in the late 1980s and early 1990s, thus rocketing the Dobie into the outer stratosphere of popularity. Still a terrific spot for film, the Dobie has plenty of foreign, independent, and well-chosen films showing each night.

Nightlife: Music and Dancing

Austin is well known for the scene on Sixth Street, roughly bounded by Red River Street to the east and Congress Avenue to the west and taking in a several-block strip of bars, restaurants, and clubs on Fifth Street. The adjacent Warehouse District, on Fourth and Fifth Streets between Congress Avenue and Guadalupe Street, is also hopping at night, and together these areas have an irresistible nighttime allure for students and twenty-somethings who pack the streets with boisterous revelry. Radiating out from Sixth Street, things mellow out considerably. Slightly east, on Red River Street, a more local scene prevails, and farther south, the South Congress neighborhood offers individual music venues and late-night eateries.

Practically speaking, clubs and bars card people religiously; so whether you consider it a hassle or a compliment, have your ID at the ready. Those under 21 will not be allowed to drink but are sometimes allowed in for the entertainment; call in advance for the official policy. Most of the venues below are open seven days; the few exceptions are noted. Many have weekday happy hours that are free or charge a nominal fee, usually $5 or less, and all run weekly specials, theme nights, and one-off deals. Whatever the entertainment, you will enjoy a haze-free view thanks to Austin's smoking ban, so smokers should be prepared

Thank You for Not Smoking

In Austin, folks used to assume that, for better or worse, smoking went hand and hand with live music, dancing, and drinking. That was until September 2005, when an ordinance was passed banning smoking in all public buildings and within 15 feet of their entrances throughout the city of Austin. While ordinances like these have passed recently in other American cities, it was of particular interest here, where strong arguments for and against were voiced. Now that the smoke has cleared, there remain only seven places in town where smokers can light up, under a grace period lasting until 2012. So if you need a smoke with your pancakes, try the **IHOP** at I-35 and César Chávez (512-478-1188; www.ihop.com; 707 E. César Chávez St.). Need a beer with your cigarette? Try the **Iron Cactus** on Stonelake (512-794-8778; www.ironcactus.com; 10001 Stonelake Blvd.) or the **Shoal Creek Saloon** (512-474-0805, www.shoalcreeksaloon.com; 909 N. Lamar Blvd.). Go upscale with a cigar and cognac at **Cool River** on Parmer (512-835-0010; www.coolrivercafe.com; 4001 W. Parmer Lane). Or take advantage of the air filtration system installed at **Trudy's** (512-454-1474; www.trudys.com; 8820 Burnet Rd., and 512-326-9899; 4141 S. Capital of Texas Hwy.).

The scene comes alive at night on Sixth Street.

to light up outside. While credit cards are accepted for sit-down drinks and meals, cash is generally used for tips, cover charges, and the $2 beer specials. Since ATM machines in this area see a lot of use, they are frequently out of cash, so consider bringing with you what you plan to spend.

For up-to-the-minute information on Austin's very active nightlife, pick up one of the free copies of the *Austin Chronicle* available around town at bookstores, breakfast and lunch spots, and sidewalk kiosks, or visit their Web site at www.austinchronicle.com. Additionally, Austin 360 at www.austin360.com is a comprehensive online guide to nightlife, movies, entertainment, and dining, and the Calendar section of the *Austin American-Statesman*, Austin's local newspaper, is accessible online at www.statesman.com and lists more of the same.

The line between music venues, bars, and restaurants is blurred in Austin, with many offering a variety of everything. Austinites love to debate the triumphs and shortcomings of the city's best-loved nightlife, but one thing is certain—the classics are classics, and the rest aspire to be.

Antone's
512-320-8424
www.antones.net
213 W. Fifth St., Austin 78701
Open: Daily

Antone's has been around the block a few times. Now on the corner of Sixth and Brazos, the club opened by Clifford Antone in 1975 had to relocate four times before landing in its current home just blocks from where it started. Throughout the years, Antone's has earned a reputation for serving up the finest blues around, and the club, not to mention the music store (see "Shopping," above) and recording label, is still a hands-down favorite among aficionados. Sadly, Antone himself passed away in May 2006, breaking the city's heart, but the music he dedicated his life to nurturing stills envelopes the club he built, and for that Austin will always be grateful.

Austin Music Hall

512-263-4146
www.austinmusichall.com
208 Nueces St., Austin, TX 78701

Large and loud, the Austin Music Hall is the best place to catch big concerts with 2,999 other music lovers. Known for its art deco interior, the Austin Music Hall is scheduled to begin major renovations in 2007, so be sure to check the Web site for updates.

The Backyard

512-263-4146
www.thebackyard.net
13101 TX 71 West, Austin, TX 78738

A huge open-air venue nestled into the Hill Country, shaded by hundreds of live oak trees, the Backyard hosts music events filled with pure magic. With multilevel decks, patios, and a grassy knoll, the Backyard is so relaxed that it feels like, well, your own backyard—except, of course, Willie Nelson, Norah Jones, the Neville Brothers, and Lyle Lovett probably wouldn't play at your house.

The Broken Spoke

512-442-6189
www.brokenspokeaustintx.com
201 S. Lamar Blvd., Austin, TX 78704
Closed: Sun. and Mon.

Pull up to the nondescript, low-slung building that houses the Broken Spoke and you won't guess that you are sidling up to a venerable Austin legend. The Broken Spoke has been hosting honky-tonk a good long time, and they've booked everyone from Tex Ritter to Willie Nelson, George Strait to Jerry Jeff Walker, and they have the pictures on the wall to prove it. The Broken Spoke sells chicken-fried steaks, burgers, and the like, which you can wash down with a Lone Star longneck before hitting the dance floor.

Cactus Café

512-475-6515
www.utexas.edu/student/txunion/ae/cactus
Texas Union Building (24th and Guadalupe Sts.), University of Texas, Austin, TX 78705
Closed: Sun.

Not many university campuses have a music venue with a national reputation for superb acoustics and a list of past performers that reads like a Who's Who of the country, folk, and singer-songwriter circuit. Then again, when that university is UT-Austin, it all makes sense. The Cactus Café opened in 1979 and has since hosted such musicians as Lyle Lovett, Lucinda Williams, Alison Kraus, the Dixie Chicks, Nanci Griffith, and Loudon Wainwright III, to name a few. A café by day with pizza, baked goods, and light lunch fare, the Cactus transforms into an intimate coffeehouse by night, serving coffee and beer. Tickets are first come, first served unless otherwise noted on their Web site. Advance tickets are available for special attractions, booked at the larger Texas Union Theatre and the much larger Texas Union Ballroom. Call the Texas Box Office (512-477-6060) for more information.

Casino el Camino

512-469-9330
www.casinoelcamino.net
517 E. Sixth St., Austin, TX 78701
Open: Daily

The only place in Austin where you get to pick the music, the Casino el Camino has ruled the realm of self-serve sounds for

Outlaws

Some of the best portraits of Texas are sung by its family of musicians, many of whom have earned national recognition for the genius of their technique, the depth of their songwriting, and the sheer amount of heart in their songs. "Outlaw" country music, which took roots in the bars and honky-tonks of Austin and bloomed prolifically throughout the 1970s, offers up some great examples.

In the 1960s a disillusioned Willie Nelson decided he'd had his fill of predictable drinking and cheating songs shined to a high gloss in Nashville studios, and quit Tennessee for Texas. In Austin he met renegades Waylon Jennings, Billy Joe Shaver, Kris Kristofferson, and Townes Van Zandt, among others, and they put their guitars and songs together and invented the genre of outlaw country.

While the name came from Jennings's 1972 song "Ladies Love Outlaws," the spirit came directly from the musicians themselves. Intent on bucking the system, they wrote raw country music influenced by the revolutionary rock and folk music of their era, and their intensely personal lyrics struck a chord with listeners. Powered by fierce individuality and abundant talent, this antiestablishment music broke into the mainstream, influencing countless musicians along the way.

Besides the pioneers listed above, Guy Clark, David Allan Coe, Jessi Colter, Joe Ely, Jimmy Dale Gilmore, Butch Hancock, Johnny Rodriguez, Kimmie Rhodes, and Jerry Jeff Walker, though they might not all be from Texas, are all classic outlaws. Stop in at any local record store and have a listen.

years. Order up a table full of burgers, hot dogs, buffalo wings—or a grilled eggplant sandwich with olive tapenade for vegetarians—and french fries, pop quarter after quarter into the legendary jukebox, and sit back and enjoy your customized evening soundtrack. That is, until someone else's intervenes.

Cedar Street Courtyard

512-495-9669
www.cedarstreetaustin.com
208 W. Fourth St., Austin, TX 78701
Open: Daily

The Cedar Street Courtyard mixes martinis with live music in its outdoor courtyard. Consider kick-starting your night with the Koffee Kerouac—a Fris vodka, Kahlua, and Bailey's creation with a shot of coffee. Or, mellow out with a Zilker—Stoli vodka shaken with Midori melon liqueur. Smoking is permitted. If the party gets rained on, things tend to move next door to Málaga Tapas and Bar (see "Dining," below), which is owned by the same folks.

The Continental

512-441-2444
www.continentalclub.com
1315 S. Congress Ave., Austin, TX 78704
Open: Daily

The Continental has been a heavy hitter in the live-music scene since it opened in 1957, but its current owner is responsible for giving it the retro look and feel that have become such a part of its identity today. While it is still known for booking great music almost every night of the week, what makes this place really popular are its rockin' happy hours, most notably on Tuesday, when the fun starts at 4 PM.

Elephant Room

512-473-2279
www.natespace.com/elephant
315 Congress Ave., Austin, TX 78701
Open: Daily

Even if it is in a basement, the Elephant Room is the high-water mark for jazz in Austin. Identifiable by the small neon sign that glows from a window at sidewalk level, the club is intimate, dim, and alluring in the way that these sorts of venues should be. Twenty different draft beers and plenty of high-quality acts make for a great alternative to the Sixth Street scene.

Elysium

512-478-2979
www.elysiumonline.net
705 Red River St., Austin, TX 78701
Closed: Mon.

While they "encourage fabulousness always," you can wear anything you'd like to this good-natured industrial Goth dance lair. Weekends (Thursday through Saturday) are reserved for live music, and Wednesday and Sunday are earmarked for popular throwback '80s theme nights.

Emo's

512-477-3667
www.emosaustin.com
603 Red River St., Austin, TX 78701
Open: Daily

Emo's has two music stages, one inside and one out, a beer garden, and a bar, which makes it well-equipped for its admitted specialty: drunken debauchery. The bands here tend to be loud, the energy high, and the patrons young. Emo's is known for top-notch, almost-nightly bookings and is certainly one venue to keep your eye on for local talent or rising stars.

Maggie Mae's

512-478-8541
www.maggiemaesaustin.com
323 E. Sixth St., Austin, TX 78701
Open: Daily

For 25 years, Maggie Mae's has been keeping Sixth Street rocking with that archetypal college town combination of beer and cover bands.

Málaga Tapas Bar

512-236-8020
www.malagatapasbar.com
208 W. Fourth St., Austin, TX 78701
Closed: Sun.

Central Texas has plenty of open-air informality and country music, day and night.

A sophisticated tapas bar with an urban, loftlike atmosphere complete with hardwood floors, exposed brick, and walls of built-in wooden wine racks. The menu includes various tastings, such as the *queso de cabra frito*—breaded and fried goat cheese cakes with a red onion marmalade, drizzled with honey—all perfectly complemented by the 50-bottle menu of wine by the glass. Candlelit tables add romance.

Opal Divine's Freehouse

512-477-3308
www.opaldivines.com
700 W. Sixth St., Austin, TX 78701
Open: Daily

Opal Divine's has one of the best selections of wine and spirits in Austin, including 65 kinds of single-malt scotch. Not to mention a very nice assortment of mixed drinks, and a range of specialty beers for those who like to mix it up. The large menu is filled with specialties like cheese steak tacos and *migas*. The establishment is named for the owner's grandmother, Opal Divine, who loved to live it up. Live music.

Reed's Jazz and Supper Club

512-342-7977
www.sgrg.com/reeds
9901 Capital of Texas Hwy., Suite 150, Austin, TX 78729
On the corner of Stonelake Blvd. near the Arboretum
Closed: Sun.

With the house band covering Billie Holiday, Cole Porter, and Duke Ellington, leather banquettes, sumptuous red-velvet curtains draped throughout the joint, and classic steak tartare on the menu, Reed's is a vintage throwback that hits the mark. The grand spiral staircase allows everyone a dramatic entrance, and if the whole scene makes you think of Rick's Café American in Casablanca, then Reed's mission is complete.

The Saxon Pub

512-488-2552
www.thesaxonpub.com
1320 S. Lamar Blvd., Austin, TX 78704

Free-flowing draft beer and nightly music, mostly singer-songwriters and Texas talent, make the Saxon Pub a terrific spot to kick back with the locals. The free happy-hour concerts Tuesday through Friday start at 6. Darts, pool, sports on the big screen, and free WiFi keep patrons busy in between sets. Great music and down-to-earth affability put the Saxon Pub on the short list of classic Austin hangouts.

Scholz Garten

512-474-1958
www.scholzgarten.net
1607 San Jacinto Blvd., Austin, TX 78701
Open: Daily

In business since 1866, this German *Biergarten* is the place to stop in, whet your whistle, and listen to some oompah music as belted out by the house Wurst Band, or maybe join the pandemonium of the crowds on game night.

WAREHOUSE DISTRICT

Stubb's Bar-B-Q

512-480-8341
www.stubbsbbq.com
801 Red River St., Austin, TX 78701
Closed: Mon.

With personality, talent, and sheer will, Christopher "Stubb" Stubblefied managed to cook his way from Lubbock, through the Korean War with the 96th Field Artillery (the last all-black army infantry), to the center of the burgeoning music scene in Austin in the 1970s. Combining two loves, BBQ and music, Stubb's restaurant was soon booking musicians like Muddy Waters, John Lee Hooker, Willie Nelson, Johnny Cash, and many others who loved

Drinks

Sometimes the best way to get to know a town is just sit down and have a drink with the locals. The following are a few suggestions, scattered about town.

Manuel's (512-472-7555; www.manuels.com; 310 Congress Ave., and 512-345-1042; 10201 Jollyville Rd.) serves prickly-pear margaritas and half-price appetizers during the daily happy hour from 4 to 7. Grown-ups might enjoy the selection at **Cork & Co.** (512-474-2675; www.cordandco.com; 308 Congress Ave.), a wine shop and tasting room with over 100 bottles, a precious few from Texas. Farther along Congress, the hip **Light Bar** (512-473-8544; www.lightbaraustin.com; 408 Congress Ave.) has a great outdoor terrace with views of downtown. While the decor may be Prohibition era, the drinks are flowing inside **Speakeasy** (512-476-8017; 412-D Congress Ave.) in the Warehouse District. On Red River Street, the patio at the hipster haven **Club de Ville** (512-457-0900;

900 Red River St.) is one of the best in Austin, and everyone is welcome. Step off busy South Congress Avenue and into the serene courtyard of the **Hotel San José** (see "Lodging," above), where everyone is welcome for drinks. Head west to South First Street and pop in at **Freddie's** or **Shady Grove** on Barton Springs, both of which offer casual drinks and food with plenty of shade trees under which to enjoy them. Just north of campus, the **Crown & Anchor** (512-322-9168; 2911 San Jacinto Blvd.) is a graduate student hangout with 32 beers on tap. Both **Asti** (512-451-1218; www.astiaustin .com; 408C E. 43rd St.) in Duval Square and **Fino** (512-474-2905; www.astiaustin.com; 2905 San Gabriel St.) are sophisticated restaurants and wine bars serving upscale trattoria food and luscious desserts for both lunch and dinner. The restaurants around Lake Austin are always a good bet for casual drinks, live music, and a view.

---

playing the outdoor venue to the sweet smell of slow-cookin' 'cue. These days, a more commercial and streamlined Stubb's is a major music venue and sells sauce in a bottle, but the old Austin favorite remains 100 percent pure Texas.

La Zona Rosa
512-263-4146
www.zonarosa.com

612 W. Fourth St., Austin, TX 78701
Open: Daily

This former Mexican restaurant now serves as a major music venue with two stages—the smaller in a club atmosphere and the larger just wide-open space—both filled nightly with big sound and wall-to-wall fans. A great place to catch an A-list act up close, but get there early 'cause everyone already knows.

AUSTIN CITY LIMITS

In 1975 local PBS affiliate KLRU, riding the wave of the city's burgeoning music scene, began taping live performances of singers, songwriters, and musicians to broadcast, calling their show AUSTIN CITY LIMITS. Simple production and an intimate stage allowed the music to stand on its own, and the combination was an immediate hit. Since its inception, the show has hosted more than five hundred artists, some well known and others less so, but all immensely talented. AUSTIN CITY LIMITS has brought a tremendous range of music to its viewers, from country and bluegrass to blues, folk, and zydeco. Watching the show is both a pleasure and an education.

It is possible to watch a live taping of AUSTIN CITY LIMITS, but only a precious few have the privilege each year. Call the KLRU hotline (512-475-9007) for details of the recording schedule and complicated ticket distribution process. The show is taped in a small studio on the sixth floor of the University of Texas College of Communication, located at 26th and Guadalupe Streets, but plans for the construction of a larger venue are being considered in earnest. Though your chances of seeing a show are slim, visitors are able to tour the studio (www.pbs.org/klru/austin; or see "Tours," below, for more details). Don't miss the fantastic AUSTIN CITY LIMITS Festival (see "Festivals," below) in September.

Festivals

Festivals are what Austin does best, and it hosts plenty of them. For specific information, check the calendars in the *Austin American-Statesman* or online at www.austin360.com.

MONTHLY

The Austin Farmers' Market (www.austinfarmersmarket.org) Saturday-morning market at the corner of Fourth and Guadalupe Streets and Wednesday-afternoon market at Whole Foods Market on Sixth Street and Lamar are not exactly festivals, but they certainly have a festive atmosphere.

FEBRUARY

Mid-Winter Music Festival (512-476-3991; www.aftm.us) A celebration of traditional, folk, and international music and dance organized by the Austin Friends of Traditional Music organization, which sponsors additional festivals throughout the year. Admission charged.

MARCH

South by Southwest (SXSW) (512-467-7979; www.sxsw.com) A conference for film, multimedia, and music with performances and presentations. Admission charged.

Star of Texas Fair and Rodeo (512-919-3000; www.staroftexas.org) Livestock show, rodeos, BBQ cook-off, and the popular kickoff event, the Cowboy Breakfast. Admission and free.

Zilker Kite Festival (512-647-7488; www.zilkerkitefestival.com) A family-friendly festival with dozens of kites dancing above Zilker Park. Free.

APRIL
Austin Fine Arts Festival (512-458-6073; www.austinfineartsfestival.org) This juried art show also showcases food and music. Admission charged.

Austin International Poetry Festival (512-349-9883; www.aipf.org) Free.

Eeyore's Birthday (512-448-5160; www.eeyores.sexton.com) This groovy event benefits nonprofit groups in Austin and is more than 40 years old. Admission charged.

Old Settler's Music Festival (www.oldsettlersmusicfest.org) International, national, and regional artists performing Americana music. Held in the Ben McCulloch Campgrounds in Driftwood, just south of Austin. Admission charged.

Saveur Texas Hill Country Wine and Food Festival (512-542-WINE; www.texaswineand food.org) Celebration of wine, food, and Central Texas with events in Austin and the surrounding Hill Country. Admission charged.

MAY
Cinco de Mayo (512-867-1999; www.austincinco.com) Commemoration and celebration of the Mexican army's victory over the French at the Battle of Puebla on May 5, 1862. A joyous cultural festival featuring events throughout the city. Free.

JUNE
Juneteenth (512-974-4926; www.ci.austin.tx.us/carver) Remembering June 19, 1865, the day that slaves in Texas first received word of the Emancipation Proclamation. A spirited citywide celebration of freedom. Visit the George Washington Carver Museum and Cultural Center (see "Museums," above) in East Austin for more information. Admission charged.

JULY
Austin Chamber Music Festival (512-454-0026; www.austinchambermusic.org) Enjoy chamber music in various venues throughout the city. Free.

Bastille Day (512-472-8180; www.frenchlegationmuseum.org) A French-fest hosted by the French Legation Museum (see "Museums," above). Free.

Zilker Summer Musical (512-479-9491; www.zilker.org) Outstanding family-friendly musicals performed outdoors. Free.

AUGUST
Austin Chronicle Hot Sauce Contest (www.austinchronicle.com) Beer, music, and lots of spicy sauce. Take a taste and feel the burn. Admission charged.

Austin City Limits Music Festival (www.aclfest.com) More than a hundred bands play to the crowds for three days straight. An Austin original. Admission charged.

Austin Latino Comedy Fiesta (512-389-0892; www.lcp.org) Stand-up and sketch comedy hosted by Latino Comedy Project. Admission charged.

SEPTEMBER
Austin Gay and Lesbian International Film Festival (512-302-9889; www.agliff.org) Edgy films tackling a wide range of topics. Admission charged.

Austin Shakespeare Festival (512-454-2273; www.austinshakespeare.org) Admission charged.

Bat Fest (512-441-9015; www.roadstarproductions.com) Lots of arts, crafts, food, music, and fun on the Congress Avenue Bridge, with proceeds to benefit Bat Conservation International. Admission charged.

Cinematexas International Short Film and Video Festival (512-471-6497; www.cinema texas.org) Competition and screenings. Admission charged.

Diez y Seis Celebration (512-974-6715) A celebration of Mexico's independence from Spain on September 16, 1821. Celebrations at Republic Square, Fifth and Guadalupe Streets. Free.

Old Pecan Street Fall Arts Festival (512-441-9015; www.roadstarproductions.com) Live music, arts and crafts, and a carnival for children. Admission charged.

OCTOBER

Austin Film Festival (512-792-4795 or 1-800-310-3378; www.austinfilmfestival.com) A multiday film festival attracting big Hollywood names and independent upstarts. Film buffs will enjoy the quality and range of the offerings. Admission charged.

Texas Parks & Wildlife Expo (1-800-792-1112; www.tpwd.state.tx.us/expo) A chance to chat about Texas parks and wildlife with the knowledgeable folks at the Park Service. Free.

NOVEMBER

Austin Celtic Festival (512-498-4908; www.austincelts.org/festival) Celtic bands from Austin and around the world. Admission charged.

Austin Powwow and American Indian Heritage Festival (512-371-0628; www.austin powwow.org) Spectacular celebration of Native American culture, the largest of its kind in the region, with food, music, and performances. Admission charged.

Dia de los Muertos (512-480-9373; www.mexic-artemuseum.org) "The Day of the Dead" is the ancient cultural tradition in which families "welcome back" departed loved ones, commemorating them through special altars and cemetery visits. Poetry readings and *calavera* processions, in which participants dress as skeletons, are especially moving. Free and admission.

DECEMBER

Armadillo Christmas Bazaar (www.armadillobazaar.com) A casual, artsy market with lots of gifts ideas. Admission charged.

Super Fest

If you are lucky enough to be in town at the right time and get tickets, Austin's music festivals rock. Maybe it's the first breezes of spring that make everyone so frisky, but South by Southwest (see above), held in March, is just one big, weeklong party. Sure, it's technically more of a conference for those in the music, film, and multimedia industries where talent is "discovered" and deals are signed, but for the bar and club owners who have to clean up after the crowd leaves, it's just one long, beer-soaked bash. In September, the AUSTIN CITY LIMITS Festival (see above) is tamer and tends to be a more local affair, but it's growing fast as word catches on.

Trail of Lights and Zilker Christmas Tree (512-974-6700; www.ci.austin .tx.us/tol)
Austin makes up for a lack of snow with a plethora of lights. Free.

Victorian Christmas on Sixth Street (512-441-9015; www.roadstarproductions.com)
Food vendors in Dickens-era costumes along with arts, crafts, and carolers. Free.

DINING

In general, Austinites are an adventurous and easygoing bunch, and the restaurants that
serve them tend to reflect this sensibility. Austin is a relatively small city, and its roots as
an overgrown college town are most apparent in its food scene, which is largely dominated
by modestly priced menus served in a relaxed atmosphere. Not surprisingly, the most represented cuisines in Austin are American, BBQ, Continental, Mexican, southern, and Tex-
Mex, and the variations and combinations of these themes seem endless. While those who
live here would warmly welcome more selection—new restaurants are quickly mobbed—
visitors still have plenty to choose from.

The secret to dining in Austin is to focus on the well-done. Whether you're in an
upscale restaurant or a neighborhood coffee shop, the charm of eating out in Austin is in
the details, with an emphasis on quality and personality. At any price level, many menus
feature creative seasonal fare accompanied by plenty of vegetables, meal-sized salads,
and hearty soups, frequently made with organic ingredients. Vegetarians and the health-
conscious will find themselves in unusually good company in Austin, where restaurant
menus tend to be diverse. Austin chefs love using locally grown or produced items, and
regional wines, cheeses, game, fruits, and vegetables are often highlighted. The many,
many individually owned and operated restaurants in Austin are very much rooted in their
neighborhoods and their city, with a large number of them supporting local causes, partic-
ipating in community events, and providing venues for local musicians and visual artists.

Now for the details. As you will undoubtedly notice, casual attire—some people wear
shorts and flip-flops throughout the better part of the year—is commonplace. Wearing
"business casual" is appropriate for most of the pricier establishments, though you won't
feel out of place should you decide to dress up for a fancy, formal meal. Families seem
especially welcome in Austin's eating establishments, most of which offer booster seats,
kids' menus, and a friendly atmosphere. Generally, credit cards are accepted, and I have
noted the occasional place where they are not. Reservations should be considered essential
at the more expensive and popular spots, and I have recommended making them if necessary. You are not allowed to smoke in any public building or within 15 feet from the
entrance to one. There are several establishments exempt from this regulation, at least
through 2012, and they are listed under "Nightlife," above. As with everything, details
change, so please call ahead to ensure your visit to one of Austin's restaurants goes
smoothly.

The restaurants below are local favorites and include those that are frequently and
enthusiastically voted onto citywide "best of" lists. Many have been around for years,
changing with tastes or remaining exactly the same. Some are uniquely Austin, and others
have a more universal appeal. Some are exquisitely appointed, with lovely stemware and
thick napkins, while others are earthy, with sticky beer-stained barstools and self-serve
plastic cutlery, but all are filled with the locals who love them. This list is by no means
exhaustive, and if your taste buds have you salivating for something specific, check out

www.austin360.com, the *Austin American-Statesman's* online listing of food, entertainment, and events, for all restaurant reviews ever written, organized by cuisine.

Restaurants with two codes have a menu that spans the price range indicated, offering, for example, a vegetarian entrée at one end of the spectrum and a premium steak at the other.

Dining Price Code

Inexpensive	Up to $12
Moderate	$12 to $25
Expensive	$25 to $40
Very Expensive	$40 or more

DOWNTOWN

In downtown Austin you are as likely to find a $100 meal as you are a $2 breakfast taco. This variety is what makes it a great place to eat for politicians, professionals, visitors, and students alike.

Café at the Four Seasons

512-685-8300
www.fourseasons.com/austin
98 San Jacinto Blvd., Austin, TX 78701
Open: Mon.–Fri. 6:30 AM–10 PM, Sat. 7 AM–10 PM, Sun. 7 AM–10 PM
Price: Very Expensive
Special Features: Reservations recommended

The Café at the Four Seasons is one of the most elegant and sophisticated dining experiences in Austin. Chef Elmar Prambs' attention to detail yields outstanding entrées such as his signature pork tenderloin schnitzel served with purple cabbage, chive spaetzle, and caramelized Gala apples drizzled with citrus sauce. Central Texas is well represented with items such as the Bella Verdi Farms Micro Greens Salad, served with creamy Dripping Springs goat cheese, forest mushrooms, and a splash of walnut vinaigrette. Vegetarians, children, and even those craving a burger are all pleasantly accommodated. The Sunday brunch (adults $49, children $21) is particularly outstanding. From the sweet pancakes and waffles to smoked meats and made-to-order omelets, sushi, and seafood, brunch is a decadent way to sample, or stuff yourself with, all the dishes the Four Seasons has to offer. Unlimited champagne and mimosas throughout the meal and a chocolate fountain, among other desserts, only add to the indulgence. The dining room is roomy, warm, and inviting, but if the weather is right, the terrace can't be beat, with cozy cushions, white umbrellas, gentle breezes, and views of Town Lake.

Clay Pit

512-322-5131
www.claypit.com
1601 Guadalupe St., Austin, TX 78701
Open: Lunch Mon.–Fri. 11–2, Sat. noon–3; dinner Sun.–Thu. 5–10, Fri.–Sat. 5–11
Price: Inexpensive to Moderate

Contemporary Indian curries, grill items, seafood, and a range of vegetarian dishes spiced with fresh ginger, cumin, garlic, and tangy tamarind chutney of varying degrees of heat are sure to please any palate. The house specialty, *Khuroos-E-Tursh*, is a moist chicken breast stuffed with seasoned spinach, mushrooms, onion, and cheese and simmered in a rich cashew-almond cream sauce that is both sweet and savory. Vegetarian options are plentiful. Prompt, friendly service and the restaurant's sophisticated interior design, complete with thick cloth napkins and pleasantly low lighting, give it an upscale feel, while large portions, modest prices, and a plentiful daily lunch buffet make Clay Pit a great value.

The Driskill Grill

512-391-7162
www.driskillhotel.com
604 Brazos St., Austin, TX 78701

Open: Tue.–Sat. 5:30 PM–10 PM
Price: Very Expensive
Special Features: Reservations recom-
  mended

Bolstered by local and national accolades, the Driskill Grill has become Austin's premiere dining experience, and its chef, David Bull, has joined the ranks of the celebrity chefs feted on Food Network. The thrill of the Driskill is the marriage of its lovely, old-time surroundings, a level of opulence not usually witnessed in Central Texas, and the innovative culinary feats of its young chef. The menu is market-driven, as in the farmer's market. Items such as heirloom tomatoes served with mozzarella and a black pepper brioche, hot smoked Bandera quail with a coriander orange curd, and the local Jameson Farms rack of lamb accompanied by a mushroom risotto are the sorts of dishes that make the Driskill Grill so very representative of Austin and the sur-rounding region. The dessert menu includes Orange Marshmallow with Earl Grey Caramel, Kumquat Preserve, Malted Milk Chocolate *Fredo*, and Vanilla Vodka Ice—all good examples of the sort of inspired creativity you can expect to the very last bite. A three-course meal is $65; six courses is $95, or $125 with wine; and the nine-course Chef's Tasting Menu is $125, or $175 paired with wine. Chef Bull's latest book is available at the Driskill and local bookstores. The attached Driskill Bar is a good place for drinks.

1886 Café and Bakery

512-391-7121
www.1886cafeandbakery.com
604 Brazos St., Austin, TX 78701
Open: Daily 7 AM–10 PM, Fri.–Sat. 7 AM–
  midnight
Price: Inexpensive to Moderate

Located in the Driskill Hotel, the 1886 Café, or as the hotel likes to call it,

Texas for Foodies

Central Texas makes some fantastic food, much of it easily found in the upscale food emporiums of Austin-based Whole Foods and San Antonio-based Central Market.

With an emphasis on quality produce and products, both Whole Foods and Central Market have tapped into the market of con-scious consumers. While doing all your gro-cery shopping here can get pricey, the elaborate deli services, self-serve soup and salad bars, a variety of prepared foods, and wonderful coffees and baked goods make them the perfect spots to grab a bite. The wide range of regional specialties, including Texas wines, makes for fun browsing. Both establishments have become destinations in their own right, places locals love to bring out-of-towners.

Central Market (512-206-1000; www.cen tralmarket.com; 4001 N. Lamar Blvd.) Ample outdoor seating and a playground make this location a family favorite. Additional location: 4477 S. Lamar Blvd., 512-899-4300. Open: Daily 8 am–9 pm.

Whole Foods Market (512-476-1206; www.wholefoodsmarket.com; 601 N. Lamar Blvd.) Shaded picnic tables and a rooftop play structure gives this location appeal. Additional location: 9607 Research Blvd., at TX 183 and Loop 360, 512-345-5003. Open: Daily 8 AM–10 PM.

"Austin's Original Socializing Parlor," serves wonderful soups, sandwiches, baked goods, and desserts amid lavish surround-ings. The all-day menu is more modestly priced than the Driskill Grill and is served until 10 PM. The Hippy Hollow, a breakfast scramble of eggs, spinach, and goat cheese; the waffles with Texas pecans, bananas, and blackberry jam; and the eggs Benedict with grilled beef tenderloin, jack cheese, and salsa on a toasted muffin are several items

The Best Burgers in Texas

One of the more popular topics of local conversation and Internet blogs is the location of the best burger in Austin. No one's talking price or service, and just about everyone is willing to overlook atmosphere. The spotlight is on that winning combination of meat, bun, and condiments. Folks here, especially old-time Austinites, feel passionately about their favorites and are willing to discuss, in minute and graphic detail, the various pros and cons of the perennial contenders. Since I wouldn't want to unduly influence your palate, I have compiled a list of the classics, arranged here alphabetically, all of which are always in the running and all standouts in their own right.

Burger Tex

512-453-8772

www.burgertex.com

5420 Airport Blvd., Austin, TX 78751

Open: Mon.–Sat. 10:40–9

What makes this place great are the "choice chuck" patties, the freshly baked buns, and the condiment bar that gives you control over your own toppings. The pool table, drop ceilings, brick walls, and faux wood laminate tables certainly create the impression you are eating in your own retro basement rec room.

Burger Tex II

512-477-8433

2912 Guadalupe St., Austin, TX 78705

Open: Mon.–Sat. 11–9

Special Features: Korean BBQ

With entirely different ownership, location, look and feel, Burger Tex II also serves a Bulgoki Burger, strips of thinly sliced beef marinated in soy sauce, ginger, and garlic marinade, giving it that saucy twang that keeps folks coming back for more.

Dirty Martin's Place

512-477-3173

www.dirtymartins.com

2808 Guadalupe St., Austin, TX 78705

Open: 11–11

Special Features: Outdoor terrace

Known simply as Dirty's, this venerable Austin institution near campus has cooked up countless burgers to feed the scores of UT students who every day buzz by the white frame drive-in looking for that perfect lunch, dinner, or late-night snack. Counter seating gives you a great view of the griddle and schooling in time-honored burger handling skills. Russet fries and thickly breaded onion rings round out an experience that some would say is a must.

The Four Seasons

512-478-4500

www.fourseasons.com/austin

98 San Jacinto Blvd., Austin, TX 78701

Open: Mon.–Fri. 6:30 AM–10 PM, Sat.–Sun. 7 AM–10 PM

Special Features: Outdoor terrace

The Four Seasons, where hamburgers are no longer on the menu, nevertheless serves roughly a hundred of its ground tenderloin and strip loin burgers a week, making it not only one of the best burger places, but also one of the best-kept secrets, in Texas. One bite of this $14 masterpiece and you'll know why this elusive burger is worth seeking out.

Frisco Shop

512-459-6279

5819 Burnet Rd., Austin, TX 78756

Open: Sun.–Wed. 7 AM–9 PM, Thu.–Sat. 7 AM–10 PM

The last of the city's famous Nighthawk chain, the Frisco Shop carries on the tradition of its signature Frisco Burger, a basic burger topped with lettuce, cheese, a dollop of their special Russian-style dressing, and a spoonful of pickle relish, all served on a toasted bun and neatly swaddled in paper.

The Best Burgers in Texas continued

Hill-Bert's
512-452-2317
www.hill-bertsburgers.com
3303 N. Lamar Blvd., Austin, TX 78705
Open: Daily 10–10
Additional Location: 5340 Cameron Rd., on the east side, just north of the I-35 and E. 51st St. intersection, 512-371-3717

The homemade whole-grain buns are toothsome and the thick patties always juicy. Add fresh condiments, crisp onion rings and fries, and a thick milkshake and you've got a winner.

Hill's Cafe
512-851-9300
www.hillscafe.com
4700 S. Congress Ave., Austin, TX 78745
Open: Mon.–Thu. 11–10, Fri.–Sat. 11–10:30, Sun. 11–9
Special Features: Free Wi-Fi; live music

After half a century of doing business in Austin, Hill's Cafe changed hands. Soon after, new owner Bob Cole received an e-mail telling him how horrible his hamburgers were. Instead of getting defensive, Bob got busy and created what was recently voted the "Best Burger in Austin." Sure it costs almost eight bucks, but who can put a price on perfection? Burgers aside, Hill's is also a standout in the live music and BBQ categories. If you go, go hungry.

Hut's Hamburgers
512-472-0693
www.hutshamburgers.citysearch.com
807 W. Sixth St., Austin, TX 78703
Open: Mon.–Sat. 11–10, Sun. 11:30–10

Hut's is one of those crowded, chock-full-of-memorabilia places that everybody loves. Diners happily overlook sticky soda spills and elbow-to-elbow seating because the great burgers always come out hot, smothered with creative toppings, and accompanied by mounds of fries or onion rings. Blue-plate specials change constantly, and the two-for-one deal offered Monday, Wednesday, and Friday at lunchtime is a hard bargain to resist. Vegetarians are surprisingly well served.

Hyde Park Bar and Grill
512-458-3168
426 Duval St., Austin, TX 78751
Open: Daily 11 AM–midnight

The half-pound sirloin burger is fantastic alone, but pair it with their fabulous fries and you have a match made in heaven. The Hyde Park Bar and Grill is renowned for its french fries. Strings of Idaho potatoes are dipped in buttermilk, dredged in seasoned flour, and fried in peanut oil just before arriving, hot and crisp, at your table. The Hyde Park Bar and Grill stays open late, making it both a neighborhood hangout and a citywide favorite for nocturnal noshing. Located in Hyde Park; the enormous fork marks the spot.

You can't miss the sign in front of the Hyde Park Bar and Grill.

continued on next page

The Best Burgers in Texas continued

Nau's Enfield Drug

512-476-1221

1115 W. Lynn St., Austin, TX 78703

Open: Mon.–Fri. 7:30 AM–4 PM, Sat. 8 AM–2:30 PM; closed Sun.

Special Features: Pharmacy

Sit at the mint green counter and spin in the salmon-colored swivel seats while you wait for your simple, juicy burger to do its time on the

grill in this old-fashioned pharmacy. If the ambience doesn't take you back to being a kid, the homemade Blue Bell shakes, malts, and crispy-on-the-outside, gooey-on-the-inside grilled cheese sandwiches just might. In addition to burgers, Nau's also serves breakfast.

Shady Grove

512-474-9991

www.theshadygrove.com

1624 Barton Springs Rd., Austin, TX 78704

Open: Sun.–Thu. 11–10:30, Fri.–Sat. 11–11

Special Features: Live music; movies

Enjoy an archetypal burger with all the fixings in this restaurant whose style is best described as 1940s burger joint meets state park lodge. While some may consider it heresy, Shady Grove also makes a nice veggie burger. Take in live music or classic movies in the pecan grove under the stars. Music Thursday nights starting at 8; call or check the Web site for lineup.

---

that make this café a great place to stop in for a taste of Texas. Breakfast is served Monday through Friday until 11 AM, Saturday and Sunday until 2:30 PM. The all-day menu is served daily from 11 AM until close.

Katz's

512-472-2037

www.katzneverkloses.com

618 W. Sixth St., Austin, TX 78701

Open: Daily

Price: Inexpensive to Moderate

Special Features: Open 24 hours

As you may have noticed from their Web site address, "Katz Never Kloses," and therein lies one of the most endearing qualities of this longtime New York–style Austin deli. Just blocks from Sixth Street and the Warehouse District, it doesn't have to be a traditional mealtime for Katz's to be busy. Breakfast is the usual array of pan-

cakes, waffles, eggs, and lox with something you will most likely find only in Texas: the kosher-style tacos—breakfast tacos served with salami, a fire dog, and potato pancakes. Hot pastrami sandwiches for lunch, Hebrew National hot dogs, potato knishes, knockwurst, and, oddly enough, Yankee pot roast for dinner, with sweet cheese blintzes for dessert. A classic deli menu. Prices are a bit steep, and some longtime residents would say the food isn't quite what it used to be, but when you need potato pancakes at 3 AM in Central Texas, Katz's just can't be beat.

Las Manitas

(see p. 81)

Noodle-ism

512-275-9988

www.noodle-ism.com

105 W. Fifth St., Austin, TX 78703

Open: Mon.–Thu. 11–10, Fri. 11–11,

Sat. noon–11, Sun. noon–9
Price: Inexpensive

Noodle-ism's soothing wonton soup or tangy *dan dan* noodles with peanut sauce can be a refreshing change of pace from Austin's beloved chicken enchiladas and baby back ribs. The menu here is flexible. Pick from one of the tantalizing Asian-style noodle dishes, or customize the contents and spiciness of one of your own. Dishes are fresh and served hot, though a lunchtime crunch can sometimes put a kink in service. The refreshing iced green tea is only slightly sweetened, a nice departure from the sugary southern sweet tea served everywhere else. Delightful black-and-white photographs of a toddler slurping soup hang on every wall; super-cute, they are sure to make you super-hungry.

SOUTH CONGRESS

Directly across Town Lake from downtown, South Austin is home to a disproportionate number of fun and funky local favorites, which are usually filled for breakfast, lunch, and dinner.

El Sol y la Luna

512-444-7770
www.elsolylalunaaustin.com
1224 S. Congress Ave., Austin, TX 78704
Open: Sun.–Tue. 7 AM–3 PM, Wed.–
    Sat. 7 AM–10 PM
Price: Inexpensive
Special Features: Live music

Long before South Congress was trendy, there was El Sol y la Luna. Since it opened in 1995, this friendly Mexican and Central American restaurant tucked into a former coffee shop in the quirky Austin Motel (see "Lodgings," above) has marched to a different drummer. The menu here is freewheeling, and the restaurant's adaptations, reinterpretations, and complete lack of self-consciousness when it comes to cooking have kept the food consistently great and the crowds happy since its inception. Soups are a big hit, with the hearty *Caldo del Sol*, a chicken and vegetable soup served with avocado and tortillas, available weekdays, and the comforting *pozole*, a hominy soup with chicken, simmering on the stove weekends. Large salads are built around beds of organic greens, with ingredients ranging from jicama to tofu. *Platos* such as the fried catfish, Mexican *barbacoa* (BBQ), and *mole* chicken are favorites. Though available only in season, the *plato Cubano*, fried plantains with sour cream, black beans, and rice, is not to be missed. While the sun has yet to set on the gentrification of South Congress, El Sol y la Luna seems unfazed and holds steady to its timeless Austin vibe.

Enoteca

512-441-7672
1610 S. Congress Ave., Austin, TX 78704
Open: Mon.–Sat. 8 AM–10 PM, Sun. 10–3
Price: Inexpensive to Moderate

Though run by the same folks as Vespaio (see below) and located right next door, Enoteca has a much more casual look and feel with small, informal, cloth-covered

Ice Cream Dream

Amy's Ice Cream (512-458-6895; www.amysicecream.com; 3500 Guadalupe St.) An Austin original, Amy's makes tons of super-premium ice cream so thick and creamy you can barely lick it, much less scoop it out of a dish with a little plastic spoon. A changing roster of flavors includes everything from the subtle mainstay Sweet Cream to Blueberry Muffin and boozy Shiner Bock. Additional locations at 1012 W. Sixth St., 512-480-0673, and 1031 S. Congress Ave., 512-440-7488. Check the Web site for farther-flung addresses.

Desserts at Enoteca on South Congress Avenue

bistro tables dotting the room, as well as seating for alfresco dining under umbrellas. The front of the restaurant features a deli case with cheeses, meats, and plenty of antipasto dishes, and shelves stocked with olive oils, capers, and other Italian essentials. As befits a relaxed European-style café, the simple all-day menu, served from 11 AM onward, features panini, pasta, pizza, salads, and daily specials. An extensive wine list leaves lots of opportunities for pairings. Dessert here is hard to resist after you've caught sight of the lovely *panna cotta* in the dessert case near the entrance. Enoteca is wonderfully atmospheric for a simple cup of morning coffee, pastry, or Sunday brunch. Squint your eyes and you could be in Europe.

Freddie's Place

www.freddiesplaceaustin.com
512-445-9197
1703 S. First St., Austin, TX 78704

Open: Daily 11–10:30
Price: Inexpensive
Special Features: Live music; movies

The big meals at Freddie's are steak-heavy—chicken-fried steaks, tuna steaks, Salisbury steaks, and even a battered and fried portabella mushroom "steak" smothered in cream gravy that won't fool a carnivore, but will have vegetarians shouting hallelujah—accompanied by such vintage side dishes as green bean casserole. Freddie's Heart Attack, an open-face sandwich with Texas toast, tomatoes, and ten slices of bacon slathered with *queso*, may have you throwing a couple extra rounds of washers (a game akin to horseshoes) in the backyard just to stabilize your cholesterol, but it's all good.

The entertainment is constant. Live music starts at 6 PM Thursday, Friday, and Saturday. The "Backyard Big Screen" is aglow with classic movies all day Monday, then again Tuesday starting at 8 PM. Football dominates Saturday, Sunday, and Monday. Add various happy-hour specials, an outdoor pool table, pets, and free-ranging children streaked with ketchup and ice cream, and Freddie's ends up being the fun-loving backyard you wish you had.

Güero's Taco Bar

512-447-7688
www.guerostacobar.com
1412 S. Congress Ave., Austin, TX 78704
Open: Mon.–Fri. 11–11, Sat.–Sun. 8 AM–11 PM
Price: Inexpensive to Moderate
Special Features: Live music

Located in the 100-year-old Central Feed and Seed building, the cavernous dining rooms at Güero's are always filled with the sound of diners munching chips and the clatter of its bustling wait staff. Güero's enormous menu is centered on classic favorites such as enchiladas, tacos, and fajitas, reshuffled into endless combinations; nightly specials keep things interesting. The popular *Huachinango*, broiled red snapper, comes with your choice of butter and garlic or a tomato sauce made with green olives and jalapeños. Handmade tortillas, a self-serve salsa bar, and a multitude of margaritas made with fresh-squeezed limes add to the cantina-like appeal. The adjacent oak grove, festooned with tiny white lights, is Güero's music venue; check the Web site for the lineup.

Magnolia Café

512-445-0000
www.cafemagnolia.com
1920 S. Congress Ave., Austin, TX 78704
Open: Daily
Price: Inexpensive
Special Features: Open 24/7
Additional Location: 512-478-8645; 2304 Lake Austin Blvd.

The place to go for gingerbread, whole wheat, buttermilk, or cornmeal pancakes

24 hours a day, seven days a week. Omelets, breakfast tacos, *huevos rancheros*, and a tantalizing version of *migas* made with what Magnolia calls "LOVE butter" (butter with fresh garlic and serrano peppers), are also available all day long. Entrées include enchiladas, quesadillas, fajitas, and tacos and are made with endless combinations of tomatoes, grilled chicken breast, spinach, spicy ground beef, avocado, catfish, and the like. There are huge salads with homemade dressings, burgers including the Jalapeño Cheese Burger and the Voodoo Bleu Cheese Burger with blackened spices, and plenty of pastas. Vegetarians and the health conscious will enjoy ample choice.

Threadgill's

512-472-9304
www.threadgills.com
301 W. Riverside Dr., Austin, TX 78704
Open: Mon.–Thu. 11–10, Fri.–Sat.
11–10:30, Sun. 10–9:30
Price: Inexpensive to Moderate
Additional Location: 512-451-5440; 6146 N. Lamar Blvd.

An Austin landmark, Threadgill's World Headquarters is built on the former site of the Armadillo World Headquarters, the legendary dance hall whose 10-year run figures prominently in local lore. Loaded with memorabilia, Threadgill's pays tribute to the history of the Austin music scene. The menu is classic stick-to-your-ribs southern cooking, with items like fried green tomatoes, chicken-fried steak, and fried okra. While the food is fine, many come for the ambience, the live music lineup, and to experience a little bit of nostalgia. The Sunday Gospel Brunch is a great time to visit, especially for families.

Uchi

512-916-4808
www.uchiaustin.com
801 S. Lamar Blvd., Austin, TX 78704

Coffee

Whether you consider coffee an indulgence or a necessity, it sure is nice to know where to find a cup when you want or need it, and, thankfully, in Austin the offerings flow freely. In addition to drinks, most cafés sell baked goods, from simple biscotti to whole cheesecakes, and many offer soups, sandwiches, salads, or other light lunch options, making them the perfect spot for a quick, healthy meal. Many use only fair-trade beans, a difference that makes a cup of coffee both taste good and feel good; once addicted, you can order beans directly from select Austin cafés on the Internet. Most are open late, some serve alcohol at night, others host live music, but almost all are filled round the clock with locals tarrying over a cup of joe. Listed here is a sampling, just to give you a taste.

Austin Java Company

512-476-1829
www.austinjava.com
1206 Parkway at 12th St. and Lamar Blvd.,
    Austin, TX 78703
Open: Mon.–Thu. 7 AM–11 PM, Fri. 7 AM–midnight, Sat. 8 AM–midnight, Sun. 8 AM–11 PM
Special Features: Free WiFi; live music; movies
Additional Locations: 1608 Barton Springs Rd.,
    512-482-9450

An overgrown college town café, Austin Java is "funky, yet refined" and specializes in imaginative coffee-based drinks. Additionally, a very substantial menu features three square meals including "flame-kissed" burgers, chicken sandwiches, and salads, pastas, soups, healthy children's choices, and lots of options for vegetarians. The breakfast menu is served all day, and French toast, pancakes, and several versions of eggs Benedict, along with a brilliant bottomless cup of coffee, make Austin Java an essential stop to meet multiple needs.

Flipnotics

512-322-9750
www.flipnotics.com
1601 Barton Springs Rd., Austin, TX 78704
Open: Mon.–Fri. 7 AM–midnight, Sat. 7 AM–1 AM,
    Sun. 8 AM–11 PM
Special Features: Free WiFi; live music

Vintage Austin in the heart of Barton Springs. A café that is as laid-back at breakfast and lunch as it is in the evening, when you can kick back in the woodsy outdoor area and order up drinks— coffee, beer, or wine—and just mellow out with all the other free-spirited Austinites. Don't feel groovy enough? Stop in at their clothing store (see "Shopping," above), where you can dig through vintage couture, cool current fashions, and displays of every imaginable accessory.

Jo's

512-444-3800
www.joscoffee.com
1300 S. Congress Ave., Austin, TX 78704
Open: Sun.–Fri. 7 AM–9 PM, Sat. 7 AM–10 PM
Special Features: Free WiFi; live music; movies
Additional Location: 242 W. Second St.,
    512-469-9003

While the middle of a parking lot may not sound like a great spot for a café, it works at Jo's. Located beside the Hotel San José on South Congress Avenue, Jo's has a walk-up window where you place and retrieve your order before searching for a vacant chair on the dog-friendly outdoor patio. You'll find friendly staff, great drinks, and super sandwiches, including the Vegetarian Wheat Roast BBQ, served piping hot with tangy sauce and chowchow relish on a bun. The downtown location has a similar menu, the same great coffee, and actual indoor seating.

Mozart's Coffee Roasters

On Lake Austin (see "Highland Lakes" in Hill Country chapter)

Progress Coffee

www.progresscoffee.com

512-493-0963

500 San Marcos St., Austin 78702

Open: Mon. 7–7, Tue.–Fri. 7 AM–9 PM,
Sat. 8 AM–9 PM, Sun. 8 –7

Special Features: Art exhibits; free WiFi; happy
hour Mon.–Fri. 5–7

Though it opened only recently, this place is so
Austin that you have to pause for a second when
you learn that its owners are actually from
Oklahoma, via San Francisco. Located just off
Fifth Street in East Austin, the café is in a converted 1942 warehouse that is both urbane and
cozy, the perfect spot to enjoy a cup made from
fair-trade, organic, shade-grown, and custom-
roasted beans. Progress serves breakfasts of granola, bagels and lox, and the like, sophisticated
salads and sandwiches for lunch, and a fun menu
of gourmet noshes at happy hour, when beer and
wine are half price.

Quack's 43rd Street Bakery

512-453-3399

411 E. 43rd St., Austin, TX 78751

Open: Mon.–Fri. 6:30 AM–1 AM, Sat. 7 AM–1 AM,
Sun. 7:30 AM–1 AM

Special Features: Free WiFi

Additional Location: 1400 E. 38½ St.,
512-538-1991

The coffee here plays second fiddle to the fabu-
lously sweet and tart key lime pie, puffy giant
éclairs, rich tiramisu, and simple snickerdoodles.
First-rate ingredients, expertly handled, make for
superb results.

Spider House

512-480-9562

www.spiderhousecafe.com

2908 Fruth St., Austin 78705

Open: Daily 8 AM–2 AM

Special Features: Live music; movies; outdoor
seating; happy hour Mon.–Fri. 4–8

Just north of campus near the intersection of
Guadalupe and 30th Streets, Spider House is a
student-oriented patio bar and café that serves
limited food but dozens of hot and cold caf-
feinated drinks, frozen fruit smoothies and
shakes, bottled beer, draft beer, a coffee martini
known as the Brown Recluse, the L'Orangina
(your choice of gin or vodka mixed the with fruity
carbonated European beverage of the same
name), a signature sangria, and numerous other
specialty drinks.

Sweetish Hill Bakery

512-472-1347

www.sweetishhill.com

1120 W. Sixth St., Austin, TX 78703

Open: Mon.–Sat. 6:30 AM–7 PM, Sun.
6:30 AM–3 PM

Additional Location: 98 San Jacinto Blvd., 512-
472-2411, open Mon.–Fri. 7:30 AM–4 PM

Originally and primarily a bakery of European-
style breads, Sweetish Hill has been wowing
Austin with the quality of its homemade
baked goods since 1975. At Sweetish Hill, they
make buttercream frostings, mayonnaise used
in delicious tuna and chicken salads, and all-
butter dough for puff pastry, croissants, and
Danish, by hand.

Open: Sun.–Thu. 5:30 PM –10 PM, Fri.–Sat.
5 PM–10:30 PM
Price: Moderate
Special Features: Reservations recommended

In 2005 Chef Tyson Cole was lauded by *Food and Wine* magazine as "one of America's best new chefs," which to many longtime lovers of Uchi's came as no surprise. Uchi's is at home in an old South Austin house painted a deep red, whose interior has been carved out to reveal vaulted ceilings, views into the kitchen, and a combination of tables and minimalist booths for diners. The items in the appetizer section of the menu are categorized as either Cool (for example, maguro sashimi and goat cheese with cracked pepper, apples, and pumpkin seed oil) or Hot (panko-fried green toma-toes). The sushi and sashimi menu includes delicate, melt-in-your-mouth tuna, baby yellowtail, snow crab, striped bass, octopus, salmon roe, and sea urchins, some raw and some cooked. If you like surprises, consider the *Omakase*, or tasting menu, which is designed for two and decided entirely by the chef. The desserts at Uchi are a must, if only for a chance to actually taste the items so temptingly described in words. Examples include the Valrhona chocolate and wasabi fondant with five-spice *tuile* and chocolate curry cookie, the hydroponic basil-Prosecco sorbet, or perhaps the homemade maple ice cream with tempura apples.

Vespaio

512-441-6100
1610 S. Congress Ave., Austin, TX 78704
Open: Mon.–Sat. 5:30 PM–10:30 PM, Sun.
5:30 PM–10 PM
Price: Moderate
Special Features: Reservations recommended

Italian for "hornets' nest," Vespaio is con-stantly buzzing, and diners swarm to this wonderful Italian trattorria, willing to wait for over an hour for the chance to sit at one of the 15 tables and dig in. From the superb, fresh handmade pastas twirled or stuffed with homemade fillings, garlic, or roasted butternut squash, pizzas caramelized in a wood-fired oven, fresh salads with tangy dressings, and a very nice antipasto selec-tion, the menu is classic Italian. While the standard menu is superb, regular diners enjoy ordering from the specials menu, fea-turing dishes like a recent version of egg-plant parmesan, with disks of fresh eggplant, lightly fried, layered with cheese, covered with a ladleful of homemade tomato sauce and served with a side of rustic gar-licky pasta. A well-thought-out wine list provides the final touch. The wonderful food aside, the sophistication but lack of pretension, fairly reasonable prices for such fare, and just that feeling of enjoying a glass of wine surrounded by the casual and com-forting din of other diners, make Vespaio a destination unto itself. Next door, Enoteca (see above) is its more casual counterpart.

East Austin

East Austin has a lot of homegrown favorites, places that have been thriving for years with terrific home-style foods and warm atmosphere. Some great examples include **Juan in a Million** (512-472-3872; www.juaninamillion.com; 2300 E. César Chávez St.), **El Azteca Restaurant** (512-477-4701; 2600 E. Seventh St.), and **Joe's Bakery & Mexican Food** (512-472-0017; 2305 E. Seventh St.) for no-frills, family-style Mexican food, and **Gene's** 512-477-6600; 1209 E. 11th St.) for a taste of New Orleans. Recently, trendy coffeehouses (see "Coffee," above) with drinks and nibbles have also been staking their claim. All give diners good reason to cross the I-35 divide to the east side.

Eastside Café

512-476-5858
www.eastsidecafeaustin.com

Las Manitas

As this book heads to press, city council members, developers, business owners, and residents are engaged in intense negotiations regarding the future of downtown Austin. While most agree that certain lots and blocks could use a face-lift, some addresses reveal enormous ideological distances between the parties, and one of them belongs to little Las Manitas Café on Congress Avenue.

Occupying a modest building on a prime piece of real estate, the beloved Las Manitas has come to represent all that is wonderful about Austin. It is a place to which everyone goes and where anyone is welcome, just as it has been for over 25 years. Not just an Austin tradition, Las Manitas is practically sacred to many. So when talk turned to relocating the café to make room for a hotel, Austinites cried foul.

Across America, mom and pop shops, diners, and restaurants have been set aside to make room for corporate storefronts, chain eateries, and parking lots. Cities have had to take a long, hard look in the mirror and ask themselves how much their icons are worth. In Austin, where everyone is hoping for a win-win solution to this quandary, the answer is "priceless."

This review of Las Manitas is offered in the sincere hope that at the time you read it the words will still be accurate; if they aren't, please consider it a memorial.

Las Manitas Café

512-472-9357
211 Congress Ave., Austin, TX 78701
Open: Mon.–Fri. 7 AM–4 PM, Sat. and Sun. 7 AM–2:30 PM
Price: Inexpensive

With open hands (MANITAS), Las Manitas welcomes everyone into this bustling family-run café and feeds them honest food with almost alarming efficiency. With an extensive menu of the usual tacos, quesadillas, flautas, and enchiladas, Las Manitas also offers daily specials such as their outstanding vegetarian tamales and CHILE RELLENOS (spicy peppers, halved, stuffed with cheese, and broiled). An Austin institution, Las Manitas serves up a whole lot of ambience, a healthy dose of history, and a damn good plate of MIGAS (eggs scrambled with onions, peppers, and fried tortilla strips), presented with a flourish and pride that just makes you feel so glad to be sitting in one of their well-worn vinyl-covered booths. Serving only breakfast and lunch, the cheerful restaurant is almost always full. This place gives a lot of love to the community—they founded a nearby Latino cultural and education center—and every day Austin diners happily give it back to them.

2113 Manor Rd., Austin, TX 78722
Open: Mon.–Thu. 11:30–9:30, Fri.
    11:30–10, Sat. 10–10, Sun. 10–9:30
Price: Moderate
Special Features: Reservations recommended

When the folks at the Eastside Café say "fresh," they mean, quite literally, "We are on our way out the back kitchen door to dig around in our on-site organic garden and pick the ingredients just for you!" Now that's fresh. And spunky. Which is exactly how one could describe many of the dishes at the Eastside Café. The menu leans toward the free-spirited and health-conscious, with the grilled ruby trout with a shitake mushroom ginger cream sauce, wild mushroom crepes with walnuts, ricotta, and jack cheese, and salmon dumplings with a spicy yellow coconut curry sauce being several examples. The chef's specials chalked on the blackboard change daily, but a recent sampling included skewered beef tenderloin tips with spicy chili rub and cilantro garlic sauce and a side dish of sliced heirloom tomatoes in lemon tarragon vinaigrette, which will make you vow to plant a garden next spring. On Saturday and Sunday, brunch is served until 3 PM, at which point dinner is served until closing.

Hoover's Cooking

512-479-5006
www.hooverscooking.com
2002 Manor Rd., Austin, TX 78722
Open: Mon.–Fri. 11–10, Sat. and Sun. 8 AM–
    10 PM
Price: Inexpensive to Moderate
Additional Location: 512-335-0300; 13376
    Research Blvd., #400

Hoover's is honest-to-goodness cooking inspired by owner/chef Hoover Alexander's mother, Dorothy, and his Texas roots, which run five generations deep. For diners this translates into great chicken-fried steak, meat loaf, charbroiled catfish, and

Elgin sausage from down the road a piece, served with mashed potatoes made from scratch and jalapeño creamed spinach, and washed down with homemade lemonade. Whether it's BBQ smothered with pickles, onions, and sauce, chicken-fried chicken breast smothered in a homemade cream gravy, or fresh fruit pie smothered in Blue Bell ice cream, Hoover's is just aching to smoother you with their comfort food the same way your grandmother might smoother you with love—in a good way! Austin loves Hoover's for its fantastic no-nonsense food served in a no-frills dining room and no-holds-barred use of the good stuff.

WEST END/CLARKSVILLE

Residential in feel and dotted with commercial centers that are home to restaurants, art galleries, and antiques shops, the West End and Clarksville are wonderful, less urban options for diners who might like to eat and take a stroll through the leafy local neighborhoods. In addition to the restaurants listed below, locals enjoy the upscale Castle Hill Café (512-476-0728; www.castlehillcafe.com; 1101 W. Fifth St.) and Jeffrey's Restaurant (512-477-5584, www.jeffreysofaustin.com; 1204 W. Lynn St.) for celebrating special occasions.

Austin Land and Cattle

512-472-1813
www.austinlandandcattlecompany.com
1205 N. Lamar Blvd., Austin, TX 78703
Open: Sun.–Thu. 5:30 PM –10 PM, Fri.–Sat.
    5:30 PM –11 PM
Price: Moderate to Expensive

Finding themselves in cattle country, many visitors to Austin set out in search of a steak. Austin Land and Cattle aims to please. Ribeye, filet mignon, top sirloin, New York strip, and the extraordinary 2-pound T-bone, served with the chef's choice of vegetables and your choice of potato or rice, are sure to satisfy any craving while setting you back close to $40. On the menu for non-red-meat eaters are chicken, seafood, and pasta dishes, and vegetarian diners will be relieved to discover that Austin Land and Cattle also serves a plump and juicy giant portobello mushroom steak. And for dessert, the tart fresh raspberry pie served with homemade whipped cream is a sweet ending.

Cipollina

512-477-5211
www.cipollina-austin.com
1213 W. Lynn St., Austin, TX 78703
Open: Mon.–Fri. 7 AM–9 PM, Sat. and Sun.
    8 AM–9 PM
Price: Inexpensive to Moderate
Special Features: Live music

Cipollina, or "little onion," is an Italian bistro, popular for morning coffee, pastry, and a quiet moment with the paper or soups, salads, sandwiches, and pizzas at lunchtime. The paper-thin-prosciutto sandwich with fresh mozzarella and basil on homemade focaccia bread spread with aioli is tasty and filling, but the pizzas really steal the show. Baked in a wood-fired oven, they are thin and crispy, with bold flavors such as bacon, gorgonzola cheese, and white truffle oil. Simple and delicious. Which is why Cipollina, despite its ample space, is frequently crowded, especially at happy hour, when the pizzas sell for only $5 apiece. A nice selection of Italian wines and a long deli case filled with dozens of homemade side dishes make Cipollina a true a neighborhood hangout.

Wink

512-482-8868
www.winkrestaurant.com
512 N. Lamar, Austin, TX 78703
Located behind the Whole Earth Provision
    Company
Open: Mon.–Wed. 6 PM–10 PM, Thu. and
    Sat. 5:30 PM –11 PM

Angelic cookies

Price: Moderate to Expensive
Special Features: Reservations recommended

Aptly named, Wink is personal, intimate, and flirty, with food so deceptively simple and earnestly pure you feel as if you are experiencing taste for the first time. Samples from a recent menu include a roasted quail with ginger quinoa, shiitakes, baby leeks, golden raisin sauce, and a sauté of monkfish with cauliflower, alba mushrooms, amaranth, and pistachio oil emulsion. Simple yet complex, unfussy yet anything but ordinary. The extensive and carefully chosen wine list only heightens the experience, and, for dessert, Wink's lemon meringue pot is a revelation. The dining room's crisp white tablecloths offset by a sweet-potato-colored wall and mobiles of semitranslucent "eyes" hanging from the ceiling, is both stylish and comfortable. Wink is simple done perfectly. Or, perfection simply done.

NORTH AUSTIN
Austin is a small enough city that "North Austin" really means only several miles north of center, a 10- to 15-minute drive, for which you will be richly rewarded with great local fare well off the beaten tourist path. The streetscape will change somewhat, so don't be surprised to find some of these gems in what might otherwise seem like nondescript shopping centers.

Fonda San Miguel
512-459-4121
www.fondasanmiguel.com
2330 W. Loop North, Austin, TX 78756
Open: Mon.–Thu. 5:30 PM–9:30 PM, Fri.–
   Sat. 5:30 PM –10 PM, Sun. 11 AM–2 PM
Price: Moderate to Expensive
Special Features: Reservations recommended

Fortunately for the rest of us, some people have vision enough to create the things we all grow to love, and such is the case with Fonda San Miguel. Started in 1975 by Tom Gilliland and Miguel Ravago, who began serving their authentic Mexican meals in a spacious stucco building, undaunted by the scarcity of ingredients north of the border at the time or the public's skepticism, Fonda San Miguel won diners over one homemade tortilla and fresh lime margarita at a time. Starters include a hot corn soup with cheese and roasted *poblano* peppers, a nopal cactus salad with chopped tomatoes and onions with *queso fresco*, and a *chile con queso* that has never, ever been violated by the addition of Velveeta. Main courses offer a choice of rotisserie broiled meats, filet of fish broiled with *achiote*, a bright and earthy spice, variations of the *chile relleno* including one with spinach, goat cheese, raisins, and pine nuts, and *Pollo Pibil*, chicken baked in a banana leaf, a Yucatan specialty. Their legendary Sunday brunches are sublime—the perfect chance to sample a huge array of dishes and delicacies to your heart's content. To celebrate its 30th anniversary, Fonda San Miguel wrote a cookbook as functional, beautiful, and enjoyable as the restaurant.

Hudson's on the Bend
512-266-1369
www.hudsonsonthebend.com
3509 Ranch Road 620 North, Austin, TX 78734
Near Lake Travis
Open: Tue.–Thu. 6 PM–10 PM, Fri.–Sat.
   5:30 PM–10 PM, Sun.–Mon. 6:30 PM–9 PM
Price: Expensive to Very Expensive
Special Features: Reservations recommended

This restaurant's got game. While the diamondback rattlesnake cakes crusted with pistachios and the espresso-chocolate-chili-rubbed elk sound exciting, it is really the ingredients of the Five Species Creature Feature Antipasto appetizer for two that pushes the limits of adventurous eating. They are: pheasant pâté, pastrami kangaroo, candied smoked salmon, venison sausage, and pecan grilled alligator, served with five separate sauces. The menu always reflects the season, as illustrated by the summertime specials of Watermelon Wild Boar and antelope served with cantaloupe, which tastes as spunky as it sounds. Needless to say, folks who love to eat fearlessly will fall in love with Hudson's on the Bend, and those who steer more toward the straight and narrow should not be deterred; Hudson's does most everything well and has a special way of making more mundane dishes seem just a tiny bit daring. The options on what they call the Way Too Many Wines List are endless, as is the view of Lake Travis.

Kerbey Lane Café

512-451-1436
www.kerbeylanecafe.com
3704 Kerbey Lane, Austin, TX 78731
Open: Daily
Price: Inexpensive
Special Features: Open 24 hours
Additional Locations: 2606 Guadalupe St.,
    512-477-5717; two others farther afield;
    check Web site

Bright, light, funky, and friendly, the Kerbey Lane Café started in 1980 in the minds of two UT grads looking for a healthy, affordable, and casual spot to eat in Austin. Over 25 years later, the idea has proved to be such a good one that there are now four area locations, each with its own distinct identity, but all serving Kerbey Lane's exhaustive menu 24/7. The food here is healthy, creative, and well-priced. The huge buttermilk, gingerbread, blueberry, or apple whole wheat pancakes are very popular, as are the French toast and their signature sticky muffin, a gooey sticky bun-muffin hybrid. On the entrée menu, the pecan crusted trout with peach vinaigrette, served with braised spinach brightened with lemon and a side of sweet potato fries, is a standout. Additionally, there are inventive sandwiches, hearty soups, meal-sized salads, and the usual Tex-Mex roster of enchiladas, quesadillas, and tacos, each with its own health-food spin. In an effort to serve super-fresh produce, Kerbey Lane has partnered with an independently owned area farm and now grows some of its own. The owners' energetic philanthropy has benefited many communities within their beloved Austin.

ATTRACTIONS, PARKS, AND RECREATION

Austinites just like being outdoors, in the year-round fantastic weather, on the miles of trails, and in the swimming holes. There are many opportunities for recreation in the city, and when you factor in the proximity of the Highland Lakes and the state parks of the Hill Country (see Hill Country chapter), the list of options grows exponentially.

Zilker Metropolitan Park and Preserve

512-867-3080
www.ci.austin.tx.us/zilker
2100 Barton Springs Rd., Austin, TX 78746
Open: Daily 5 AM–10 PM
Admission: Free
Parking: $3 during peak season

Ornithomimus *in the Hartman Prehistoric Garden of the Zilker Botanical Garden*

Zilker Park is Austin's playground. The 351-acre urban park just south of Town Lake and the Colorado River encompasses the Zilker Botanical Gardens, Zilker Nature Preserve, and Barton Springs Pool. It is dotted with sports fields, picnic tables, children's playgrounds, and a miniature railroad, the Zilker Zephyr. The park hosts many of the city's music, arts, and cultural events, including the *Austin City Limits* Music Festival and the Zilker Park Kite Festival. Miles of hike-and-bike trails traverse the park and connect with those of its neighbor, Town Lake. Zilker Park is a stop on the free Tour the Town weekend bus service. Parking is free on weekdays; on Saturday, Sunday, and holidays from March through Labor Day there is a $3 fee per car, collected at any gate, and valid throughout the day at any parking lot within Zilker Park.

Zilker Botanical Garden
512-477-8672
www.zilkergarden.org
2220 Barton Springs Rd., Austin, TX 78746
Open: Daily 7–7
Admission: Free

Verdant terraced gardens, winding stone paths, and great views of the city and hills make this a pleasant place to stroll. Educational components prove there's more to the garden than just smelling the roses. The "Green Garden" features native and adapted plants and flowers best suited to the Central Texas climate, while the Hartman Prehistoric Garden conceals a life-size bronze sculpture of *Ornithomimus*, the dinosaur whose tracks were discovered here in 1992, nestled in among plants representing the Cretaceous period.

Tumbling water at Zilker Botanical Garden

Bridge over the Colorado River at dusk

Zilker Nature Preserve (302 Nature Center Dr.) An expansive 60-acre preserve with meadows, a trickling stream, and an outstanding view of Austin from the Overlook Trail, located just west of Loop 360.

Barton Springs
512-476-9044
www.ci.austin.tx.us/parks/bartonsprings
2101 Barton Springs Rd., Austin, TX 78704
Located inside Zilker Park
Open: Daily 8 AM–10 PM
Admission: Adults $3, juniors (12–17 years) $2, children $1. Movie night: Adults $2, children 50 cents.

The hot Texas sun can be a great equalizer. Barton Springs attracts just about everyone in Austin with a swimsuit and a few dollars to pony up for a chance to cool off. It has always been a gathering place. Native Americans believed it held healing powers, and the Spanish, impressed and inspired by it, setting up temporary missions here in the 1730s. The springs became a city park in 1917, and dams were added in 1929 and 1932, creating the swimming area. Today, Barton Springs is still a constant and bracing 68 degrees, a fact people approach with strategies ranging from dipping a toe in the cool dark water to belly flopping off the diving board. The expansive, grassy lawn rimmed with trees is a big draw. Unless you are a dog-lover, consider paying the fee for entrance to the gated portion of the springs, where the water is deep and the grassy knoll clean. The shallow free-and-open-to-the-public section below the dam tends to be overrun with canines fetching, splashing, and frolicking with their owners. And while the dog population runs high, the Barton Springs salamander has declined to the point of critical endangerment in this, its only known habitat. The little lungless salamander is now a protected endangered species, which means that Zilker Park's managers, scientists, and various environmental agencies are doing all they can to support its survival.

Zilker Zephyr
Open: Mon.–Fri. 10–5, Sat.–Sun. 10–7
Admission: Adults $2.75, children $1.75

This miniature train makes a leisurely 25-minute loop through the park, past Barton Springs and Town Lake before heading back to the playground in front of the Barton Springs Pool entrance.

Austin Nature and Science Center
512-327-8181
www.ci.austin.tx.us/ansc
301 Nature Center Dr., Austin, TX 78746
Open: Mon.–Sat. 9–5, Sun. noon–5
Admission: Donation

The Austin Nature and Science Center is the sort of hands-on place that appeals to children. You can dig up bones in the Dino Pit, be an "eco-detective" on the path around the nearby pond, use a science lab, and see some native Texas animals up close, courtesy of the center's program to care for animals who cannot be returned to the wild.

Right across the street the SPLASH! Into the Edwards Aquifer interpretative center at the old Barton Springs Pool Bathhouse (512-478-3170; 2201 Barton Springs Rd.) does a nice job of explaining the fragility of the region's underground ecosystem through interactive exhibits.

Mexican Free-Tailed Bats
Bat Conservation International
512-347-9721
www.batcon.com
Congress Ave. Bridge (spanning Town Lake), Austin, TX 78701

When the city of Austin reconstructed the Congress Avenue Bridge in 1980, its architects unwittingly created a perfect bat habitat. Before long, close to a million migratory Mexican free-tailed bats began using the nooks and crannies under the bridge decking as their summer home. From April to October, the bats live, give birth, and raise their young under the bridge, taking flight each night at dusk to scour the greater metro area for tens of thousands of pounds of insects *per night*; they head back to Mexico at the first nip of winter winds. Once Austin's biggest nuisance—early on there was talk of poisoning the colony— the bats are now its most innovative form of pest control, not to mention one of its most asked-about attractions.

The best time to see the bats is in August. For information about observing the colony from the *Austin American-Statesman* parking lot, 305 S. Congress Ave., or the *Bat Boat*, a nightly cruise run by Lone Star Riverboat (see "Tours," below), call the Bat Hotline at

512-416-5700, category 3636. Another great vantage point is the Shoreline Grill, 98 San Jacinto Blvd., www.shorelinegrill.com, 512-477-3300; reservations recommended.

Umlauf Sculpture Gardens
512-445-5582
www.umlaufsculpture.org
605 Robert E. Lee Rd., Austin, TX 78704
Open: Wed.–Fri. 10–4:30, Sat.–Sun. 1–4:30
Admission: Adults $3.50, seniors $2.50, students $1, children under 6 free

A native of Michigan, Charles Umlauf moved with his wife, Angeline, to Texas in 1941 when he took a teaching position with the fledgling University of Texas art department. Forty years and dozens of awards and accolades later, he retired, and in 1985 he and his wife donated their home, studio, and 168 pieces of art to the city of Austin. In 1991 a new museum was built on neighboring land, and today visitors are invited to tour both its interior and grounds. Themes of children, mothers, and docile animals dominate Umlauf's works, and the resulting sculptures tend to be sweet, tender, and lyrical—an especially nice fit for the lush gardens in which they are displayed.

West Austin

Deep Eddy Pool
512-472-8546
www.ci.austin.tx.us/parks/pools
401 Deep Eddy Dr., Austin, TX 78701
At Lake Austin Blvd, just west of MoPac
Open: Daily. Times vary throughout the year, but generally 10–9; call or check the Web site for details.
Admission: Adults $3, juniors (12–17 years) $2, children $1. Movie night, adults $2, children 50 cents.

Take a Dip: Quick Getaways

Hamilton Pool (512-264-2740, managed by the Travis County Parks 512-854-7275; 24300 Hamilton Pool Rd., Dripping Springs, TX 78620) With its grotto and 45-foot waterfall, Hamilton Pool is the centerpiece of this nature preserve. A well-marked trail leads from the parking lot to the pool. Bring your own food and water and arrive early, as the park closes when it reaches capacity. The park is approximately 30 miles west of Austin. From the TX 71 and US 290 intersection take TX 71 to FM 3238/Hamilton Pool Rd. Open: Daily 9–5:30, subject to water quality; call for daily recorded report. Admission: $8.

Krause Springs (830-693-4181; 404 Krause Springs, Spicewood, TX 78669) Open: Daily. Admission: Adults $4, children $3. Camping: Adults $8, children $5. A privately owned park with a large spring-fed swimming hole on Little Cypress Creek. With one of the nicest swimming holes around, combined with tent camping, Krause Springs is a great place to spend a hot day or two. From Austin take TX 71 west to Spicewood and follow signs.

Built in 1916, the concrete expanse of Deep Eddy Pool was the first outdoor pool in Texas and once part of a larger resort area including rental cottages, bustling concession stands, and a Ferris wheel. While all those amusements are long gone, the main attraction remains —the water. The pool is spring-fed, with areas for laps, wading, and just splashing around. The fantastic combination of swimming and a movie make the family-friendly Splash Party Movie Night a big hit in the summertime. The Friends of Deep Eddy (www.deepeddy.org), a crew of dedicated volunteers, have recently undertaken a thorough restoration of the 1936 bathhouse aimed at bringing it back to its former glory. Amenities such as family restrooms, wheelchair and stroller-accessible ramps, and more landscaping will keep the pool and its environs as well-used and well-loved in the future as they are now.

SOUTH AUSTIN

Austin Zoo
215-288-1490
www.austinzoo.org
10807 Rawhide Trail, Austin, TX 78736
The zoo is located just off US 290, between Austin and Dripping Springs. From South
    Austin take US 290 west, past its intersection with TX 71, until you see signs.
Open: Daily 10–6; no admittance after 5 PM
Admission: Adults $7, seniors $5, children $4; train tickets $2.50

The Austin Zoo is really more of an "educational sanctuary" dedicated to the rescue and rehabilitation of animals and education of the public. The zoo was originally known as the Good Day Ranch, a fitting moniker, since 90 percent of the animals at the zoo are rescued, in many cases from the unfortunate "roadside attraction" outfits that dot Texas's highways. There are lions, bears, monkeys, exotic birds, zebras, emus, and Texas longhorns, a little petting zoo, and a sweet miniature train, which takes visitors on a 2-mile journey through the surrounding countryside. The zoo is neither large nor elaborate, but well intentioned; consider the price of admission a donation to a worthy cause.

Lady Bird Johnson Wildflower Center
512-292-4100
www.wildflower.org
4801 La Crosse Ave., Austin, TX 78739
Take MoPac south, past Slaughter Lane, then follow signs, taking a left onto La Crosse
    Avenue.
Open: Tue.–Sat. 9–5:30, Sun. noon–5:30
Admission: Adults $7, seniors and students $6, children $3, children 4 and under free

The Lady Bird Johnson Wildflower Center is a lovely swath of nature in the midst of the growing Austin suburbs. Proving that it is never too late to follow a dream, on her 70th birthday, December 22, 1982, Lady Bird Johnson and her friend, the actress Helen Hayes, started the center to protect and preserve North America's native plants and diverse natural landscapes. Lady Bird is quoted as once saying "Ugliness is so grim, a little beauty can help create harmony." Always one to follow words with action, Lady Bird was a tireless environmentalist, promoting the simple idea that we are all custodians of beauty as nature intended it. The center will soon be brought under the auspices of the University of Texas, but its mission of educating visitors about the environmental impact and economic value of native plants will surely remain unchanged. While its lovely gardens are populated by

Potted succulent at the Lady Bird Johnson Wildflower Center

plants and flowers native to Texas, diligently tended by the center's staff and volunteers, the center, through its Web site and hotline, is a clearinghouse of invaluable information to gardeners throughout the U.S. and Canada. Beyond flowers, the center also models both new and recycled ideas, such as its rainwater harvesting system, which diverts water from the roofs of its structure into several cisterns, supplying 10 to 15 percent of the center's annual water demand. The Wildflower Café (open Tue.–Sat. 10–4, Sun. 1–4) serves drinks, sandwiches, and treats, and the gift shop, Wild Ideas (512-292-4300 or 1-877-945-3357), has nifty nature-themed items.

North Austin

Pioneer Farms
512-837-1215
www.pioneerfarms.org
1400 Pioneer Farms Dr., Austin, TX 78754
Located in northeast Austin. Take I-35 to the Braker Lane exit, then left on Dessau Road.
Open: Wed. and Fri. 10–2, Sun. 1–5
Admission: Adults $8, children $6

Pioneer Farms is a collection of pre–Civil War structures, plus some new ones made to look old, arranged on a parcel of land to re-create some of the look and feel of pioneer life. Within each barn, home, and shop, volunteer interpreters dressed in period costumes go about their work cooking, blacksmithing, spinning cotton into thread, making cheese, and woodworking. The General Store sells reproduction toys. Die-hard history buffs might enjoy taking a class at Pioneer School ($15–$25). Topics range from Dutch-oven cooking to the efficiency of the foot-powered lathe.

RECREATION

A tremendous online resource for all outdoor recreation in Texas is www.texasoutside.com.

Baseball
Round Rock Express (512-255-2255; www.roundrockexpress.com; 3400 E. Palm Valley Blvd., Round Rock, TX 78664). The thrill of minor league baseball. The Express play at the Dell Diamond, located on US 79 in Round Rock, just north of Austin.

Bicycling

Bicycling, both road and mountain biking, is big in Central Texas, especially in Austin and the Hill Country. Rentals are available through **Bicycle Sport Shop** (512-477-3472; www.bicyclesportshop.com; 517 S. Lamar Blvd., Austin, TX 78704. Additional location: 512-345-7460; 10947 Research Blvd.) and University Cyclery (512-474-6696; www.universitycyclery.com; 2901 N. Lamar Blvd., Austin, TX 78705).
Helpful Web sites include:

Austin Cycling Association (www.austincycling.org)

Austin Ridge Riders (www.austinridgeriders.org)

Bicycle Texas (www.bicycletexas.com)

City of Austin (www.ci.austin.tx.us/parks/trails)

Cycle Texas (www.cycletexas.com)

Texas State Park System (www.tpwd.state.tx.us/exptexas/bike)

Bird Watching

Austin is a great spot to catch a glimpse of rare, migratory, and native birds. Online, **Texas Parks and Wildlife**, www.tpwd.state.tx.us, and the **Travis County Audubon Society**, www.travisaudubon.org, offer a wealth of information. See "Suggested References" in the Information chapter for a selection of bird-watching guides.

Cyclist in Austin

Boating, Canoeing, and Kayaking

Canoes, kayaks, and paddleboat rentals are available on Barton Creek or Town Lake.

Austin Canoe and Kayak (512-719-4386 or 1-888-828-3828; www.austinkayak.com; 9705 Burnet Rd. #102, Austin, TX 78758) Open: Mon.–Fri. 10–6, Sat.–Sun. 10–5. Price: $25–$35 a day.

Capital Cruises (512-480-9264; www.capitalcruises.com; 209 Barton Springs Rd., Austin, TX 78704) Canoes, kayaks, paddleboats, and swan boats. Price: $10–$25 an hour. Open: Mar.–Oct. Mon.–Fri. 10–dusk, Sat.–Sun. 9–dusk.

The Rowing Dock (512-459-0999; www.rowingdock.com; 2418 Stratford Dr., Austin, TX 78746) Located just west of Zilker Park on Town Lake. Open: Mon.–Fri. 6:30–noon and 4–8, Sat.–Sun. 8–8. Price: $10–$25 an hour.

Zilker Park Boat Rentals (512-478-3852; www.zilkerboats.com) They are located in Zilker Park, though you will not be able to see their stand from the road. From the main entrance to the park, make a left and drive around the field to the parking lot and follow signs. Open: Mon.–Fri. 9–dark, Sat.–Sun. 11–dark, weather permitting. Price $10 an hour or $40 a day.

Camping

Pecan Grove RV Park (512-472-1067; 1518 Barton Springs Rd., Austin, TX) In the heart of South Austin, Pecan Grove is perfect for those who like to camp close to takeout coffee and burritos. **Emma Long Metropolitan Park** is a favorite, as is **McKinney Falls State Park**, just south of the city. **Camp Ben McCulloch** (512-858-2084) in Driftwood, southwest of the city, was once a reunion camp for Confederate veterans and is now a historic site, campground, and host of the annual Old Settler's Music Festival (see "Festivals," above). The various state parks in the Hill Country, Krause Springs, and the public and private parks surrounding the Highland Lakes offer a variety of camping options (see individual entries in Hill Country chapter).

Climbing

Austin Rock Gym (512-416-9266; www.austinrockgym.com; 4401 Freidrich Lane, Suite 300, Austin, TX 78744. Additional location: 8300 N. Lamar Blvd., Suite 102B, 512-416-9299) Two gyms, each with excellent facilities and climbing instructors. Price: $13–$25.

Cypress Valley Canopy Tours (512-264-8880; www.cypressvalleycanopytours.com; 1223 Paleface Ranch Rd., Spicewood, TX 78669) Gliding canopy tours in the Hill Country 30 minutes west of Austin. Tour participants use steel zip lines to travel between treetop platforms among old-growth cypress. Price: $60–$125.

Mountain Madness Rock Climbing School (512-329-0309; www.mtmadness.com; P.O. Box 162643, Austin, TX 78716) Weekend classes held at Enchanted Rock State Natural Area near Fredericksburg. Price: $100 for one day, $160 for two.

Disc Golf

Disc Golf is based on the rules of golf. Players throw a Frisbee-like disc toward a basket hanging approximately 2 feet from the ground, in an effort to "sink" the disc. Points are

Hiking, Biking, Running, Strolling

While Zilker Park provides plenty of opportunities for recreation, outdoor enthusiasts will also enjoy the other gems of Austin's extensive system of parks, hike-and-bike trails, and greenbelts. The city's Parks Department Web site has excellent maps of the greenbelts; see www.ci.austin.tx.us/parks/trails for more details. The following list is not exhaustive, but includes highlights. All these listings offer activities appropriate for any ability level.

Barton Creek Greenbelt (www.ci.austin.tx.us/parks/trails) This enormous greenbelt, spreading south from Zilker Park then west of Loop 360, includes climbing walls, swimming areas, hike-and-bike trails, and abundant natural scenery.

Bright Leaf Park (512-459-7269; www.brightleaf.org; Crestway Dr.) A 200-acre natural area located in central northwest Austin, north of Camp Mabry, offering guided hikes only.

Mayfield Park (512-974-2000; www.ci.austin.tx.us; 3808 W. 35th St.) Twenty-two peaceful acres with easy-to-navigate trails located beside Laguna Gloria.

McKinney Falls Sate Park (512-243-1643; www.tpwd.state.tx.us; 5808 McKinney Falls Pkwy.) Straddling the banks of Onion Creek, McKinney Falls is 13 miles southeast of Austin off US 183 and offers swimming, hiking, fishing, camping, and picnicking. When the river is high, the falls are lovely, but drought can lessen them to a trickle.

Mount Bonnell (3800 Mt. Bonnell Dr.) The 785-foot-high mount is a popular place to watch the sun set over the hills. Climb the steep stairs and behold the wide views of Town Lake and the West Lake Hills.

Shoal Creek Greenbelt connects with the Town Lake Hike and Bike Trail (see below) and continues for 4 miles following Shoal Creek. The disc golf course in Pease Park is very popular with twenty-something Austinites.

Town Lake Hike and Bike Trail (www.ci.austin.tx.us/parks/trails) This hike-and-bike trail runs along both shores of Town Lake and the Colorado River and is dotted with drinking fountains and rudimentary restrooms. A favorite trail for runners and dog walkers.

Veloway (4801 La Crosse Ave., Austin, TX 78739) A 3-mile paved loop designed specifically for bikers and inline skaters. The trail traverses parkland, and its entrance point is across from the Lady Bird Johnson Wildflower Center.

added for extra throws over par, and the course tends to be 18 holes, though some are 9 and others 27. Disc golf is extraordinarily popular in Austin; of the five free courses scattered throughout the city, two of the most popular are **Pease Park** in the Shoal Creek Greenbelt and **Zilker Park** (see "Attractions, Parks, and Recreation," above). Find out all you need to know about disc golf in Texas online at www.texasdiscgolf.org.

Fishing

Fishing in Central Texas is excellent, though developed or privately owned shoreline can make it difficult to find a spot to sink your lure in Austin. **Emma Long Metropolitan Park** on Lake Austin is a popular fishing spot, as are the **Highland Lakes**. Check www.texasoutside.com, www.txfishing.com, or www.austinkayakfishing.com. You don't need a license to fish from shore in a Texas state park.

Football

Longhorns (512-471-3333 or 1-800-982-2386; www.texasxports.com; Texas Memorial Stadium, 2100 San Jacinto Blvd.) Austin doesn't have a pro team, but it does have the University of Texas Longhorns. In 2006, after 36 years of waiting, the Longhorns roped in a Rose Bowl win, sending regional fans into a state of extended ecstasy. Hook 'em Horns!

Austin Wranglers (512-491-6600; www.austinwranglers.com; the Erwin Center, 1701 Red River St.) The Wranglers are the newest members of the professional Arena Football League.

Golf

Avery Ranch Golf (512-248-2442; www.averyranchgolf.com; 10500 Avery Club Dr.) Excellent public golf course in northwest Austin. Price: $40–$70.

Lakeway Golf Club (512-261-7172; www.lakewaygolfclub.com; One World of Tennis Square) Semiprivate club and a local favorite. Price: $65–$90.

Ice Hockey

Austin Ice Bats (512-927-7825; www.icebats.com; 14200 I-35 North) Where there's ice, there's hockey. The minor league Ice Bats are major fun for kids and hockey enthusiasts.

Swimming

People have been dipping their toes in the water around Austin for centuries. If you're looking to cool off in the city, try **Barton Springs** or **Deep Eddy Pool** (see Attractions, Parks, and Recreation, above). Outside the city, **Hamilton Pool** ("Take a Dip," above), a natural grotto and waterfall, is about a 45-minute drive, as is **Hippie Hollow** (see "Highland Lakes" in Hill Country chapter), everyone's favorite nudist hangout on Lake Travis. **Krause Springs** ("Take a Dip," above) in Spicewood also has camping.

Tours

Whether by foot, boat, amphibious vehicle, or Segway, touring Austin outside a car can give you a whole new perspective. The **Austin Visitors Center** (www.austintexas.org;) runs many worthwhile tours, all of which are listed on its Web site. For example, **AdeoTours** (www.adeo tours.com) uses MP3s for a self-guided audio tour of Austin on one of two themes, Culture or Music Venues, while the **Austin Overtures** tour (www.austinovertures.com) guides guests through town in its bright pink van with star-shaped hubcaps; check Web sites for details.

Austin City Limits Tour (512-471-4811; www.pbs.org/klru/austin; Communications Building B, corner of 26th and Guadalupe Sts., University of Texas) Studio tours available each Friday at 10:30 AM. Free.

Alien Scooters (512-444-8687; www.alienscooters.com; 1122B S. Lamar Blvd., in Lamar Plaza) Hour-and-a-half eco-friendly tours of Austin on electric bikes that recharge using green energy. Price: $27.50.

Austin Duck Adventures (512-477-5274; www.austinducks.com; in front of the Visitors Center, 209 E. Sixth St.) Drive around Austin in an amphibious British Alvis Stalwart before splashing into Lake Austin. Price: Adults $21.95, seniors $19.95, children $13, plus tax.

Lake Austin

Austin Steam Train (512-477-8468; www.austinsteamtrain.org) Restored vintage trains run from Austin south to Manor and from Cedar Park to Burnet in the Hill Country. Trips seem best suited to die-hard train aficionados. Price: Adults $14–$27, seniors $13–$24, children $10–$17.

Capital Cruises (512-480-9264; www.capitalcruises.com; 209 Barton Springs Rd.) Sightseeing cruises leave Sat. and Sun. at 1; bat-watching cruises leave nightly 30 minutes before sunset. Check Web site for dinner cruise details. Reservations recommended. Price: Adults $8, seniors $6, children $5.

Gliding Revolution (512-296-2666; www.glidingrevolution.com) These tours on a Segway, the self-balancing, motorized two-wheel contraption, are rumored to be great fun, but be prepared for plenty of stares. Two-and-a-half-hour tours start at 9:30, 11, 3, and 6:30 and lead participants around the city or Town Lake, with a special Bat Tour at dusk. Price: $65.

Haunted Texas Tours (512-853-9826; www.hauntedtexas.com; 617 Congress Ave.) Tour paranormal Austin. Price: $15.

Historic Hyde Park Homes Tour (512-330-2228; www.hydeparkhomestour.org) is an architectural tour of Hyde Park held annually on Father's Day weekend and commencing at the Ney Museum. Admission: Adults $15, children $7.50; adults $12, children $5 if tickets are purchased in advance.

Lake Austin Riverboats (512-345-5220; www.austinriverboats.com; 3700 Lake Austin Blvd.) Relaxing riverboat tours; call for details.

Lone Star Riverboat (512-327-1388; www.lonestarriverboat.com; S. First St. Bridge) This old-fashioned paddle-wheel riverboat cruises around Town Lake for a relaxing 90 minutes. There are also week-

Stevie Ray Vaughan Memorial

A tribute to the Austin bluesman whose life was cut short tragically when he died in a helicopter crash in 1990 at the age of 35, the statue of Stevie Ray Vaughan was placed on the south shore of Town Lake by the city of Austin in 1993. At the time of his death, Vaughan had released five albums and won three Grammy Awards, with an additional two awarded posthumously. He was a revered musician, and tracks from the solo albums FAMILY STYLE and THE SKY IS CRYING, along with those recorded with his band Double Trouble, COULDN'T STAND THE WEATHER, SOUL TO SOUL, TEXAS FLOOD, and LIVE AT CARNEGIE HALL, are radio mainstays. Vaughan left a legacy of heartfelt music to his fans; for Austin his statue is an expression of love and respect for all its musicians.

end Bat Watching/Sunset cruises; call for departure times. Reservations recommended. Open: March–Oct. Sat.–Sun. at 3. Price: Adults $9/$8, seniors $7/$6, children $6/$5.

SegCity (512-402-9299; www.segcity.com; 621 E. Sixth St.) More tours on that funky self-balancing machine, the Segway. Three 3-hour tours daily, departing at 9 AM and 1 and 7 PM. Price: $65.

Texas State Capitol (512-463-0063; www.tspb.state.tx.us; Congress Ave., Between 11th and 14th Sts.) Free guided tours Mon.–Fri. 8–4:30, Sat. 9:30–3:30, Sun. noon–3:30. Admission: Free. See "Historic Places," p. 41.

Texpert Tours (512-383-8989; www.texperttours.com) A variety of tours throughout Austin and the Hill Country hosted by Austin's own Howie Richey, whose knowledge of wacky stories and odd facts is astounding. Departures at 9 AM and 2 and 7 PM most days. Price: $50.

University of Texas Tower Tours (512-475-6633, 877-475-6633; www.ut.edu; Texas Union Information Center, corner of 24th and Guadalupe Sts.) For the best view of the UT campus and surrounding Austin, take a tour of the tower. Reservations are recommended; hours vary with the seasons. Open: Sat. and Sun. Admission: $5.

Tubing

Without a doubt, tubing is one of the more popular outdoor activities in Central Texas, and New Braunfels is the best place to experience it (see chapter 7, Nearby and In Between).

Mission San Francisco de la Espada

4

San Antonio

Pride and Joy

There is something special about San Antonio. You notice it when you are there, and it stays with you when you leave. Even Mark Twain felt it, naming San Antonio one of America's "unique cities" along with Boston, New Orleans, and San Francisco. Both a crossroads and a destination, San Antonio has attracted people for centuries, and its roots are deep and widespread. It is in many ways the birthplace of Texas; as a noted Texas historian and journalist once said, "Every Texan has two homes, his own and San Antonio."

ROOTS

Native Americans were the first settlers of the area, drawn to the banks of the San Antonio River, or, as they called it, the Yanaguana, meaning "refreshing waters" or "clear waters." Indeed, San Antonio's raison d'être is water, flowing from the San Antonio and San Pedro Springs into the San Antonio and San Pedro Rivers, supporting the lush ecosystem of the surrounding Olmos Creek basin. Tools and other artifacts found in this region attest to over 11,000 years of human habitation, and it is known that Native Americans used this area as a popular meeting and camping spot and a productive area for hunting and gathering. Though drilling, damming, and diverting have altered the location, flow, and personalities of the area's waterways, it is still easy to envision the practicality, charm, and charisma the water held for those who encountered it. Gurgling springs, the rushing river, and the surrounding vegetation are the center around which the city's history, most of its contested issues, and civic pride have revolved.

While it is unclear exactly when the first explorers of European origin entered the region, what is known is that on June 13, 1691, a group of Spanish priests, en route to visit missions in East Texas, paused to camp at the clear-running river's edge, beside a group of welcoming Native Americans. The day happened to be the Feast of Saint Anthony of Padua, and the priests, so taken with the area's beauty, decided to name it San Antonio de Padua. In the late 1700s, the French were eyeing Texas, and the Spanish moved to put down deeper roots. Between 1709 and 1722, Spanish *entradas*, organized expeditions, started to search the region for strategic spots to claim in advance of any French incursions. By 1718, the Spanish had staked a claim in San Antonio and founded the San Antonio de Béxar Presidio. In the same year, Franciscans, anxious for citizens and converts, established the first of the five missions they would build in the area, including the

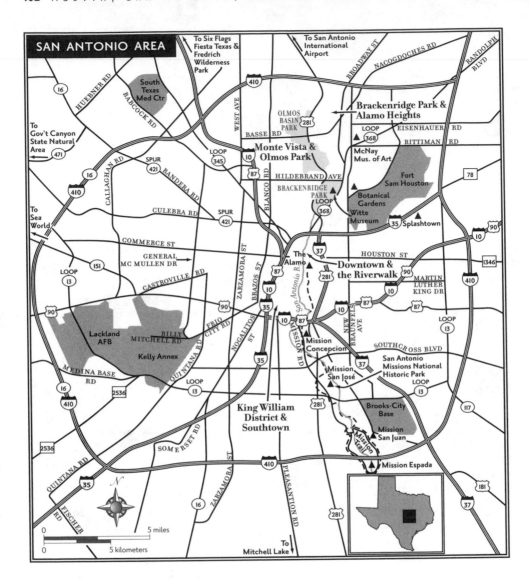

Alamo. The inhabitants of the missions, in turn, built seven *acequias,* a series of interconnected irrigation ditches and aqueducts, linking the missions and transporting water from the San Antonio River and the San Pedro Creek to the outlying farmlands, an outstanding feat of engineering for its day. In 1731, the village of San Fernando de Béxar was chartered by Canary Islanders, who went on to establish the San Fernando de Béxar Cathedral, and in 1772 the small town, by this time called San Antonio de Béxar, was made the capital of Spanish-ruled Texas.

When the Republic of Texas was formed in 1836, just months after the legendary battle of the Alamo, San Antonio was chartered as the seat of Bexar County. Located near a hotly contested border, San Antonio endured several Mexican invasions, and its population declined significantly until the Civil War in 1861. After the Civil War, San Antonio became a nexus of distribution, supplying the cattle-trail drives and serving as a gateway to the Southwest. Five railroad routes passed through between 1877 and 1900, setting the city on track to participate in the economic growth and modernization of the nation and hastening immigration. By the 1920s just over 161,000 residents called San Antonio home, making it the largest city in the state. The city was already a diverse mix of Tejanos, Mexicans, German Americans, and Anglos from the American South when the Mexican Revolution 1910 fueled substantial Mexican immigration, enhancing the city's already intimately intertwined history with Mexico.

THE RIVER

Over time, each group in each era has left its mark on San Antonio. From the food and architecture, to historic sites and festivals, San Antonio is a fascinating interplay of cultures and history. One of the city's most recognizable landmarks—the lovely Riverwalk— is also one of its newest, though its story begins in the 19th century.

Back then, San Antonians relied on the river for drinking, swimming and bathing, hydropower, and irrigation. By 1890, the need for more and more fresh water had grown urgent, and many artesian wells were drilled into the Edwards Aquifer. Snatching water directly from its source meant an inevitable decline in water flow on the surface, and by 1896 the spring-fed river was in jeopardy, its current reduced to a gloomy trickle dotted with garbage. The social consequences were steep for the diverse community of residents who would flock to the river to swim and picnic along its shady banks. The final blow came, with a swift chop, in 1904, as city workers used axes to fell two beloved willow trees in the

Bridge over the Riverwalk

name of river "cleanup." After enraged citizens turned out in droves to berate their city and its misguided plan, officials responded with promises to beautify and protect the waterway. Civic associations formed and began to push for revitalization of both the river and the public life that had flourished along it. In 1912 local architect Harvey L. Page designed a plan for reinforcement of a 13-mile stretch of river using what are known as "Surkey seawalls," to be traversed by decorative bridges and lined with benches.

Mother Nature, it seems, had other plans. Six major floods between 1914 and 1921 destroyed any progress on the plans, testing the city's resolve. Some even suggested simply covering the river with concrete and using it as a sewer, an idea met with little enthusiasm. Then came the Big One. On September 10, 1921, while the city slept, an enormous flood swept through the area, killing 50 people, steeping downtown in 2 to 10 feet of water, and making it crystal clear to the entire city that water must first be managed before it can be enjoyed. So the Olmos Dam was constructed in 1926, and a cut-off channel, allowing excess water to bypass downtown, completed in 1929—projects that together provided flood control. Then, a young architect, Robert H. Hugman, stepped forward with an ingenious plan. Designed specifically to showcase the river, his proposal of narrow pedestrian walkways, shops, and restaurants built to hug the bends and curves of the waters flowing 20 feet below street level was inspired by the old cities of Spain. Unfortunately, the Great Depression derailed this new plan, and a few new flower beds were planted along the river instead.

In 1936, the 100th anniversary of the Republic of Texas, a rush of civic pride washed over the city; by 1939 construction had begun on Hugman's plan for the Paseo del Rio, the San Antonio Riverwalk. The Work Progress Administration (WPA) managed the project, and on March 13, 1941, the WPA gifted the completed Riverwalk, with 17,000 feet of side-

Musicians on the Riverwalk

A welcome sight on a hot city day

walks, 31 stairways, and 4,000 plantings, to the city of San Antonio. Although 50,000 people came out to cheer for its dedication on April 21 of that year, the Riverwalk didn't come
into its own until the 1968 Hemisfair, during which it finally became an icon of the city.

PRIDE AND PRESERVATION

By 1930 both Houston and Dallas had surpassed San Antonio in population and economic
clout. Geographically, San Antonio remained within the boundaries of its original Spanish
charter until 1940, when the automobile hastened suburban growth.

Economically, San Antonio relies on military bases, educational institutions, and its
medical complexes for stability. Good weather, access to health care, and a large veteran
community, not to mention outstanding golf, have made San Antonio a popular retirement
area. Another big segment of its economy is tourism, and San Antonio is well aware of the
value of its many cultural and historic sites, neighborhoods, and festivals. With a rich
history to care for, San Antonio has been a leader in preservation; the San Antonio
Conservation Society, founded in 1924, has become a force to be reckoned with. Strict
preservation codes, tempered by tax incentives for rehabilitation and preservation, have
enabled individual buildings, even entire neighborhoods, to retain their unique features
and identities. Festivals such as the San Antonio Annual Livestock Show and Rodeo in
February, the wildly popular Fiesta San Antonio in April, the Tejano Conjunto Festival in
May, and the Texas Folklife Festival in June bring out the city's best. A dynamic and diverse
city, with lots of personality, and a river running through it, San Antonio is the pride and
joy of Texas.

Gargoyles on the Smith Young Building in downtown San Antonio

NEIGHBORHOODS

Many of San Antonio's sights, historic and cultural, can be found in the compact downtown surrounding the Riverwalk. Once you procure parking, this area is very easy to navigate on foot. Outside downtown, driving to and from the recommendations listed in this book is a nice way to explore the city's unique neighborhoods.

Downtown and the Riverwalk

"Downtown" is the area roughly contained by McCullough Avenue to the north, I-35 to the north and west, I-37/US 281 to the east, and West Durango Boulevard to the south. It is urban, with traffic, noise, and limited parking. Visitors can easily eat, sleep, and sightsee exclusively in this area.

King William District and Southtown

The King William District is the neighborhood south of Durango Boulevard, bounded by the river to the west and South Alamo Street to the east. German immigration to the neighborhood in the 1840s earned it the nickname "Sauerkraut Bend." Originally a fashionable area with large, single-family homes, the area slumped in the 1920s, and by the 1940s many of the homes had been converted to apartments. Located just a stone's throw from downtown, the neighborhood caught the spirit of renovation and preservation in the 1950s; in 1967 it earned the distinction of being the first Historic Neighborhood District in Texas. Today, the neighborhood is a lovely mix of restored larger homes, more modest abodes, atmospheric B&Bs, several small businesses, art studios, and popular restaurants all nestled under huge pecan trees.

Architectural detail in the King William district

Directly east, the area south of South Alamo Street is known as Southtown. This neighborhood of art galleries and studios is particularly interesting to wander through during festive "First Fridays" (see "Galleries," below), when establishments stay open late.

Brackenridge Park and Alamo Heights

From downtown, Broadway heads north past Brackenridge Park on its way to Alamo Heights. While the area surrounding Brackenridge Park and its attractions maintains an urban feel, Alamo Heights, San Antonio's original suburb and now its own city, is much more residential, with large homes and upscale dining and shopping clustered around the

Enjoying a boat ride on the San Antonio River

intersections of Broadway, North New Braunfels Avenue, and Austin Highway south of Northeast Loop 410 near the McNay Art Museum.

Monte Vista and Olmos Park

Neighboring Alamo Heights to the west, this once exquisite neighborhood has an uneven look and feel today, with lovingly restored mansions side by side with those that have fallen on hard times. A down-to-earth side of San Antonio, the neighborhood is the home to some well-loved restaurants and B&Bs.

TRANSPORTATION

Getting Around San Antonio

Public transportation offers an enjoyable way to get around in San Antonio. The city's public bus system, VIA (210-362-2020; www.viainfo.net), runs a network of routes throughout the city, and two are particularly useful to visitors. First, four VIA streetcars, reproductions of vintage open-air models, crisscross downtown along four different routes taking in most area attractions. Second, the No. 7, "Sightseer Special," ferries visitors to far-flung sites and attractions. All VIA buses are handicapped accessible. Fare: 80 cents a ride, or $3 for a convenient one-day pass.

Or try a water taxi! Rio San Antonio (210-244-5700 or 1-800-417-4139; www.riosan antonio.com) provides both river taxi and tour services (see "Tours," below) on the San Antonio River. You can purchase tickets from the drivers onboard, at a kiosk, or online. Fare: $4 one way, $10 for a 24-hour pass, and $25 for a three-day pass.

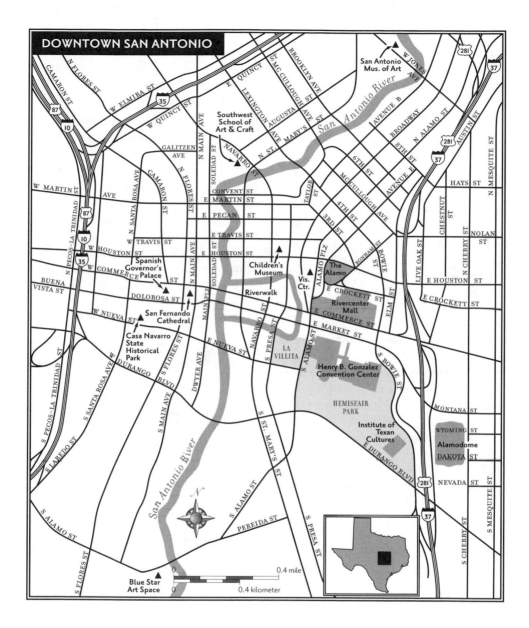

DOWNTOWN SAN ANTONIO

LODGING

Since much of the activity in San Antonio revolves around the Riverwalk, it is no surprise that many visitors spend the night as close as possible to the water. While the area is dominated by large chain hotels, boutique hotels just blocks away offer variety. One of San Antonio's best-kept secrets is its network of bed and breakfasts scattered throughout the historic neighborhoods, just minutes from the city center. The San Antonio B&B Association, or SABBA (www.sanantoniobb.org), is a self-regulating group that ensures standards are kept up. To offer extra incentive, and to compete with hotels along the

Riverwalk, many B&Bs offer free WiFi and parking, modernized baths, and sometimes discounts if you are traveling on a weekday or for business. Unlike chain hotels, however, B&Bs frequently require a two-day minimum on weekends, possibly more during holidays such as Fiesta (see "Festivals," below).

When choosing an area of town, keep in mind that the Riverwalk tends to stay open late for dining and drinking, and people like to visit San Antonio to have a good time. If you are used to city sounds, the resulting noise level may not bother you, but if you require silence to sleep, you might consider a hotel in a quieter neighborhood several blocks removed or a B&B with strictly enforced quiet hours. In addition, downtown hotels often charge hefty parking fees; be sure to inquire when making your reservation.

Guests with limited mobility may find the larger hotels to be the best fit, especially those along the Riverwalk, where they may have elevator access to the walk itself. The city's B&Bs are located in older homes that can not always be retrofitted appropriately, but that said, if a certain property catches your eye, by all means call and inquire, as special arrangements can sometimes be made.

The codes here reflect the hotels' advertised rates; keep in mind that they tend to rise in peak season and fall in off-season.

Lodging Price Code

Inexpensive	Up to $100
Moderate	$100 to $150
Expensive	$150 to $250
Very Expensive	Over $250

DOWNTOWN AND RIVERWALK

Drury Inn and Suites–Riverwalk
210-212-5200 or 1-800-378-7946
www.druryhotels.com
201 N. St. Mary's St., San Antonio, TX 78205
Price: Expensive
Special Features: Free Internet in rooms; free WiFi in lobby; handicapped access; pets welcome; pool

Located in a renovated 1920s building, the Drury occupies a lovely spot along the Riverwalk somewhat removed from the most congested areas and is a solid value for this area of San Antonio. Most of its rooms have a view, though whether of the river or the rooftops depends on what you pay. The decent-size rooms and two-room suites tend to be exceptionally clean and comfortable, with high ceilings and wood-trimmed windows, and the hotel as a whole has a casual, friendly air about it. Freshly popped popcorn and fountain drinks are available at no charge in the lobby from 3 PM to 10 PM daily, and adults are given vouchers for three free drinks during the "Manager's Reception," held nightly from 5:30 to 7. In the morning, the complimentary breakfast buffet is substantial, with eggs, sausage, waffles, cereals, and fruits. The Drury is a favorite of families and convention-goers, both of whom tend to be a bit noisy in their exuberance. The hotel's elevator provides direct access to the Riverwalk, perfect for strollers or wheelchairs.

Emily Morgan
210-225-5100 or 1-800-824-6674
www.emilymorganhotel.com
705 Houston St., San Antonio, TX 78205
Price: Expensive
Special Features: Handicapped access; pool; WiFi $9.95

The Emily Morgan is the grande dame of hotels in San Antonio. A tall, wedge-shaped Gothic-revival building built in the 1920s—a former medical facility whose exterior is festooned with ailing gargoyles—directly across from the Alamo, the Emily has been updated inside with modern decor and stylish bathrooms. While all of the smallish rooms are cozy and stocked with Aveda bath products and luxurious linens, some have down pillow-top mattresses and Jacuzzi tubs. Still, older hotels have their idiosyncrasies, and in this one you can expect a few, such as fickle showerheads and a noisy heating system. In addition to the extra expense for Internet access, the valet parking will set you back roughly $20 a day, and you will have to purchase breakfast, as it is not included. Overall, the Emily is a wonderful slice of history and charm for travelers who prefer boutique hotels to big chains and expect quirks.

Hawthorn Suites San Antonio/River Walk
210-527-1900 or 1-800-527-1133
www.hawthorn-riverwalk.com
830 N. St. Mary's St., San Antonio, TX 78205
Price: Inexpensive to Moderate
Special Features: Free WiFi; handicapped access; pool

As you will quickly discover, many establishments in San Antonio love to include the famous Riverwalk in their name, regardless of where they are located. The Hyatt-owned Hawthorn Suites is situated, quite literally, on the Riverwalk, just farther north than you may have expected—a block north of the Southwest School of Arts and Crafts, to be exact, and nowhere near the restaurants and attractions. Those who enjoy a little peace and quiet, however, should take heart; the Hawthorn Suites is situated on a flourishing stretch of the river with lovely views of lush greenery, birds, and flowers. The hotel has oversized studio suites with refrigerators and microwaves, a large patio/deck off the breakfast room with ample space for relaxing, a small pool for cooling off, and a larger-than-average complimentary breakfast buffet served each morning until 10:30. It isn't unnecessarily fancy, just new, clean, very functional, and spacious, a good value and

perfect for families. Those who enjoy exercise will find that walking along the Riverwalk into downtown makes for a pleasant 20-minute stroll. The adventurous can try the River Taxi ($4 a person), which runs twice hourly from the landing below the hotel, while those who need wheels can either take their car or call a cab for the brief ride downtown.

Hotel Contessa
210-229-9222 or 1-866-435-0900
www.thehotelcontessa.com
306 W. Market St., San Antonio, TX 78205
Price: Expensive to Very Expensive
Special Features: Handicapped access; pool; WiFi $9.95

This 12-story, all-suite hotel and conference center is a newcomer to the Riverwalk, having opened in December 2005. Decor is simple and modern, with details that nod to the Mediterranean or the American Southwest, executed in colors chosen from a soothing earth-tone palette. Each spacious room has a separate parlor (with sleeper sofa) and bedroom, with comfy mattresses and crisp linens, and flat-screen televisions. All the rooms are non-smoking. The Contessa is designed with lots of open space, and noise can travel throughout it, especially on weekends, so consider requesting a room on one of the upper floors if you're a light sleeper. The exercise room is small but adequate, as is the rooftop pool, which comes with super views. Prices vary depending on the view, one of which is of Marriage Island, just behind the property, where San Antonio's first Catholic Mass was held in 1691 and couples still say their nuptial vows today.

Hotel Valencia
210-227-9700 or 1-866-842-0100
www.hotelvalencia.com
150 E. Houston St., San Antonio, TX 78205
Price: Very Expensive

Special Features: Handicapped access; free
   WiFi

Modern and hip, this hotel isn't just a
building, it's architecture. Designed by
dMd Associates of Los Angeles, the hotel is
stylish, sophisticated, dramatic, and dimly
lit. The Valencia is on busy Houston Street
near the Majestic Theatre, so be prepared
for some noise. The down comforters and
pillows are thick and luxurious, and the
sparse, uncluttered decor is so refreshing it
has some guests heading straight home to
remodel. Lest your expectations start to
skyrocket, be prepared for service that can
be uneven, extras, such as dips into the
minibar and snacks that add up quickly,
and parking that might be a challenge if you
aren't prepared to pay almost $40 a day for
valet service. Outdoor space is limited, with
no pool and a tiny "balcony" in some rooms
that may best be described as a ledge. A new
hotel, the Valencia is still ironing out the
kinks, but copious luxuries and quality
touches such as the seven layers of Egyptian
cotton linens on each bed are promising
signs. Have a drink at the bar (see "Nightlife," below) and decide for yourself.

La Mansión Del Rio

210-518-1000 or 1-888-444-6664
www.omnihotels.com
112 College St., San Antonio, TX 78205
Price: Very Expensive
Special Features: Handicapped access;
   pool; WiFi $9.95

This 1852 Spanish colonial–style structure,
once a Catholic school, exudes historic
charm in its hacienda-style courtyards,
lush vegetation, and bubbling fountains.
Room sizes vary, ranging from spacious to
cozy, and each is unique, with details such
as exposed ceiling beams and brick walls.
La Mansión Del Rio is an older hotel, but
its eccentricities capture the look and feel
of old San Antonio, and its fantastic location in the heart of the Riverwalk makes it a

favorite among travelers. The on-site
restaurant, Las Canarias, has a champagne
Sunday brunch buffet (10–3, adults $38,
children $19.95) that is sheer extravagance.
Dine in a riverside veranda, on a tiled patio
with gently swaying palms, or inside in the
atmospheric dining rooms.

Menger Hotel

210-223-4361
www.mengerhotel.com
204 Alamo Plaza, San Antonio, TX 78205
Price: Expensive
Special Features: Free Internet in rooms;
   WiFi in lobby; pool; bar; restaurant

Just across from the Alamo, the Menger
Hotel, built in 1859, is so steeped in history
that there are even tales of ghosts haunting
its halls. As with most historic hotels, the
Menger's front entrance is grand while its
rooms are small, especially by today's standards. Updated bathrooms are also tiny and
lack the coffeemakers and blow-dryers
we've all become accustomed to. On the
plus side, the beds are comfy, the rooms
cozy, the location fantastic, and the courtyard and poolside relaxing. Past guests
include Mae West, Babe Ruth, and Teddy
Roosevelt, so you can rest easy knowing
you're in good company. Another perk is
the Menger Bar (see "Nightlife," below),
built in 1887 as a replica of the taproom
inside the House of Lords in London and
the venue from which T.R. reportedly rustled up his Rough Riders; it's still a fun
place for a drink.

The Painted Lady Inn

210-220-1092
www.thepaintedladyinn.com
620 Broadway, San Antonio, TX 78215
Price: Moderate to Expensive
Special Features: Free WiFi

The Painted Lady Inn's rooms, the Mae
West, the Amelia Earhart, and the Oscar
Wilde, to name a few, are smart and very

La Mansión del Rio Hotel along the Riverwalk

The Menger Hotel beside the Alamo

individual, with a sense of style and personality that reminds visitors of a time when style was personal. This Victorian inn is sandwiched between two solid concrete buildings on a busy street, and its well-insulated interior is impervious to the sounds of traffic on Broadway. This was once a boardinghouse, and the rooms for guests are all on the first floor, flanking the broad central hall. The inn is friendly, relaxed, and comfortable, with high ceilings, antique beds, thoroughly modern baths, videos and DVDs for loan at night, and hot muffins delivered to your room in the morning. The six-block walk to the Riverwalk is not necessarily scenic, but considerate owner and manager Jacob can help you map an agreeable route.

Riverwalk Vista

210-223-3200 or 1-866-898-4782
www.riverwalkvista.com
262 Losoya St., San Antonio, TX 78205
Price: Moderate to Expensive
Special Features: Free Internet

The Riverwalk Vista is completely unlike any other hotel in San Antonio. Part B&B, part boutique, and park Riverwalk venue, it strikes a wonderful balance for travelers looking for personality, style, and location. Each of the hotel's 17 rooms feels like a bedroom in a city loft. Enormous 4-by-10-foot windows let in plenty of light, wood floors add charm, and some of the rooms have exposed brick walls. Chic and sparsely decorated, the rooms have wooden beds, down comforters, and leather chairs that work beautifully with their warm earth-tone walls and black-and-white artwork. The spacious common rooms are likewise decorated, and the overall effect is very 1930s and 1940s. Modern slate-tiled showers, a 26-inch flat-screen TV, and Teddy the Bear waiting on each bed round out the amenities. The breakfast is not as elaborate as you might find at a comparably priced

B&B, and the fridge should be treated more like a hotel minibar than one at a B&B, whose extras tend to be complimentary. Overall, a good choice for lovebirds, business travelers looking for a break from the monotony of the chain hotels, and guests who appreciate individuality.

KING WILLIAM DISTRICT AND SOUTHTOWN

Brackenridge House

210-271-3442 or 1-800-221-1412
www.brackenridgehouse.com
230 Madison St., San Antonio, TX 78204
Price: Moderate to Expensive.
Special Features: Free WiFi; pool

The Brackenridge House is imbued with the sense of southern hospitality that emanates from its friendly owners Bennie and Sue, whose roots in San Antonio go way back. The neatly kept rooms in this historic home are individually decorated with cheerfully painted walls, well-chosen antiques, and colorful carpets over hardwood floors. Some rooms have quilts, others have kitchenettes, but they all have claw-foot tubs, microwaves, mini-refrigerators stocked with complimentary beverages, and chocolates left out for your enjoyment. In the morning, breakfast is a three-course affair, served with fancy crystal and china in the dining room, after which you might enjoy lounging by the outdoor pool. Children and pets are welcome to stay in the spacious backyard Carriage House.

Gardenia Inn

210-223-5875 or 1-800-356-1605
www.gardenia-inn.com
307 Beauregard St., San Antonio, TX 78204
Price: Inexpensive to Moderate
Special Features: Free WiFi

Nestled on a leafy street in the heart of the King William District, the Gardenia Inn, built in 1905, is a Greek revival–style home with a stunning veranda. The interior

The table, set for breakfast, at the Gardenia Inn

features gleaming woodwork set against crisp white walls with richly colored rugs, upholstery, and artwork. Rooms tend to be well-sized, light, and airy, with Old World details such as lustrous wood floors, antique beds, and deep claw-foot tubs, coupled with the modern amenities of climate control, high-speed Internet, and cable televisions. The Gardenia Inn is unusual in that two rooms, the Rose Cottage Carriage House and the Desert Blossom Suite, can sleep four and five guests respectively, making the inn a wonderful alternative for families or friends traveling together; and children are welcome. The hearty breakfasts are to be enjoyed with gusto, as the thoughtful innkeepers have adapted the recipes to make them as healthy as they are delicious; other dietary needs are accommodated as well.

The Ogé House
210-223-2353 or 1-800-242-2770
www.ogeinn.com
209 Washington St., San Antonio, TX 78204

Price: Expensive
Special Features: Free WiFi

The Ogé House (Oh-jay), built in 1857, is a lovely mansion on the banks of the San Antonio River in the King William District and is both listed in the National Register of Historic Places and designated a Texas Historical Landmark. Once the home of Texas Ranger, cattle rancher, and businessman Louis Ogé, the Ogé House embodies the grandeur of bygone Texas, with tall ceilings and windows, verandas on each of its three stories, and fireplaces in many of its rooms. The same owners operate several other luxurious, though much smaller, B&Bs throughout the area; see www.nobleinns.com for more details.

A Yellow Rose Bed and Breakfast
210-229-9903 or 1-800-950-9903
www.ayellowrose.com
229 Madison St., San Antonio, TX 78204
Price: Moderate
Special Features: Free WiFi

The home you see when you walk up to A Yellow Rose is the owner's; the guest rooms are tucked back behind, each with its own door to the porches and garden. The rooms are large—especially the roomy Carriage House Suite, which has two separate beds—clean, entirely comfortable, and have an air of familiarity. With large bathrooms, comfy sitting areas, books to peruse, and large beds for lounging, A Yellow Rose feels like a retreat indeed. Whether strolling the leafy neighborhood in the evening, just blocks from South Alamo Street, or sitting in the chairs on the porch with one of the resident cats, you feel you have a home away from home at the Yellow Rose.

MONTE VISTA AND OLMOS PARK

Bonner Garden
210-733-4222 or 1-800-396-4222
www.bonnergarden.com
145 E. Agarita Ave., San Antonio, TX 78212
Price: Moderate to Expensive
Special Features: Free WiFi; pool

Bonner Garden, built in 1910 and modeled after a 17th-century Italian villa, is filled with history and character. Once home to Texas artist Mary Bonner, the building has been lovingly restored by a succession of owners and is now run by Margi and Jim Herbold. Bonner's artwork and that of her French mentor hang throughout the house. Each of the home's six rooms has its own personality; the Studio, with exposed stone walls and hand-carved Mexican furniture, is both rustic and cozy, while the Portico Room has crisp, white woodwork and an airy ceiling mural. Outdoors, large shade-trees and a refreshing European-style swimming pool make this a great place to hide from the heat.

Ruckman Haus
210-736-1468 or 1-866-736-1468
www.ruckmanhaus.com
629 W. French Place, San Antonio, TX 78212
Price: Inexpensive to Moderate
Special Features: Free WiFi

The Ruckman Haus is a comfortable crafts-man-style B&B tucked away on a quiet side street off San Pedro Avenue. Its owners, the very affable Ron and lovely Prudence, are as gracious as can be, and their thoughtfulness is evidenced throughout the home. Rooms are decorated thematically; the pretty blue and yellow French Room, for example, is light and airy with gleaming hardwood floors, and the large Sun Room has its own rooftop deck. Guests are welcome to help themselves to an evening glass of wine in the kitchen, read in the living room, or relax on the small stone patio. From complimentary beverages in room refrigerators to thick towels and soft luxurious linens, the Ruckmans have thought of every detail. With generous home-cooked breakfasts, including real cream for your coffee, it's easy to feel right at home. Special rates are extended to visitors traveling alone on business, and many, once they've had a taste of life at Ruckman Haus, never return to the chain hotels. A real treat and a terrific value.

OUTER SAN ANTONIO

Hyatt Regency Hill Country Resort and Spa
210-647-1234 or 1-800-233-1234
www.hillcountry.hyatt.com
9800 Hyatt Resort Dr., San Antonio, TX 78251
Price: Very Expensive
Special Features: Bar; golf; handicapped access; pool and water features; restaurants; spa; WiFi $9.95

The Hyatt has created a self-contained resort with a distinctly Hill Country feel just minutes west of downtown San Antonio. With amenities like a spa, a golf course, a 4-acre water park, pools, numerous restaurants, a slow manmade river for tubing, and pristinely manicured grounds, this place is made for those who like to combine relaxation and recreation, especially families. With so much here to do, you may find you check in and never go out, spending day after day at the pool just lazing around. Once you've worn yourself out, retire to the guest room with its funky jewel-toned fabrics, wooden furniture, and bed with many pillows, to sleep off the experience. If you visit the Hyatt Hill Country Resort and Spa, be sure to wear your pants with deep pockets; with all the additional fees, this place can get pricey. But special packages such as the Family Getaway for $249 per weekday night help take the edge off.

The Westin La Cantera Resort
210-558-6500 or 1-800-937-8661
www.westinlacantera.com
16641 La Cantera Pkwy., San Antonio, TX
    78256

Price: Very Expensive
Special Features: Free WiFi in the lobby; handicapped access

Built high on a hill on the site of a former limestone quarry—la cantera—this resort is 20 minutes from downtown but in a world all its own. The resort's two world-class golf courses (see "Fore!" below), including the challenging and spectacular Palmer Course, are a big draw, and the patrons who come to play are quite serious about their game. Consequently, the mood doesn't feel quite as relaxed as at the Hyatt. Six pools, tennis courts, spa services, and three hot tubs round out the offerings. For accommodations, you can choose between a typical Westin guest room in the main complex or a casita, "little house," in Casita Village. All rooms feature a super-comfy bed, luxurious bath products, and complimentary Starbucks coffee.

CULTURE

Most of San Antonio's sights can be found in three neighborhoods of the city—the Riverwalk, King William District, and Brackenridge Park—but don't miss the Mission Trail, the route linking the four historic missions on the outer edges of the city.

Historic Places

The Alamo
210-225-1391
www.thealamo.org
300 Alamo Square, San Antonio, TX 78205
Open: Mon.–Sat. 9–5:30, Sun. 10–5:30
Admission: Free, donations accepted
Special Features: Gardens; gift shop

The Alamo began as an idea when Antonio de San Buenaventura y Olivares, a participant in the entrada to establish missions in Texas, visited a spot just west of the San Pedro Springs on April 13, 1709, and dreamt of building a mission there. That dream was realized nine years later on May 1, 1718, when he erected a small hut of brush and grapevines, said Mass, and named his creation the Mission San Antonio de Valero. In 1719, the mission relocated to the east of San Pedro Springs; it was later uprooted and moved once more to the spot now occupied by St. Joseph's Church in San Antonio, where it was destroyed by floods in

The Alamo

Detail of the front of the Alamo

1724. Finally, in 1744, the mission was built along the banks of the San Antonio River, only to be abandoned when Mexico secularized the missions in 1793. From these chaotic beginnings and amid rising tensions between area Anglos and Mexicans, the mission's function morphed from sanctuary for converts to an enclave of combatants. When the Mexican cavalry occupied the mission in the early 1800s, its was referred to as the *pueblo del Alamo—alamo* being the Spanish word for cottonwood, so-called perhaps for the trees along the river—and the name stuck.

On October 2, 1835, turf wars between Mexicans and Anglos reached a boiling point when Mexicans demanded the town cannon from the nearby settlement of Gonzales, and were told, in no uncertain terms, "Come and get it." Needless to say, the Mexicans did and promptly lost the first battle of the Texas Revolution. Emboldened by success, a hastily gathered group of barely 200 male colonists (and dozens of women and children), including the legendary Davy Crockett, Stephen F. Austin, William Travis, and the famous knife fighter Jim Bowie, seized San Antonio and settled into the abandoned mission, the Alamo, to wait for inevitable Mexican retribution.

On February 23, 1836, an estimated 4,000 Mexican troops under the command of the formidable Gen. Antonio López de Santa Anna besieged the Alamo, capturing it after 13 days of constant battle and the deaths of all defenders. While the participants lost the Alamo and their lives (though some women and children were released), their actions became the stuff of legend. The event galvanized support for the ultimately successful revolution against Mexico, for which the phrase "Remember the Alamo" became a rallying cry. Or so the story goes. As with any historically significant battle, especially one as dramatic and pivotal as this, the facts are still debated. What remains is what the Alamo has come to represent: collective courage in the face of insurmountable odds.

Visitors may be surprised by the size of the Alamo. Rather than an imposing fort, the Alamo is a small structure whose architecture is indicative of its religious roots. Built from local rock, its intricately carved exterior is a light, sandy beige color that reflects the bright Texas sun. The Daughters of the Republic of Texas, women whose Texas roots run as deep as the aquifer, are particularly proud of their role as custodians of the structure; they maintain it with care and demand utmost respect. Nearby, the Alamo IMAX Theater (see "Cinema," below) shows an informative film about the siege year-round, while the San Antonio Living History Association stages dramatic reenactments.

Memorial to those who died at the Battle of the Alamo in 1836

Riverwalk Accessibility

The Riverwalk is recessed below street level, and getting to it can be a challenge for anyone with restricted mobility. Strollers, wheelchairs, and walkers are simply impossible to manage on the steep, sometimes slippery, steps. If you are planning some of the details of your trip in advance and online, consider printing a copy of the "Accessible Riverwalk" map found on www.sanantoniovisit .com, under the "Coming to Visit?" then "Maps" sections.

While elevators dot the Riverwalk, some particularly convenient locations include: Crowne Plaza Hotel, Hawthorne Suites Hotel, Hilton del Rio, Holiday Inn Riverwalk, Hotel Contessa, the Hyatt, La Mansión Del Rio, Rivercenter Mall, the Westin, and in front of the Aztec Theater.

The Mission Trail
www.nps.gov/saan
National Park Service
2202 Roosevelt Ave., San Antonio, TX 78210
Open: Daily 9–5

Allow at least three hours to visit the entire park, 1½ to 2 hours at the Mission San José and the park's Visitor Center located there, then 30–40 minutes at each of the other three parks. The missions are approximately 2 miles apart, a short drive, but too far to walk. Bicycle tours are available (see "Tours," below).

The Missions in San Antonio were built in the 1700s as part of Spain's efforts to colonize its northern frontier, Texas. The idea was to build self-sustaining communities, patterned after villages in Spain, that would provide support for continued colonization as well as formal education for Native Americans in the ways and religion of the country that now considered them subjects. While some Native Americans met the idea with resistance, others acquiesced, and construction began. The five expansive San Antonio missions were built in just 13 years, with presidios, or military outposts, established nearby for protection.

One of the extraordinary features of the missions are the *acequias*—aqueducts and irrigation ditches—running between them. While the Pueblo in New Mexico had already designed and built aqueducts, this technology would have been unknown to the nomadic Native Americans in Central Texas. Desperate to irrigate the arid land, the Franciscan missionaries, familiar with the aqueducts built by the Romans and the Moors, designed the system, part of which is still in use and can be seen at various locations along the Mission Trail, including Espada Park near Mission San José.

With housing, water, and farming in place, the missions functioned relatively well from 1745 to the 1780s. Over time, though, attacks and looting by Native Americans, lack of recruits, and disease took their toll; in 1794 a decree from the government ordered the secularization of all missions, disbanding their communal structure.

Throughout the years, the missions have endured the passing of time, weather, and some misguided attempts at restoration. Though many of the details you see today are actually painstaking reproductions, the sheer beauty and scale of the endeavor is impressive.

Today, the individual missions are active parishes, with many of the descendants of the original parishioners among their members. Though visitors are welcome to attend Mass, the Park Service reminds guests to be respectful of weddings, funerals, or other functions, which may temporarily close the venue for several hours.

Mission Concepción
210-534-1540
807 Mission Rd., at Felisa, San Antonio, TX 78210

A stone church bookended by a pair of bell towers, Mission Concepción is a spectacular example of Spanish colonial architecture, with intricate details, artwork, and design adaptations that illustrate the close relationship between the Native American, Spanish, and Mexican artisans who built it. Colorful and detailed frescos once covered both the front and interior of the church. While only a handful have survived the 250 years since they were created, those that do are a testament to the craftsmanship and artistry of their makers. Mission Concepción was host of many religious festivals, celebrations, pageants, and processionals, all designed to school new Spaniards in the ways of Christianity.

Mission San Francisco de la Espada
210-627-2021
10040 Espada Rd., San Antonio, TX 78214

Mission Espada was the first mission in Texas, originally founded in East Texas in 1690 and moved to San Antonio in 1731. The present-day building, completed in 1756, is clearly recognizable by its graceful *espadana* (bell tower) with three bells, which rises above its unique arched doorway; be sure to ask a park ranger about the mystery of its design. The

Mission Concepción

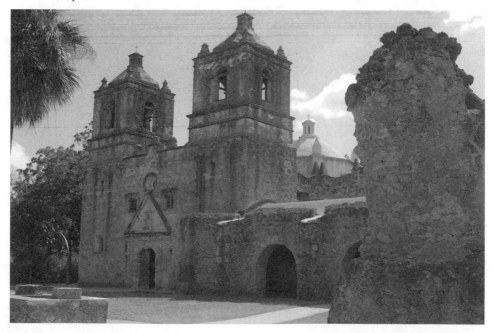

Mission San José

wooden cross beside the door, as the story goes, was borne by parishioners processing and praying for rain. The diminutive and detailed chapel is intimate and tranquil. Mission Espada's *acequia madre* (the main aqueduct) and nearby Espada Dam, built in the 1730s, are both still in use.

Mission San José

210-932-1001

6701 San José Dr., San Antonio, TX 78214

Mission San José, just a few miles south of the Alamo, was founded in 1720 by Father Antonio Margil de Jésus. Its complex of bastions, a granary, and a church, surrounded by stone walls, was completed in 1782. Elaborate design features, such as the enormous and intricately carved wooden doors, touching statuary, and ornate *La Ventana de Rosa*, the Rose Window, created in 1775 in the mission's sacristy, earned Mission San José the reputation of "Queen of the Missions." A thriving community of three hundred souls in its heyday, Mission San José was a model of success for the other missions.

It is still a very active parish, and visitors are welcome to attend Mass. On Sunday, the noon "Mariachi Mass" is very popular; doors close once seats are filled, so plan on arriving early.

Mission San Juan Capistrano

210-534-0749

9101 Graf Rd., San Antonio, TX 78214

Mission San Juan was founded in 1716 in what is now East Texas and moved to its present location in 1731. This mission is best remembered for its remarkable productivity, with orchards and gardens in its adjacent *labores* (farmlands designated for the mission's use)

Mission San Juan Capistrano

The dramatic facade of San Fernando Cathedral

and herds of sheep and cattle. By the mid-1700s, Mission San Juan was a major supplier of produce not just to the local area, but to markets as far away as Louisiana and Mexico.

Navarro State Historic Site

210-226-4801
www.tpwd.state.tx.us
228 S. Laredo St., San Antonio, TX 78207
Open: Wed.–Sun. 10–4
Admission: Adults $2

This complex of white limestone, clay, and adobe structures that was once home to prominent Tejano businessman, statesman, and writer José Antonio Navarro will be of interest to anyone wanting to dig a little deeper into the complexities of Texas history. Navarro, who was born in 1795 and died in 1871, witnessed the most significant years in Texas history. He was one of the signers of the Texas Declaration of Independence in 1836 and known as a tireless defender of Tejano rights. The historic site is operated by the State Park Service, with expert guides on hand to answer any questions.

San Fernando Cathedral

210-227-1297
www.sfcathedral.org
115 W. Main Plaza, San Antonio, TX 78205
Open: Daily, first Mass at 6:15 AM; closing times vary
Admission: Free, donations accepted

Established in 1731 by just over a dozen families from the Canary Islands, and completed in 1749, the cathedral that was designed to be in the center of town has certainly been the center of drama over the years. Jim Bowie was purportedly married here. Santa Anna used it as a lookout post and from its walls raised the flag that signaled the start of the battle of the Alamo. The huge Gothic revival–style cathedral you see today, built in 1868, integrates the original structure into its plan. In 1871 the original massive dome ceiling collapsed and was later rebuilt. In the 1930s, remains uncovered on-site thought to be those of Bowie, Davy Crockett, and William Travis were laid to rest in a marble casket at the back of the church. After Texas joined the United States in 1845, the strong ties between San Fernando and the community it served survived, and they are still vital today, making the cathedral one of the most important, lasting Hispanic institutions in a rapidly changing city and state.

San Fernando is host to music, concerts, and interdenominational events and doubles as a community center and social services headquarters. In order to preserve the historic structure and add much-needed space for functions, San Fernando is currently raising funds for a massive renovation project scheduled to begin in the near future. A parish church, San Fernando conducts hundreds of baptisms, weddings, and funerals each year: If your visit coincides with one, the church respectfully asks that you return at a different time. The best time to visit just might be attending Mass; see the Web site for details.

Spanish Governor's Palace

210-224-0601
www.sanantonio.gov/parks

Spanish Governor's Palace

105 Plaza de Armas, San Antonio, TX 78205
Open: Mon.–Sat. 9–5, Sun. 10–5
Admission: Adults $1.50, children 75 cents

A National Historic Landmark, the Spanish Governor's Palace was actually the residence
and headquarters of the presidio captain who was to watch over the Mission San Antonio
de Valero—the Alamo. Built in the early 1700s, the building is the only surviving example of
a Spanish aristocratic home in the United States. A small white stucco building, with very
low ceilings and doorways, the abode is graceful in its simplicity; a small courtyard, fountain, and period furnishings lend themselves to the atmosphere, as does *La Compañía de
Cavallería del Real Presidio de San Antonio de Béxar*, the living history group that gives performances on the final Sunday of each month. Acquired by the city of San Antonio in the
1920s, the home is currently under the auspices of the city's Parks and Recreation
Department.

La Villita

210-207-8610
www.lavillita.com
418 Villita St., San Antonio, TX 78205
Open: Daily 10–6
Admission: Free

Perched above the San Antonio River is the city's first neighborhood, La Villita, "little village." First the Coahuiltecan Indians settled here. Later Spanish soldiers built huts, which
were washed away in a flood in 1819 and replaced with more substantial dwellings made of
stone, adobe, and brick. In 1836, General Santa Anna used the area for his cannons in the
battle of the Alamo. In the late 1800s, Germans and French immigrated to the area and
brought with them their own architectural style, hence the Victorian elements still seen in
La Villita. In the early 20th century the neighborhood fell into disrepair, but by the late
1930s talk of the Riverwalk project brought renewed interest in San Antonio's historic
past, and La Villita was preserved as the urban center grew around it. These days, La Villita
is called an artist community, though it feels more like one gift shop after the next. The
area is pleasant, a welcome detour from the city's busy streets, and it's Arneson Theatre is
well known for hosting music and cultural performances.

Museums

Institute of Texan Cultures

210-458-2330
www.texancultures.utsa.edu
801 S. Bowie St., San Antonio, TX 78205
Open: Tue.–Sat. 10–6, Sun. noon–5
Admission: Adults $7, seniors and children $4

Originally designed as a collection of exhibits for the Texas pavilion of the Hemisfair
held in San Antonio in 1968, the Institute of Texan Cultures (ITC) is now best described
as an education center highlighting the contributions of the state's vastly diverse ethnic
groups and, as their mission statement states, "the dynamics between cultural history and

scientific discovery." Though it was supposed to have only a six-month run, the effort was so well received that the ITC has remained open to this day, now under the auspices of the University of Texas at San Antonio. The focus of the ITC is education; its exhibits, while fairly low-tech and not particularly flashy, are engaging, thoughtfully put together, and rich with historical detail. The esoteric surprises are fun, such as the small exhibit on the Wendish immigrants to Texas, from what is now borderland between Germany and Poland. The staff is particularly knowledgeable and happy to answer questions. The institute hosts the fantastic Texas Folklife Festival every year in June (see "Festivals," below).

McNay Art Museum
210-824-5368
www.mcnayart.org
6000 N. New Braunfels Ave., San Antonio, TX 78209
Open: Tue.–Fri. 10–4, Thu. 10–9, Sat. and Sun. 10–5
Price: Free, but a $5 donation suggested

The wonderful McNay Art Museum, the first modern art museum in Texas, is located in art-lover Marion Koogler McNay's Spanish colonial revival–style mansion. Upon her death in 1950, she bequeathed the mansion, the gorgeous 23 acres on which it sits, the extensive art collection housed within it, and two-thirds of her fortune to the city of San Antonio, which opened the entire estate as a museum in 1954. A serious collector, Mrs. McNay had a wonderful eye; the museum houses some real gems, most of them American or European pieces from the 19th and 20th centuries. There are bold paintings by Paul Gauguin and Vincent van Gogh, watercolors by Mary Cassatt and Winslow Homer, and collections of pieces in various mediums that McNay acquired on trips to artist colonies in New Mexico in the 1930s. Over the years, gifts by various collectors have added major paintings by Georgia O'Keeffe and sculptures by Auguste Rodin and Alberto Giacometti, among others. In 1984 Robert L. B. Tobin donated a collection of eight thousand books, many on the theater arts, which are now part of a research library that bears his name. The Blanche and John Leeper Auditorium was completed in the early 1990s, paving the way for performances and concerts to be held at the museum. In many ways, the McNay is best known for the breadth and depth of the outstanding national exhibitions it is able to attract and host in its galleries in a given year. All told, a lovely museum, inside and out.

Pensive statue in front of the McNay Art Museum

At the corner of Market Square, the much-anticipated **Museo Americano Smithsonian** (210-458-2300; 101 S. Santa Rosa Blvd.) has yet to open.

San Antonio Children's Museum

210-212-4453

www.sakids.org

305 E. Houston St., San Antonio, TX 78205

Open: Tue.–Fri. 9–2, Sat. 9–6, Sun. noon–4 Sept.–May; Mon.–Fri. 9–5, Sat. 9–6, Sun. noon–4

Admission: $6.95

After a day of "Please eat nicely with your fork, we're in a restaurant," "Please don't touch that, honey, this is a museum," and "Please don't climb on that, it is very fragile and of great historical significance," doesn't a museum for kids sound great? At the San Antonio Children's Museum kids can pretend to be a pilot, a dentist, a frontloader operator, and a chef. They can power an elevator, open a bank account, and play chess with pawns the size of a toddler. If you're lucky, you'll catch one of the museum's many special events or weekly activities involving playing with food, hands-on exploration, and unrestricted creative movement. This time all you have to do is just sit back and watch!

San Antonio Museum of Art

210-978-8100

www.samuseum.org

200 W. Jones Ave., San Antonio, TX 78215

Open: Tue. 10–8, Wed.–Sat. 10–5, Sun. noon–6

Admission: Adults $8, seniors $7, students $5, children $3, children 3 and under free; Tue. 4–8 free

---

Quirky Museums of Texas Past

There are several museums in San Antonio that, depending on your interests, may intrigue.

Buckhorn Saloon and Museum (210-247-4000; www.buckhornmuseum.com; 348 E. Houston St.) Open: Memorial Day to Labor Day 10–6, Labor Day to Memorial Day 10–5. Admission: Adults $11, seniors $10, children $8. If you're not into alcohol and taxidermy this place may not appeal, but if you are, it's neat. The entrance is at the bar, and from there you can wander, drink in hand, into the museum, where all sorts of Wild West memorabilia share billing with the mounted heads of a wide variety of animals. Just in case you didn't think it was odd enough, check out the Curio Store.

O. Henry House Museum (corner of Laredo St. and Houston St.) Open: Hours vary. Admission: free. A glimpse into the world of William Sidney Porter, who lived in this 1886 Queen Anne–style cottage from 1893 to 1895; but die-hard O. Henry fans will find the O. Henry Museum in Austin more satisfying.

Texas Pioneer and Ranger Museum (210-822-9011; www.texasranger.org; 3805 Broadway) Open: Mon.–Sat. 10–5, Sun. noon–5. Admission: Adults $5, seniors $3, children $1. This tatty museum stuffed with photos, artifacts, and tidbits of information on Texas pioneers, trail drivers, and rangers isn't a must-see, but its quirky charm is sure to appeal to some. Next door to the Witte Museum and housed in a deco-style WPA building from 1936, the low-tech digs don't dampen the spirits of the museum's employees; if you bite, they'll reel you in.

The San Antonio Museum of Art (SAMA) inhabits the large industrial, almost fortresslike facilities of the former Lone Star Brewery. The bulk of the museum's holdings results from the combination of two major collections, one bequeathed by Gilbert M. Denman Jr. and the other the Stark-Willson Collection. The SAMA is noted for its outstanding collection of ancient Egyptian, Near Eastern, Greek, and Roman art; it is the largest collection of antiquities in the United States. Remarkable ivory carvings, detailed mummy masks, a flask with snake-shaped threads at its opening, and a camel cosmetic case are all good examples. The museum's Nelson A. Rockefeller Center for Latin American Arts has over 10,000 pieces in its collection. Pre-Columbian art, mostly from the first millennium A.D., is well represented, and there is plenty of Spanish colonial art, particularly that which is religious in nature. For some, though, it is the pieces of folk art that really stand out—such as a fascinating display of colorful jaguar masks used in religious rituals during pre-Columbian days, through the colonial era, and still used in the villages of southern Mexico during certain celebrations—and that illustrate the staying power of imagery and its adaptability under outside influences and changing times.

Southwest School of Art and Craft

210-224-1848
www.swschool.org
300 Augusta St., San Antonio, TX 78205
Open: Mon.–Sat. 9–5, Sun. 11–4
Admission: Free

The home of the Southwest School of Art and Craft was built in 1851 as the Ursuline Convent and Academy and is part of an effort to renew Texans' interest in the Catholic Church. The Ursuline Academy remained until 1965, when it relocated, selling a portion of its property to the San Antonio Conservation Society, who in turn invited the Southwest School of Art and Craft to take up residency in the early 1970s. Creative and possessing an appreciation of the property's beauty and significance, the school extensively renovated the complex while retaining its lovely sense of calm and quiet dignity. Today, close to a quarter of a million visitors come to the school each year to enjoy its exhibits and events. Some four thousand adults and children draw, paint, tape, glue, and sculpt in classes offered throughout the year, with eight thousand more children doing the same through the school's extensive outreach programs.

The school's gardens, courtyards, and chapel are calm and serene. The graceful buildings were created using a technique known as *pisé de terre*, in which bricks are made by forcing clay, rock, and straw into wooden forms, allowing them to dry, then skim-coating with plaster—the inspiration for modern-day rammed-earth construction. The results are solid and thick, resisting the heat of the sun, and, when combined with creaky wooden floors, make for a very atmospheric interior. The structures are designated as a Texas Historic Landmark and are on the National Register of Historic Places. The Copper Kitchen Café (210-224-0123; open Mon.–Fri. 11:30–2) serves simple meals, and its dining rooms have an austere beauty that harks back to convent days; the Gift Gallery (210-224-1848, ext. 315; open Mon.–Fri. 10–5) has unique artistic gifts; the Visitors Center Museum (210-224-1848; open Mon.–Sat. 10–5 and Sun. 11–4) offers docent tours of the property Mon.–Fri. 10–3; and the annual Fiesta Arts Fair is a much-anticipated kickoff event for Fiesta San Antonio in April (see "Festivals" below).

Witte Museum

210-357-1900
www.wittemuseum.org
3801 Broadway, San Antonio, TX 78209

HemisFair Park

The Hemisfair, held April through October 1968 and planned to coincide with the 250th anniversary of the founding of the city, was an international exposition celebrating the shared cultural heritage of San Antonio and Latin America, organized around the theme of "Confluence of Civilization in the Americas." Canada, Mexico, Italy, Spain, France, and Japan were quick to host large exhibits; and some effort, including sponsorship from local foundations, had to be made in order for exhibits representing Nicaragua, Honduras, Guatemala, El Salvador, and Costa Rica to be realized. The Institute of Texan Cultures (see below) was constructed for this event, and its exhibits highlighting the contributions of various ethnic groups to the formation of modern Texas were a huge hit.

The construction of the fairgrounds was mired in controversy, as the land used was part of the "old city," home to 120 buildings in various states of upkeep and residents with an attachment to their neighborhood. Fair planners were able to have the area designated an urban renewal site and secured federal funding for the project. In the end only 22 of the original structures survived and were incorporated into the park, the rest destroyed; all the residents were relocated. The Tower of the Americas, a technological feat at its time, was built, and the Riverwalk was extended a quarter-mile to link the park to the greater downtown neighborhood. Though over 6 million visitors enjoyed the park during the Hemisfair, the park failed to become the cultural or recreational center of the city as planners had hoped. The Institute of Texan Cultures excepted, many of the buildings now serve other functions; for example, what was the United States' exhibit hall is now a federal courthouse.

Today, the park consists of 5 acres of grass, trees, and gardens crisscrossed with paths and dotted with fountains, and an enormous wooden play structure for children. **The Instituto Cultural Mexicano** (210-227-0123; www.institutodemx.org; 600 Hemisfair Plaza) hosts films, music, salsa, merengue, and tango dance classes and is home to the small Casa Mexicana Gallery (210-227-0123; open Mon.–Fri. 9:30–5; admission free), which displays works of contemporary artists from Mexico. The **Tower of the Americas** (210-223-3101; www.toweroftheamericas .com; open Sun.–Thu. 10–10, Fri.–Sat. 10 AM–11 PM) has just undergone an $11 million makeover designed to ignite more interest among both residents and visitors. The observation deck, **Flags Over Texas** (admission: adults $5, seniors $4, children $3), is now open for spectacular views of the city, and the 4-D theater, **Skies Over Texas** (admission: adults $6, seniors and children $5.50), will challenge your sensitivity to vertigo. At its pinnacle, the newly opened rotating restaurant **Eyes Over Texas** (210-223-3101; www.toweroftheamericas .com; open Sun.–Thu. 11–10, Fri.–Sat. 11–11; price: expensive), is run by Landry's, with a seafood-centric menu and friendly, if somewhat slow, service. The ground floor café is open for coffee or cold drinks.

Tower of the Americas, with a storm brewing

Shopping

There are plenty of knickknack and souvenir shops in the neighborhood surrounding the **Riverwalk** and **Market Square/El Mercado** (210-207-8600; www.marketsquaresa.com; 514 W. Commerce St.; open daily in summer 10–8, winter 10–6), with plenty of Mexican imports for sale.

For clever and quirky gifts, try the gift shops at any of the area museums, and for handcrafted arts make a trip to the gift shop of the **Southwest School of Art and Craft** (see above). **Southtown** is a good neighborhood for gallery-gazing.

Market Square: El Mercado

Open: Mon. and Wed.–Sat. 10–5, Tue. 10–8, Sun. noon–5
Admission: Adults $7, seniors $6, children $5. Tue. 3–8 is free.

Remarkably, San Antonio's natural history museum was born through the perseverance of a local schoolteacher. The teacher, Ellen Schulz, managed to raise $5,000 in the 1920s and purchase a large group of specimens, which were then put on display at the high school. An appeal to the city for assistance in building a proper museum yielded public funding and a $65,000 donation from a Mr. Witte, who requested that the planned museum be built in Brackenridge Park and named for his parents. The Witte Museum subsequently opened its doors in 1926. In the 1970s the museum hired an art historian as director, and its focus began to shift, leading to the purchase and renovation of an old brewery to house its rapidly expanding collection of art and culminating in the formation of the San Antonio Museum of Art (see above) in 1981, an entity that would become independent in 1994.

Refocused on its original mission, the Witte is now a museum dedicated solely to the history, cultures, and science of South Texas and is most interesting to children and their families. Full-scale dinosaur skeletons, including the enormous triceratops at the center of the gallery, detailed dioramas depicting what life may have been like for Native Americans in the Lower Pecos region, and displays of live bees, spiders, and snakes will all appeal to the curious. The colorful H-E-B Science Tree House features hands-on science exhibits such as an Archimedes' screw, the ancient, ingenious tool used for moving water uphill, and rudimentary machines demonstrating the principles of sound, electricity, and gravity. Many of the museum's most interesting and intriguing pieces are in storage, since the collection has long outgrown its exhibition space, a quandary the museum hopes to remedy through the major overhaul and expansion planned for 2007. The remodeling will allow the museum to refocus the collection yet again, on heritage, natural resources, and ecology.

Performing Arts

San Antonio has fantastic theaters that are historic and atmospheric; most are multipurpose performing arts centers.

The Alameda (210-299-4300; www.thealameda.org; 318 W. Houston St.) A center for Latino arts and culture, the Alameda is currently in the middle of renovations but will bring more theater, opera, dance, film, and music to San Antonio again soon.

Alamo City Men's Chorale (210-495-7464; www.acmc-texas.org) Local gay men's chorus harmonizes in lovely holiday concerts and enthusiastic performances at the annual Pride Concert.

Arneson Theatre (210-207-8610; www.lavillita.com/arneson; 418 Villita St.) The Arneson hosts events in its outdoor amphitheater on the banks of the Riverwalk at La Villita. Diverse offerings include the **Alamo Irish Festival** (www.harpandshamrock.org) in March and the **Fiesta Noche del Rio** (www.alamo-kiwanis.org/noche/fiesta), an August celebration of song and dance from Mexico, Spain, Argentina, and Texas, put on by the Kiwanis Club, with all proceeds benefiting local charity.

ARTS San Antonio (210-226-2891, 210-224-9600; www.artssanantonio.com; 222 E. Houston St., Suite 400) ARTS San Antonio brings comedy, musicals, and dance performances from classical to contemporary, with most taking place at the centrally located Convention Center.

Carver Community Cultural Center (210-207-7211; www.thecarver.org; 226 N. Hackberry St.) The Carver Center began as an African American public library in 1929, when segregation mandated separate facilities. The center soon grew into an epicenter of the arts, with performances by many of the greats, such as Ella Fitzgerald, Louis Armstrong, Charlie "Bird" Parker, and Cab Calloway. These days, the Carver is a historic venue in which to catch big-name national and international stars of dance and music, especially jazz.

Church Bistro and Theatre (210-271-7791; www.churchbistroandtheatre.com; 1150 South Alamo St.) Easily recognized by its burnt-orange awnings and stubby mission-style twin bell towers, the Church has undergone extensive renovations to restore a great deal of its 1912 character. The pressed-tin ceilings have been repaired and freshly painted, and the stained-glass windows, once covered with shutters, now glow in the sunlight. The Church celebrated its grand opening with a production of David Sedaris's popular *Santaland Diaries*, a show that set the tone for this smart yet offbeat spot. The theater stages shows Friday and Saturday nights, with an occasional Sunday matinee (see Web site for current listings). Parenthetically, the Church may or may not be haunted; ask to see Polaroid photos taken in 1990 or, if you are visiting around Halloween, consider attending the Sanctuary Ghosts event. The theater also serves meals; stop in for lunch or dinner (see "Dining," below).

Empire Theatre (210-226-3333; www.majesticempire.com; 226 N. St. Mary's St.) Nine feet of water poured into this theater during the flood of 1921, damaging much of its gilded 1890s interior. Over time, the Empire declined, and it closed in the 1970s. Rescued by the city with the help of Las Casas Foundation, the nonprofit organization responsible for saving some of San Antonio's most historic and treasured cultural institutions, the Empire reopened in 1998, restored to its original glory. Due to its outstanding acoustics, the Empire Theatre hosts mostly music.

Guadalupe Cultural Arts Center (210-271-3151; www.guadalupeculturalarts.org; 1300 Guadalupe St.) The Guadalupe, as it is known, aims to "preserve, promote, and develop the arts and culture of the Chicano/Latino/Native American peoples for all ages and backgrounds" through the performing arts. And it certainly does. Among other things, the organization presents the city's annual CineFestival and Tejano Conjunto Festival (see Festivals, below).

Josephine Theatre (210-734-4646; www.josephinetheatre.org; 339 W. Josephine St.) The Josephine is a small local theater with a lot of chutzpah. When the future of the theater company's 1947 art deco digs became uncertain in 2003, the spunky little company raised enough money to buy the building and continued right along producing their high-energy, feel-good musicals on weekends.

Jump-Start Performance Company (210-227-5867; www.jump-start.org; 108 Blue Star) Located in the Blue Start Art Complex, the performances at Jump-Start are definitely energizing. Jump-Start recently staged *The Return of the Shrew*, a contemporary takeoff on *Taming of the Shrew* that involved lots of outrageous outfits and madcap escapades, as do most of their productions. Each year, Jump-Start and writer Sandra Cisneros pair up to host a special event, always a mélange of entertainment, refreshments, and well-chosen words; see the Web site for details.

Magik Children's Theatre (210-227-2751; www.magiktheatre.org; 420 S. Alamo St.) This is a terrific theater for children and families. Daytime and evening shows (adults $10, seniors $9, children $8) change monthly, and a brand-new Shakespeare in the Park series is sure to become an annual event.

Majestic Theatre (210-226-3333; www.majesticempire.com; 224 E. Houston St.) The impossibly ornate Majestic Theatre was built in 1929, sadly closed in the 1970s, then triumphantly renovated and reopened in 1989. The home to the San Antonio Symphony (see below), the Majestic has an enticing roster ranging from Broadway shows to ballet, classical, and contemporary music.

San Antonio Dance Umbrella (210-212-6600; www.sadu.org; 106 Auditorium Circle, Suite 105) This city organization promotes, encourages, supports, and hosts all aspects of dance in San Antonio. Its comprehensive Web site lists all dance performances throughout the city.

San Antonio Living History Association (210-273-1730; www.sanantoniolivinghistory.org; 5310 San Pedro Ave.) A group of dedicated volunteers performs action-packed reenactments of historic battles, including the one for the Alamo. The events are interesting, free, and infrequent.

Blue Star Arts Complex
210-227-6960
www.bluestarartspace.org
116 Blue Star, San Antonio, TX 78204
Open: Daily. Individual gallery hours vary; check Web site.

The Blue Star Arts Complex, Blue Star for short, is both a building and a community. Blue Star the building is a historic 1920s warehouse that has been renovated, retrofitted, and readapted to serve as a residential, commercial, and art space, with lofts, studios, and several galleries. This effort was pioneered in 1985 by a community of artists and volunteers bound by their dream of providing exhibition space for contemporary artists; it made a big splash when it opened, and the ripple effects of revitalization were felt throughout its neighborhood, the King William District, and neighboring Southtown. Though Blue Star has matured into a sophisticated and sought-after contemporary art venue, one now run by a professional staff, it retains much of the earnestness of its grassroots days. With local, national, and international artists represented across the gamut of painting, etching, photography, and performance art—and its own on-site brew pub, the Blue Star Brewing Company (see "Nightlife," below)—Blue Star shines brightly in South San Antonio.

San Antonio Symphony (210-554-1010; www.sasymphony.org; 222 E. Houston St., Suite 200) For many years after its inception in 1939, the San Antonio Symphony traveled a bumpy road fraught with financial difficulties and changing leadership. Today the path is smoother, and music lovers can now enjoy the symphony's sharp performances in the sumptuous, historic Majestic Theatre.

San Pedro Playhouse (210-733-7258; www.sanpedroplayhouse.com; 800 W. Ashby at San Pedro Ave.) Actors at the San Pedro Playhouse have been onstage in this Greek-revival mansion in San Pedro Park for more than 70 years, putting on everything from *Hair* to *Hamlet*.

Sunken Garden Theatre (210-735-0663; www.sanantonio.gov/sapar/sunkenintro.asp; 3875 N. St. Mary's St.) Another abandoned area quarry put to good use, the Sunken Garden Theatre is located in Brackenridge Park, next to the Japanese Tea Garden. A lovely open-air venue for comedy, Shakespeare, and music performances.

Texas Talent Musicians Association (210-222-8862; www.tejanomusicawards.org). A nonprofit organization dedicated to promoting more understanding and appreciation of Tejano music, in part through its largest event, the Tejano Music Awards. The list of past winners reads like a Who's Who of the Tejano music scene.

Cinema

Alamo Drafthouse
210-677-8500
www.drafthouse.com
1255 SW Loop 410 in the West Lakes Shopping Center, San Antonio, TX 78227

The San Antonio branch of this Central Texas–based cinema chain is every bit as fun as the ones in Austin. Great flicks, with great food brought right to your seat. Everything from angus burgers to fried pickles. First-run movies all the time and special events like Anime Monday, films for the younger set on Baby Day Tuesdays, Weird Wednesday, and, on the last Thursday of the month, that essential flick shown by all great movie houses, *The Rocky Horror Picture Show.*

Alamo IMAX Theater
210-247-4629 or 1-800-354-4629
www.imax-sa.com
849 E. Commerce St. in the Rivercenter Mall, San Antonio, TX 78205

The larger-than-life drama of the siege of the Alamo comes alive on this six-story screen accompanied by six-track stereo sound. Highly recommended for those whose Texas history has gotten a little rusty.

Aztec on the River
210-227-3930, 877-432-9832
www.aztecontheriver.com
Corner of Commerce St. and N. St. Mary's St., San Antonio, TX 78205

A recent massive renovation of this 80-year-old building, decadent in its day and no less so now, has restored the theater right down to its 1925 Mighty Wurlitzer organ. There are some free entertainment features—the lobby itself is worth a peek—but the big draw here is the "edutainment," which takes the form of films such as *Amazing Caves* (www.amazing caves.com) and *Mystery of the Maya* (www.bigfilms.ca). The perfect air-conditioned family-friendly rest stop.

The Bijou at Crossroads
210-496-2221
www.santikos.com
4522 Fredericksburg Rd., San Antonio, TX 78201

The Santikos family has been bringing movies to San Antonio for over 80 years; they currently operate a variety of venues (including a drive-in), many of which serve hors d'oeuvres, burgers, gourmet pizzas, and spanakopita, the Greek spinach dish. Wine tasting every third Thursday. See Web site for a full list of theaters.

Galleries

Tightly knit Southtown (www.southtown.net) has a growing number of galleries and creative shops, all within easy walking distance from one another. **El Sol Studios** (210-226-9700; 936 S. Alamo St.) is a modest art gallery with cards and other creative items. **Garcia Art Glass** (210-354-4681; www.garciaartglass.com; 715 S. Alamo St.) sells vividly colored handblown art glass. The highly respected **San Angel Folk Art Gallery** (210-226-6688; www.sanangelfolkart.com; 110 Blue Star) displays a very nice selection of folk art pieces created by artists living in the United States, Mexico, and Europe. **Stone Metal Press** (210-227-0312; www.stonemetal-press.com) displays works on paper with a studio in the **Gallista Art Studios** (210-212-8606; www.gallista.com; 1913 S. Flore St.) and a gallery in the Blue Star Arts Complex (see below).

Open Galleries

First Friday Art Walk is an open gallery night that takes place the first Friday evening of the month and revolves around South Alamo Street, between Durango and Probandt, in the heart of Southtown. Galleries tend to open between 6 PM and 10 PM, and admission is free. Check www.southtown.net for details.

NIGHTLIFE: MUSIC AND DANCING

Nightlife in San Antonio is quite tame; simple pleasures such as sitting out under the stars, sipping a drink on the patio of just about any restaurant along the Riverwalk, are sure to make for a relaxing evening. Strolling the sidewalks of the historic King William District, gallery hopping on First Fridays (see "Galleries," above), or just lingering over dessert at a local bistro are activities San Antonians enjoy on nights out. Visitors will find that the city offers a nice selection of live music, from jazz ensembles to *conjunto* music, energetic performing arts organizations, and dynamic festivals whose exuberant celebrations can last well into the evening. For variety's sake, locals don't think twice about driving the 30 miles north on I-35 to historic Gruene for dinner and dancing in Gruene Hall (see Nearby and In Between chapter). For up-to-the-minute information on San Antonio's nightlife, pick up a copy of either the *San Antonio Current* or *San Antonio Express-News*, or access the information online at www.sacurrent.com and www.mysanantonio.com.

Blue Cactus Café
210-490-7330
www.thebluecactuscafe.com
13525 Wetmore Rd., San Antonio,
   TX 78247
Open: Sun.–Thu. 11–9, Fri.–Sat. 11–11

A new restaurant located in a century-old former general store and post office, the Blue Cactus Café is family run and family friendly. There are games, books, blocks, a big play structure out back, and tic-tac-toe at the table for children, while adults will enjoy live music on the weekends. Come early for dinner and make a night of it.

Blue Star Brewing Company

210-212-5506
www.bluestarbrewing.com
1414 S. Alamo, San Antonio, TX 78210
Open: Mon.–Thu. 11 AM–midnight,
    Fri.–Sat. 11 AM–1 AM

Located in the Blue Star Arts Complex, the Blue Star Brewing Company (BSBC) has a similar, albeit more polished, warehouse feel with high ceilings, exposed brick, lots of wood, and enormous stainless steel vats of brew. The pub grub menu has appetizers of onion rings, mushrooms, or calamari dipped in the brewery's own beer batter and fried, plus burgers, pizzas, and fish-and-chips. A half-dozen handcrafted beers are brewed on site, from the mild golden lager and amber ale to the full-bodied King William Ale and the deep, rich signature stout. For nondrinkers, the homemade pints of root beer and cream soda are sweet stand-ins. Tuesday nights mean big-band jazz starting at 8, and on First Fridays (see "Galleries," above) the BSBC features local art on its walls and hosts concerts "live from the deck."

The Bonham Exchange

210-271-3811
www.bonhamexchange.net
411 Bonham St., San Antonio, TX 78205
Open: Fri. 4 PM–3 AM, Sat. 8 PM–2 AM, Sun.
    4 PM –2 AM

A gay/lesbian bar and club known for over-the-top celebrations, booty-shaking contests, and hot dancers.

Casbeer's

210-732-3511
www.casbeers.com
1719 Blanco Rd., San Antonio, TX 78212
Open: Tue.–Thu. 11–11, Fri. 11 AM–
    midnight, Sat. 5–1

From blues and lounge music to local singer-songwriters, gospel to homegrown honky-tonk, Casbeer's has a wide-open roster of music offerings, all of which go quite nicely with their famous cheese enchiladas (see "Dining," below).

Cowboys Dancehall

210-646-9378
www.cowboysdancehall.com
3030 NE Loop 410 at I-35 and Loop 410,
San Antonio, TX 78218
Open Wed. and Fri. 8 PM–2 AM, Thu. 7 PM–
    2 AM, Sat. 8 PM–3 AM

A warehouse-sized combination dance hall and indoor rodeo. From the George Strait and Dwight Yoakam concerts to the live pro bull riding shows, Cowboys is country western through and through. Check Web site for concert and event schedule.

Dolores Del Rio

210-223-0609
106 Riverwalk, San Antonio, TX 78205
Open: Mon.–Wed. 11:30–2:30 and 6–10,
    Thu. 11:30–2:30 and 6–10:30, Fri.
    11:30–11, Sat. 6–11, Sun. 6–10

This tiny Italian restaurant (see "Dining," below) provides the perfect backdrop for the jazz combos who frequent its small stage, and the perfect foil to the noisy wide-open patios of the Riverwalk. A cozy place to spend a rainy evening or a sticky summer's night. If you're lucky, you might get to see the unbelievably talented belly dancers who sometimes perform here.

John T. Floore Country Store

210-695-8827
www.liveatfloores.com
14464 Old Bandera Rd., Helotes, TX
Open: Thu.–Sun.
Take Bandera Road northwest to Helotes,
    just past Loop 1604.

A Honky Tonk northwest of town, Floore's has had patrons singing, dancing, and whooping it up with folks like Willie Nelson and Patsy Cline for over 60 years. Floore's isn't as old as the historic dance hall in Gruene (See Nearby and In Between chapter), but it is much bigger and the boot scootin' is every bit as fun. Free family dances on Sundays.

Conjunto Music

As the Spanish moved across Texas in the early 1800s, they organized dances and concerts featuring the violins, guitars, and PITOS (a wind instrument) specific to their musical traditions. By the 1860s, the rhythms of the waltzes and polkas of the European court had drifted from Maximillian-ruled Mexico north into Texas and were added to the developing style of MÚSICA TEJANA, or Tex-Mex music. Then Germans arrived to live and work in South and Central Texas and northern Mexico, bringing with them the diatonic button accordion, the instrument that would revolutionize the music of the area.

Since the accordion allowed for a single musician to play both melody and harmony with one instrument, the popularity of the violins and PITOS diminished. By the late 1880s, the TAMBORA DE RANCH (goatskin drum) and the BAJO SEXTO (12-string guitar) were added to the accordion to give more depth and complexity to the sound. By the 1900s, MÚSICA NORTEÑA was played all over ranches and farms of South Texas and northern Mexico and at the fandangos, or get-togethers, featuring eating, dancing, and gambling, closely identified with working-class Tejanos.

In the early 1900s, as Tejanos moved to cities, they took their accordions with them and continued to play CONJUNTO at home, parties, and neighborhood events. During the 1930s virtuoso Narciso Martínez, known as the father of modern CONJUNTO, and San Antonian Santiago Jimenez popularized the genre through recordings and radio broadcasts. The legendary Tejana singer of this era, Lydia Mendoza, also known as the "queen of Tejano," sang her way to fame in the plazas of San Antonio.

In the 1940s and 1950s, singer Valerio Longoria layered lyrics over the accordion, playing what would become known as CANCIONES RANCHERAS. These "ranch songs" were nostalgic pieces whose lyrics of love, loss, and simpler times resonated deeply with listeners. As CONJUNTO matured, it never strayed far from its Tejano roots. Touring and playing for large groups along the migrant trail between Mexico and the United States in the 1950s and '60s, Tony de la Rosa added amplifiers to what had by then become the standard quartet: accordion, BAJO SEXTO, bass, and drums.

In more recent memory, individual musicians have left their mark. Paulino Bernal, Roberto Pulido, and Rubén Vela each added his own innovations in the 1960s. Leonardo (Flaco) Jimenez, son of Santiago Jimenez, took the music to more mainstream audiences throughout the United States and Europe to much acclaim. The very open-minded Esteban Jordán stretched the limits of the genre, and his followers, such as Inocencia and Emilio Navaira and Río, have added saxophones, keyboards, and synthesizers, creating the new sounds of CONJUNTOS ORQUESTA.

San Antonio has long been the epicenter of CONJUNTO music in Texas, and each May the Guadalupe Cultural Arts Center brings some of the biggest names and greatest talents to the city for the spectacular Tejano Conjunto Festival (see Festivals, below). The event draws crowds of thousands of fans and features an outstanding lineup of top-notch musicians, including such luminaries as Fred Zimmerle, Eva Ybarra, Lupita Rodela, Laura Canales, as well as some of the musicians mentioned above. Conjunto music is sometimes referred to as MÚSICA ALEGRE, or happy music; after just a few notes you'll know why.

Piano player at Jim Cullum's Landing

The Landing

210-223-7266

www.landing.com

123 Losoya St., Hyatt Regency Hotel, San
   Antonio, TX 78205

Open: Daily 3–1

Popularized through the Public Radio
International syndicated jazz broadcast
Riverwalk, Live from the Landing, the seven-
piece Jim Cullum Jazz Band (JCJB) has been
making outstanding music in San Antonio
since 1963. JCJB plays Monday through
Saturday starting at 8 PM; reservations are
recommended for weekend performances.
The local jazz group Small World takes the
reins on Sunday night. If you can't make
the performance, you can catch it on KSTX
89.1 FM Saturday at 7 PM and Sunday at
noon, or listen online at www.riverwalk
jazz.com.

Luna Fine Music Club

210-804-2433

www.lunalive.com.

6740 San Pedro Ave., San Antonio, TX
   78216

Open: Wed.–Sat. 8 PM–2 AM

With a very '40s feel, Luna pairs top-notch
musicians with a slightly more upscale
ambience than other area clubs. The
acoustics of the club benefit the blues, jazz,
Latin, soul, swing, and world music equally,
making it a music-lover's delight.

Poly Esther's

210-220-1972

www.polyesthers.com

212 College St., San Antonio, TX

Open: Sun.–Thu. 8 PM–2 AM, Fri.–Sat.
   8 PM–4 AM

With three levels, there is lots of room to dance to either current music or throwbacks to the '70s, '80s, or '90s.

Rosario's

210-223-1806

www.rosariossa.com

910 S. Alamo St., San Antonio, TX 78205

Open: Sun. 11 AM–8 PM, Mon. 11 AM–3 PM,
Tue.–Thu. 11 AM– 10 PM, Fri.–Sat. 11–11

Arrive early, order dinner, eat at your leisure, and then join the margarita-fueled throngs on the dance floor for live salsa, pop, or contemporary Latin music. The combination of free live music every Friday night, a great Southtown location, and fantastic food all week long (see "Dining," below) are just some of the many reasons to stop in at Rosario's.

Sam's Burger Joint

210-223-2830

www.samsburgerjoint.com

330 E. Grayson St., San Antonio, TX 78215

Open: Mon.–Thu. 11–11, Fri.–Sat. 11
AM–midnight

Near the I-35 and I-37 intersection, Sam's mixes it up all week with swing dancing on Monday, poetry slams on Tuesday, blues on Thursday, and hard rocking all weekend. No need to eat before you go; Sam's sells enormous, juicy burgers.

Sunset Station

210-222-9481, tickets 210-474-7640

www.sunset-station.com

1174 E. Commerce St., San Antonio, TX
78205

Built in 1902 as a Southern Pacific Railroad depot, Sunset Station is located in the St. Paul Historic District near the Alamodome. The structure has been extensively renovated and is now a multipurpose entertainment venue, with an old-time saloon and plenty of space for the wide-ranging, big-name concerts it is known for hosting. Also popular are the Gospel Brunches, which start each Sunday morning at 10 and feature a full southern-style buffet. Check the Web site for event details.

Drinks

Azúca

210-225-5550

www.azuca.net

713 S. Alamo St., San Antonio, TX 78205

Open: Dining Mon.–Thu. 11–9:30,
Fri.–Sat. 11–10:30; bar Mon.–Thu. 4–11,
Fri.–Sat. 4–2

Price: Moderate

An indoor/outdoor experience of the food, music, and drinks of Central and South America and the Caribbean. From the reinterpreted classic entrées served for lunch and dinner, to the salsa and merengue dancing into the evenings, Azúca is a fun place to spend an evening in Southtown.

Beethoven Halle und Garten

210-222-1521
www.beethovenmaennerchor.com
422 Pereida St., San Antonio, TX 78210
Open: Tue.–Sat. 4–11

This *Biergarten* revels in German culture, with plenty of German beers and live music during Gartenkonzerts, Octoberfest, and First Fridays. Cash only.

Broadway 50/50

210-826-0069
www.broadway5050.com
5050 Broadway, San Antonio, TX 78209
Open: Sun.–Thu. 11 AM–1 AM, Sat.–
    Sun. 11 AM–2 AM

Burgers, beer, cocktails, pool, and live music. Hang with the crowd or hang back at a table for two.

Cappyccino's

210-828-6860
www.sawhost.com/cappy
5003 Broadway, San Antonio, TX 78209
Open: Mon.–Wed. 11–10, Thu. 11–11,
    Fri.–Sat. 11 AM–midnight

This bistro and bar in the tony Alamo Heights neighborhood is a popular spot for a light meal, evening drinks, or coffee and dessert. Nearby, Cappy's restaurant (see "Dining," below) is a relaxing spot for a refined dinner.

The Davenport

210-354-1200
200 E. Houston St., San Antonio, TX
    78205
Open: Mon.–Sat. 2–2, Sun. 6 PM–2 AM

Right downtown, the Davenport has two floors, one for chatting over martinis and the other for dancing and flirting. A huge selection of liquor and a comfortable, unpretentious vibe make the Davenport popular with locals.

Esquire Tavern

210-222-2521
155 E. Commerce St., San Antonio, TX
    78205
Open: Mon.–Sat. 9 AM–1 AM, Sun.
    noon–midnight

The cheapest, and probably most worn, place downtown in which to sip a longneck elbow-to-elbow with anyone from anywhere. This historic bar is still a local haunt, with a nice little patio overlooking the river and jukebox full of Texas tunes.

La Tuna

210-224-8862
100 Probandt St., San Antonio, TX 78204

A few blocks south of Southtown, La Tuna is an open-air chat fest with music on the weekends. Though it's primarily a bar with a good selection of beer, La Tuna is oddly popular with families who come to while the evening away at the picnic tables under the trees and soak in the down-to-earth atmosphere.

The Menger Bar

210-223-4361 or 1-800-345-9285
www.mengerhotel.com
Menger Hotel, 204 Alamo Plaza, San
    Antonio, TX 78205
Open: Mon.–Sat. 11 AM–midnight, Sun.
    noon–11

Take a break from the margaritas on the crowded Riverwalk and duck into the dimly lit Menger Bar for a stiff shot of whisky in the shadow of the Alamo. Rumor has it that here Teddy Roosevelt offered free drinks to men who would, after tying on a few, readily join his Rough Riders and head off to fight in the Spanish-American War. Built in 1887, with a design based on the taproom in London's House of Lords, the bar is quiet and relaxed, with dark cherrywood paneling, beveled glass mirrors from France, and other Victorian embellishments.

Silo Elevated Cuisine

210-864-8686
www.siloelevatedcuisine.com
1133 Austin Hwy., San Antonio, TX 78209
Open: Lunch daily 11—2:30; dinner Sun.—
   Thu. 5:30—10, Fri.—Sat. 5:30—10:30

Whether or not you decide to go upstairs for dinner (see "Dining," below), the full bar on the ground floor is a sophisticated place for drinks.

Swig Martini Bar

210-476-0005
www.swigmartini.com
111 W. Crockett St. #205, San Antonio, TX 78205
Open: Mon.—Sat. 2—2, Sun. 4—2

This swanky martini bar serves specialty martinis, cocktails, live music, and that thrill of yesteryear, cigars. While the decor sets a vintage 1940s feel, the high price of drinks is very now. An upscale look, but the down-to-earth attitude makes most everyone feel welcome.

Vbar

210-227-9700
www.hotelvalencia.com
Hotel Valencia Riverwalk, 150 E. Houston
   St., San Antonio, TX 78205
Open: Daily 4—2

Very cosmopolitan Vbar is just the spot to enjoy a little tapas, sip a cocktail, and take in the scenery—both the river and fellow well-dressed patrons. A place to see and be seen. Such details as curtains of metal bead chains, leather stools, fun music, and a stone terrace directly on the Riverwalk keep the mood light.

Zen Bar Ultralounge

210-271-7472
www.zenbar.com
221 E. Houston St., San Antonio, TX 78205
Open: Mon.—Sat. 5—2

Since the following defies categorizing, it is here, in a box all its own.

The Cove

210-227-2683
www.thecove.us
606 W. Cypress St., San Antonio, TX 78212
Open: Daily 7:30 AM—midnight
Price: Inexpensive
Special Features: Bar; basketball court; car wash; children welcome; laundromat; live music; outdoor terrace; playground; pool table; video games

Everyone likes to slip into the Cove. The funky, heartwarming spot near San Antonio College has become known as much for its great food, friendly service, and outstanding live music as for its odd mix of additional offerings. The Cove has an extensive, healthy, and well-priced menu; eating a grilled-fish taco served with cilantro coleslaw and a signature POBLANO cream sauce is a terrific way to pass the time while doing your laundry. That's right, laundry. The Cove's 34 washers and 30 dryers get lots of use. Almost as much use as the basketball court out back, or the child-friendly playscape, or the self-serve four-bay car wash. The Cove has everything you've never thought of, plus a pool table, video games, art on the walls, and wine and cheese tastings. At night, the nice long beer list takes center stage during "happy time" (Tue.—Fri. 3—7) when all domestics are $1.75. Things heat up around 8, when music lovers show up for the live blues, jazz, and acoustic folk concerts. The Cove is a San Antonio classic; stop in for some hospitality and go home full, clean, and satisfied.

A dramatic use of crimson red paint inside this trendy bar is tempered with serene Buddhas and gurgling fountains, not to mention any number of drinks, both stirred and shaken.

FESTIVALS

San Antonio is bursting at the seams with festivals, cultural events, market days, and music. Some may be worth planning a trip around, and others may just happen to coincide with your visit. These events always bring out the best in vivacious and community-minded San Antonio.

MONTHLY

Houston Street Fair and Market (210-841-3217; www.houstonstreetfairandmarket.com) Last Saturday of the month, noon–6. Food, face painting, music, storytellers, and an art fair make this event especially family friendly. Park for free, beginning at noon, in the city's St. Mary's Street parking garage at 400 N. St. Mary's at Travis Street. Free.

JANUARY

Riverwalk Mud Festival (210-227-4262; www.thesanantonioriverwalk.com) Celebrating the annual draining of the San Antonio River for cleaning, this festival features parades, pie, pub crawl, and mud.

Martin Luther King Jr. March (210-207-2098; www.sanantonio.gov/mlk) While most cities have special events on this weekend, San Antonio has one of the largest. Free.

FEBRUARY

San Antonio Stock Show and Rodeo (210-225-5851, 877-637-6336; www.sarodeo.com) A 16-day extravaganza of food, music, and rodeo performances. Admission charged.

Mardi Gras (210-227-4262; www.thesanantonioriverwalk.com) Colorful barges and a variety of music along the river are the hallmarks of Mardi Gras in San Antonio. Held the weekend before Ash Wednesday. Free.

MARCH

Remember the Alamo Weekend and **Dawn at the Alamo** (210-273-1730; www.sanantonio livinghistory.org; Alamo Plaza) Reenactment and interpretation of the events at the Alamo, both commemorative and educational. Free.

St. Patrick's Day (210-227-4262; www.thesanantonioriverwalk.com) Various events including parades on both street and river, and the "Dyeing o' the River Green." Free.

Watercolor Month (210-222-2787; www.sanantonio.gov/art) Watercolors of all sizes, styles, and subjects on display in galleries, museums, and other venues throughout town. Free.

APRIL

Fiesta San Antonio! (210-227-5191; www.fiesta-sa.org) One of the country's oldest traditions of sheer cross-cultural fun and the city's signature event. Food, art, fireworks, carnivals, sports, and music you can't help but dance to bring out some three million revelers to this weeklong, citywide party. Admission charged.

King William Fair (210-271-3247; www.kwfair.org; 1032 S. Alamo St.) Held at the end of April, this fair encompasses several blocks of Madison, King William, and Washington Streets. With food booths, juried arts and crafts vendors, a children's area with pony rides and blow-up bouncy structures, and a parade. A great way to spend some time in the lovely King William District. Free.

MAY

Cinco de Mayo (210-207-8600) Commemoration and celebration of the Mexican army's victory over the French at the Battle of Puebla on May 5, 1862. A joyous cultural festival featuring events in Market Square and throughout the city. Free.

Tejano Conjunto Festival en San Antonio (210-271-3151; www.guadalupeculturalarts.org; Guadalupe Campus and Rosedale Park) A week of live music from traditional *conjunto* to progressive *Tejano* and everything in between, played by extremely talented musicians, in some cases living legends. Food, games, and dancing. Admission charged.

JUNE

Texas Folklife Festival (210-458-2330; www.texasfolklifefestival.org; HemisFair Park) A major four-day cultural extravaganza representing more than 40 ethnic groups, with plenty of food, dancing, music, and crafts to go round. The 2006 celebration had nine performance stages booked solid for the duration of the festival, with such acts as Scottish bagpipe bands, Lebanese, Flemish, and German folk dancers, Mexican ranchero songs, Latin jazz, and Chinese dragon dancers, all from groups with strong Texas roots. Food is as wide-ranging, from Czech *kolaches* to Polish *pierogis* to homemade flour tortillas. A truly amazing display of diversity. Admission charged.

Juneteenth (www.juneteenthsanantonio.com). Remembering June 19, 1865, the day that slaves in Texas first received word of the Emancipation Proclamation. A spirited citywide celebration of freedom. Admission charged.

JULY

Fourth of July (www.sanantoniovisit.com) In San Antonio, Independence Day festivities center on Market Square, the Riverwalk, and blow-out celebrations at the local theme parks. Admission and free.

San Antonio Conjunto Shootout (210-207-8600; www.ci.sat.tx.us/sapar; City of San Antonio Parks and Recreation) A *conjunto* battle of the bands, held in Market Square with food, refreshments, and dancing. Free.

Contemporary Art Month (210-222-2787; www.sanantonio.gov/art; Office of Cultural Affairs, 318 W. Houston St., Suite 301) The only monthlong contemporary arts festival in the nation, with more than 400 exhibitions in galleries, museums, neighborhoods, and studios. Admission and free.

Cactus Pear Music Festival (www.cpmf.us) A chamber music festival in San Antonio and the Hill Country towns that steps in where the San Antonio Symphony leaves off for the summer. Admission charged.

Pridefest (www.alamopridefest.org) Local gay/lesbian groups celebrate this nationally recognized event with a block party and parade in HemisFair Park. Free.

AUGUST

Ford Canoe Challenge (210-227-4262; www.sanantonioriverwalk.com) Participants race canoes from the Chamber of Commerce, around the Convention Center Lagoon, through the River Center Mall Lagoon, and back to the Chamber of Commerce. Free.

SEPTEMBER

FotoSeptiembre USA (210-737-8255; www.safotofestival.com; Office of Cultural Affairs, 318 W Houston St., Suite 301) One of the largest photography festivals in the country, with exhibits, workshops, and multimedia presentations. Admission and free.

Texas Football Classic (210-207-3663 or 1-800-884-3663; www.alamodome.com) Ten of the top high school football teams in the state duke it out at the Alamodome. Admission charged.

Jazz'SAlive (210-212-8423; www.saparksfoundation.org; City of San Antonio Parks & Recreation Department and San Antonio Parks Foundation) Outstanding performances from the nation's top jazz entertainers and local talent. Travis Park. Free.

Diez y Seis Events (210-223-3151; 1327 Guadalupe St.) A celebration of Mexico's independence from Spain on September 16, 1821. Three days of parades, dance, and rodeos. Free.

Valero Texas Open at La Cantera (210-345-3818; www.golfsanantonio.org; La Cantera Golf Club, 16641 La Cantera Pkwy.) One of the oldest professional golf tournaments and an official PGA tour event. Admission charged.

OCTOBER

A Festival of Films (210-736-FILM; www.afestivaloffilms.com) This two-day festival produced by Texas independent filmmakers features independent films and workshops for filmmakers. Admission charged.

International Accordion Festival (210-573-6984; www.internationalaccordionfestival .org; La Villita) A three-day festival of dancing, food, and accordions. Free.

AT&T Championship (210-698-3582; www.pgatour.com. 210-349-5151; www.oakhillscc .com; Oak Hills Country Club, 5403 Fredericksburg Rd.) An official Senior PGA Tour golf tournament. Admission charged.

Cinefestival 2006 (210-271-3151; www.guadalupeculturalarts.org; 1300 Guadalupe St.) International film festival featuring Chicano/Latino/indigenous films at the historic Guadalupe Theater, with panels, workshops, retrospectives, and sidebar programs offered in conjunction. Admission charged.

NOVEMBER

El Dia de los Muertos (210-432-1896; www.sacalaveras.com; Office of Cultural Affairs, 318 W. Houston St., Suite 301) "The Day of the Dead" is the ancient cultural tradition in which families "welcome back" departed loved ones, commemorating them through special altars and cemetery visits. Poetry readings and *calavera* processions, in which participants dress as skeletons, are especially moving. Admission and Free.

San Antonio New World Wine & Food Festival (210-223-2881; www.nwwff.org) A celebration of food, wine, and San Antonio's position as culinary and cultural gateway to Mexico and Latin America. Admission charged.

Holiday River Parade and Lighting Ceremony (210-227-4262; www.thesanantonioriver walk.com; Paseo del Rio Association and the City of San Antonio) Held the day after

Altars for the El Dia de los Muertos, the Day of the Dead

Thanksgiving, this twilight river parade lights up the Paseo del Rio. The more than 122,000 lights stay on until New Year's Day. Admission charged.

DECEMBER

Hecho a Mano/Made by Hand (210-271-3151; www.guadalupeculturalarts.org; 1300 Guadalupe St.) An arts and crafts market featuring ceramics, jewelry, woodwork, fiber arts, clothing, metalwork, and more. Admission charged.

Bazar Sábado (210-978-8100; www.samuseum.org; San Antonio Museum of Art, 200 W. Jones St.) Mexican folk art on display and for sale. Admission charged.

MasterCard Alamo Bowl (210-226-2695; www.alamobowl.com; Alamodome) College football featuring teams from the Big Twelve and Big Ten conferences. Admission charged.

Celebrate San Antonio (210-212-8423; www.sanantonio.gov/sapar; City of San Antonio Parks & Recreation, San Antonio Parks Foundation) New Year's Eve fireworks, live music, food, and family activities. South Alamo Street between Durango and Market Streets, La Villita, and HemisFair Park. Free.

DINING

In a culture of chain restaurants and fast food, San Antonio has a satisfying number of homegrown restaurants and old-time establishments that have been favorites forever, as well as exciting new eateries that diners are always eager to try. In general, the Riverwalk is a mix of high-end restaurants, some of which are real culinary gems, and more predictable eateries catering to out-of-town visitors. In an effort to preserve the historic nature of the Riverwalk, the city of San Antonio has recently sought to limit the number of chain restaurants that can operate on its famed waterside in favor of highlighting local eateries. And you certainly don't have to go far to find restaurants with character and history. Just blocks away, the business section of downtown San Antonio is home to some much-loved standbys, which pack in the locals on lunch breaks. Visitors looking for a memorable dining experience may want to travel the short distance to the artsy King William District or the Alamo Heights neighborhood, where a drop in prices and a rise in diversity of both cuisine and clientele make dining more interesting.

In San Antonio, people like to eat out in style. For pricier establishments "business casual" is generally appropriate, and I have noted where a jacket is required. Families are welcome, particularly at the city's many casual restaurants, which are often family-run themselves and quite kid friendly. Generally, credit cards are accepted; I have noted the occasional place where they are not. Unlike Austin, which has banned smoking in all public areas, San Antonio permits smoking in bars, hotel meeting rooms, and restaurants that have met city code requirements by providing a walled-off section to confine smoke. Be specific about your needs when making reservations, which should be considered essential, and are sometimes even required, at the more expensive and popular spots. Details change, so call ahead to ensure your meal goes smoothly.

The restaurants below are local favorites and those that are frequently and enthusiastically cited "best of" citywide. San Antonians are justifiably proud of the uniqueness of their city, and they love frequenting the restaurants that contribute something special to the city's culinary scene.

Restaurants with two codes have a menu that spans the price range indicated, offering, for example, a vegetarian entrée at one end of the spectrum and a premium steak at the other.

Dining Price Code

Inexpensive	Up to $12
Moderate	$12 to $25
Expensive	$25 to $40
Very Expensive	$40 or more

DOWNTOWN AND RIVERWALK

The many convenient eateries lining the Riverwalk are perfectly enjoyable places to stop in; some are even destinations unto themselves. Several of the best restaurants downtown cater to the business lunch crowd.

Biga on the Banks

210-225-0722
www.biga.com
203 S. St. Mary's St., San Antonio, TX 78205
At the intersection with Market St.
Open: Sun.–Thu. 5:30 PM–10 PM, Fri.–Sat. 5:30 PM–11 PM
Price: Moderate to Expensive
Special Features: Reservations recommended

Chef/Owner Bruce Auden, four-time James Beard award nominee, hit it big with Biga. *Gourmet* magazine recently named it one of the top five restaurants in Texas. The atmosphere is modern yet comfortable, and the clean lines, graceful curves, and warm earthy colors of both the decor and the food mix well with the crisp zenlike white accents. Auden's menu changes daily, but you can expect to see dishes in which the ingredients of the American Southwest are given a decidedly Asian interpretation. Entrées such as sesame tempura-crusted swordfish served with orange cumin ama-ranth, a toss of mango watercress, and a splash of red pepper ginger sauce or the Hunan-style BBQ veal chop with a side of tangy cilantro noodles, bok choy, and black bean sauce illustrate the point nicely. The popular hot and crunchy sweetbread appetizer and the sticky toffee pudding with English custard hint at Auden's roots in Britain. With all entrées priced over $20 and appetizers starting at $8, Biga isn't for everybody everyday, but it is a boon for foodies, those celebrating special occasions, and anyone looking for a memorable meal.

Boudro's

210-224-8484
www.boudros.com
421 E. Commerce St., San Antonio, TX 78205
Open: Sun.–Thu. 11–11, Fri.–Sat. 11 AM–midnight.
Price: Moderate
Special Features: Reservations recommended

Located on the Riverwalk, with both indoor and outdoor seating, Boudro's is one restaurant that manages to keep both visitors and locals happy with its cheerful, modern atmosphere and tasty food. The flavors here are big and bold, with hot chilies and Cajun spices used liberally. The guacamole appetizer, made at your table, is as fresh as can be and always a big hit. The big juicy steaks, Gulf Coast seafood, and the not-to-be-missed prickly-pear margaritas are all a taste of Texas, and the lime chess pie is a knockout. While dinner with drinks, dessert, and tip can easily put you over the $40 per person mark, the lunch menu will set you back just a fraction of that. Altogether, Boudro's is a predictably delicious local favorite for dinner as well as a solid value for a midday meal on the Riverwalk.

Dolores Del Rio

210-223-0609
106 Riverwalk, San Antonio, TX 78205
Open: Mon.–Wed. 11:30–2:30 and 6–10,
Thu. 11:30–2:30 and 6–10:30, Fri.
11:30–11, Sat. 6–11, Sun. 6–10
Price: Moderate
Special Features: Live music; reservations
recommended

An intimate cave of a club right on the
Riverwalk, Dolores Del Rio, despite its
touristy surroundings, caters mainly to in-
the-know locals who go for the tasty garlic-
infused country Italian cuisine, the cozy,
round, candlelit tables, and the live music.
There is music seven nights a week, some
of it folk or rock/blues, but very often a jazz
duo or trio, with the likes of Bett Butler,
Fred and Sylvia, Aaron Prado, and piano
favorite Barry Brake (of Jazz Protagonists
fame) performing. The music is so good
that jazz legends Spot Barnett and (Mambo
Kings bandleader) Luis Gasca have been
known to stroll in and listen for the evening
when they're in town. The home cooking
and, strange as it sounds, belly-dancing
during the breaks successfully create that
artsy atmosphere that all clubs strive for.

Mi Tierra Café

210-225-1262
www.mitierracafe.com
218 Produce Row, San Antonio, TX 78207
Open: Daily
Price: Inexpensive to Moderate
Special Features: Open 24 hours

This Tex-Mex bakery and restaurant
demurely calls itself a café, but it should be
called Mi Tierra World. Festive hats and
decorations stream from the ceiling, mariachi bands cycle through, and the waiters
with overflowing trays of food weave their
way in and out of the crowd. The restaurant
is open 24 hours a day, offering a slightly
overpriced menu packed with Tex-Mex
favorites, and is always bustling, and has
been since it opened in 1941. The bakery,
on the other hand, is very reasonably
priced, and the lines move quickly. In
addition to baked goods such as the tradi-

Treats at Mi Tierra Café

tional pumpkin or sweet potato *empanadas* (turnovers) or *churros* (a fried stick of dough often dusted with sugar), there is a pineapple biscuit, their own creation, which is best likened to a scone, and a pecan praline that is not to be missed. Take a minute to ogle the pastries, cookies, and treats at what feels like a milelong counter, then order a wide selection to sample as you wander the nearby Market Square.

Organics at the Radius Café

210-271-2805

www.radiuscafe.org

106 Auditorium Circle, San Antonio, TX 78205

Open: Daily 11 AM–2 PM

Price: Inexpensive

Special Features: Live music; free WiFi

North of Alamo Square, after Presa becomes Jefferson and near the intersection of Avenue A, is the innovative and interesting Radius Café. Not a café, per se, Radius is a collective effort of arts- and education-oriented nonprofits who have decided to conserve space, energy, and money by living together under one roof. The building itself is a sleek, modern retrofit of an old Studebaker dealership, with wide-open spaces to encourage the unobstructed flow of ideas. Sharing space with an art gallery and a music venue, Organics, an actual café, serves a very limited menu of simple and satisfying soups, sandwiches, and salads, most of which, naturally, are made with organic ingredients. Your heart and conscience will rest easy knowing that Organics avoids high fructose corn syrup and hydrogenated oils and happily uses organic fair-trade coffee and tea.

Le Rêve

210-212-2221

www.restaurantlereve.com

152 E. Pecan St., San Antonio, TX 78205

Open: Tue.–Sat. 5:30 PM–11 PM, last seating at 8:30. Closed end of August to Labor Day weekend.

Price: Very Expensive

Special Features: Reservations and jackets required

Andrew Weissman's menus, dictated by the seasons and the creativity of the chef, have earned Le Rêve recognition as one of the best restaurants—some, *Gourmet* magazine included, would say *the* best restaurant—in Texas. A James Beard Award nominee in 2006, Chef Weissman's classic French cuisine is meticulously prepared and marvelously presented, so much so that the restaurant cautions to allow between and hour and a half and two hours for a meal at Le Rêve. Some past offerings have included an hors d'oeuvres of foie gras accompanied by Texas Hill Country peaches, and a salad of roasted peppers, quail eggs, and artichokes. One of many *plats de résistance* was sautéed duck breast with thyme-infused roasted pears. Sample desserts are a sweet *tres leches* cake with coconut ice cream and a delicate lemon curd tart with soft citrus meringue. The Tasting Menu ($100, or $150 with wine) will put you in the very capable hands of the chef. Le Rêve has very specific ideas about maintaining the integrity of the environment to allow for the maximum gastronomic fulfillment. To this end, cell phones must be turned off, men must wear collared shirts and jackets, and reservations are required. Though Le Rêve is certainly not on anyone's short list for daily dining, it is a marvelously decadent place for a very, very special occasion. In a word: Dreamy.

Schilo's

210-223-6692

424 E. Commerce St., San Antonio, TX 78205

Open: Mon.–Sat. 7 AM–8:30 PM

Price: Inexpensive

Special Features: Live music

Schilo's serves the sort of food necessary to survive hard labor and cold German winters—hearty and economical pea soup, plump kielbasa, pungent krauts, plates of rye bread with butter, and thick, dark beers. In sunny, urban San Antonio an old-style German deli may seem out of place, until you learn that the Schilo family arrived in San Antonio via Poland and Germany in 1914 and have been feeding the good people of this city since 1917. In that time, many of the recipes have remained the same, and the prices seem barely to have matched inflation. In a part of town where a decent breakfast can be hard to come by, Schilo's is a real find, and the dishes like the Papa Fritz Breakfast ($5.65), with its two eggs, bratwurst, your choice of hash browns or grits, biscuits or muffins, and coffee, should give you enough calories to keep chugging right through lunch. Weekend evenings means German music from 5 to 8, so get ready to enjoy some accordion. If you are searching for a bit of historic San Antonio, step into Schilo's, split a pitcher of frosty homemade root beer in one of the well-worn wooden booths, and spend a little time just soaking it all in. In case you need to ask a local for directions, Schilo's is pronounced "she-lows," not "shy-lows."

Sip

210-222-0149
160 E. Houston St. (at St. Mary's), San Antonio, TX 78025
Open: Mon.–Thu. 7–6, Fri. 7 AM–9 PM, Sat. 8–8
Price: Inexpensive

Coffee addicts will appreciate the strong aroma of freshly brewed coffee and rich Italian espresso that greets them upon entering Sip. A stone's throw from the Majestic Theatre, removed from the activity of the Alamo, and without a river view in sight, Sip is a coffee spot that, in addition to pastries and treats, offers light fare, an abbreviated breakfast menu, and a simple lunchtime menu of salads and grilled panini sandwiches. Pick up a Box Lunch (sandwich, green salad or chips, and a cookie) for $6.95, slip down to the peaceful section of the Riverwalk just below Houston Street, and enjoy your meal on a bench at water's edge. Don't forget to bring a coffee to sip.

Twin Sisters Bakery & Café

210-354-1559
124 Broadway St, San Antonio, TX 78205
Open: Mon.–Fri. 8 AM–3 PM
Price: Inexpensive
Additional Location: 210-822-2265;
    6322 N. New Braunfels Ave. Open:
    Mon.–Fri. 7 AM–9 PM, Sat. 7 AM–2 PM,
    Sun. 9 AM–2 PM

With two locations just where you need 'em, smack in the middle of downtown and few blocks behind the Witte Museum in the Alamo Heights neighborhood, Twin Sisters is a funky and good-natured homegrown bakery and café that serves up light breakfasts and huge lunches to crowds of repeat customers and grateful tourists. With an emphasis on healthy food, Twin Sisters makes oodles of salads, sandwiches, burgers, soups, and stir fries, some of which are vegetarian, all of which are tasty. So, if you feel you are falling short of your daily recommended amounts of whole grains, fruits, or vegetables, stop in at Twin Sisters and leave satisfied. Very popular at the business lunch hour; avoid a wait by arriving either before or after.

KING WILLIAM DISTRICT AND SOUTHTOWN

King William District and Southtown have some much-loved restaurants that possess as much character and charm as the neighborhood itself.

Church Bistro and Theatre
210-271-7791
www.churchbistroandtheatre.com
1150 S. Alamo St., San Antonio, TX 78205
Open: Lunch Mon.–Fri. 11–2, Dinner
    Fri.–Sat. 5–11; Sun. 9 AM–3 PM
Price: Moderate to Expensive
Special Features: Theater performances

Built in 1912 and used as a house of worship until 1966, this former Methodist church dominates the corner of Wickes and South Alamo Streets. The bistro serves a weekday lunchtime buffet of comfort foods, including lasagna, chicken and dumplings, and meat loaf, and the $36.95 dinner theater includes a buffet meal and a show, though you can catch just the show for $20. The Garden of Eden Salad, "baptized" with a maple walnut dressing, is particularly divine.

Guenther House
210-227-1061 or 1-800-235-8186
www.guentherhouse.com
205 E. Guenther St., San Antonio, TX 78204
Open: Mon.–Sat. 8 AM–4 PM, Sun. 8 AM–
    3 PM
Price: Inexpensive
Special Features: On-site gift shop

Carl Hilmar Guenther came to America seeking fortune and found it when the flour mill he built in the mid-1800s, Pioneer Flour Mills, prospered. Guenther House is the home Guenther built for his family in 1860s; a popular restaurant and gift shop live here today. Though Guenther House serves a lovely lunch, including its Champagne Chicken Enchiladas, another reason diners are milling about outside waiting for a table is the baked goods on the all-day breakfast menu. The buttermilk biscuits with sausage gravy, the Southern Sweet Cream Waffles, served with or without strawberries and whipped cream, and the enormous cinnamon rolls and sticky buns are all crowd-pleasers. Guenther House's art nouveau interior and outdoor garden seating are both special and casual, making it a crowded, family-friendly favorite; you may want to consider eating here off-hours to avoid a long wait.

Mad Hatters Tea House and Cafe
210-212-4832
www.MadhattersTea.com
322 Beauregard St., San Antonio, TX 78204
Open: Mon.–Fri. 7 AM–9 PM, Sat. 9–9, Sun.
    9–6
Price: Inexpensive

Tucked in a side street, the Mad Hatters is a lovely spot for tea and a tête-à-tête, either outside at a bistro table under shade umbrellas or in the armchairs dotting the cheerfully painted and eclectically

Cowgirl hat in San Antonio

A side of chips and salsa

decorated interior. The inventive menu represents the spirit of the place. Imagine appetizers of grilled bacon-wrapped artichoke "lollipops" and entrée salads including the tea-smoked chicken breast salad with chili roasted pecans and tea vinaigrette, or the warm pork tamale salad with a creamy chipotle dressing. Don't be fooled by the humdrum name of the grilled spinach and chicken salad sandwich—it is a signature dish and a favorite of devotees. Saturday breakfast is especially popular; they often run out of the eggs Benedict early. Not surprising, the Mad Hatters loves tea parties, and you can order high tea, afternoon tea, or kids' tea served on a three-tiered tea service, each for $18.

El Mirador

210-225-9444
www.elmiradorsatx.com
722 S. St. Mary's St., San Antonio, TX 78204
Open: Mon.–Thu. 6:30 AM–9 PM, Fri.–Sat.
6:30 AM–10 PM, Sun. 6:30 AM–2 PM
Price: Inexpensive to Moderate

Family-owned and -operated since 1967, El Mirador is deeply rooted in San Antonio and is a citywide favorite. Owners Don Julian and Doña Maria hail from Salinas and Victoria, Texas, and Guanajuato, Mexico, respectively, and their family recipes exemplify Tex-Mex cuisine. Diners who grew up eating the handmade tortillas at El Mirador now bring their children to experience the outstanding chicken enchiladas served with a choice of chili, *mole*, or *frescadilla*, a sauce made of spinach, tomatillos, and green chilies. The *sopa tarasca* is a hearty blend of tomatoes and beans and is both creamy and savory and a meal unto itself, as is almost any soup featured on the revolving menu of homemade family favorites. Eat inside their casual and cheerful dining rooms or outside on a patio so lush with vegetation you'll hardly notice it juts out into a parking lot. The on-site Puro Social Club is members only, but the purchase of a cigar buys you entrée for the duration of your smoke. If you have one meal in San Antonio, the combination of food, friendliness, atmosphere, and value should put El Mirador on your short list.

Rosario's

210-223-1806

www.rosariossa.com

910 S. Alamo St., San Antonio, TX 78205

Open: Sun. 11 AM–8 PM, Mon. 11 AM–3 PM,
   Tue.–Thu. 11–10, Fri.–Sat. 11–11

Price: Inexpensive

Special Features: Live music

From the minute you tuck into the chips and salsa, you'll notice something different. For instance, instead of the ubiquitous red salsa, Rosario's serves a signature tangy chipotle version that rings true to its roots deep in Mexico. Everything on the menu is super-fresh and homemade, with a modern sensibility. The *Enfrijoladas Santa Clara*, chicken enchiladas with a zippy cumin chili sauce, and the fish tacos are just two of the many favorites that have diners returning again and again. The restaurant is usually hopping with professionals just off work and stopping in for drinks, families with children of all ages, tourists and residents alike. While it can get a bit loud, Rosario's is also the sort of place where you can have a wonderfully intimate meal surrounded by the din of happy diners. Consider arriving early to avoid a wait, and as the menu gently reminds diners, good food takes time, so allow for a leisurely meal; the outstanding results, at modest prices, will make you happy you did. Reservations recommended. Live music Friday evenings (see Music and Dancing, above). See Web site for details.

BRACKENRIDGE PARK AND
ALAMO HEIGHTS

Just a short drive from downtown, Brackenridge Park is less urban, yet home to several one-of-a-kind restaurants with a city feel. Farther north, Alamo Heights is even more polished.

Cappy's

210-828-9669

www.sawhost.com/cappy

5011 Broadway, San Antonio, TX 78209

Price: Inexpensive to Moderate

Open: Mon.–Fri. 11–2:30 and 5:30–10, Sat. 11–3 and 5:30–11, Sun. 10:30–3 and 5–10

This neighborhood restaurant, located in a brick building dating from the 1930s in the Alamo Heights neighborhood, serves an upscale menu at fairly modest prices. For starters, try the zesty Truffled Potato Stack, with thin homemade fries tossed in white truffle oil and grated parmesan. The Mustang Chicken, which packs a punch with fresh horseradish and Dijon cream, served with pecan rice, and the classic southern pecan-crusted catfish are so popular they are served for both lunch and dinner. The chef's prix fixe dinner option includes an appetizer, salad, and entrée, a terrific deal for $34. The casual, cheerful interior and leafy patio only enhance the dining experience. Nearby, Cappyccino's (see "Drinks," above) is a great out-of-the-way place for evening drinks.

Janie's Pie Factory

210-826-8715

www.janiespiefactory.com

1832 Nacogdoches Rd., San Antonio, TX 78209

Open: Tue.–Fri. 10–6, Sat. 10–4.

Price: Inexpensive

Located on Nacogdoches Road near the corner of North New Braunfels in Carousel Court, Janie's Pie Factory is a mecca for pie lovers, where the dessert is sold whole or by the slice. Janie's won the American Pie Council's National Pie Championship in 2005 with its fantastic apple pie. Janie's also sells quiches and casseroles to go, should you find yourself in need of enough chicken Tetrazzini or Texas Zucchini Bake to serve four.

Enjoy a well-balanced meal at the left-leaning (literally) Liberty Bar

Liberty Bar
210-227-1187
www.liberty-bar.com
328 E. Josephine St., San Antonio, TX 78215
Open: Mon.–Thu. 11:30–10:30, Fri.–Sat.
   11:30 AM–midnight, Sun. 10:30–10:30
Price: Inexpensive to Moderate

Located on a nondescript street, tucked under an elevated highway, and leaning, as a result of flood damage years ago, quite literally and rather dramatically to the left, the Liberty Bar doesn't seem to have much going for it. Prejudgments would be premature; for the Liberty Bar, these quirky details are very much part of its charm. Find a space in the crowded parking lot, step inside, walk past the fresh bread slicing station, glance at the specials on the chalkboard, and prepare yourself for a wonderful meal. While the setting may be casual, the food is refined—not expensive, fussy, or extravagant, just very simply inspired and wonderfully cooked. Items such as roasted hazelnut with prosciutto, apples, and Pecorino cheese, and *chile relleno en nogada* (a poblano pepper in walnut sauce) illustrate the menu's inclination toward dishes cooked Mediterranean-style with fresh herbs and vinaigrettes or with sauces inspired by the flavors of Mexico. Emancipate your taste buds with lamb burgers, mesquite-grilled smoked pork sausages, pot roast sandwiches, and homemade fettuccine with garlic. Vegetarians will find plenty of options to choose from. The weekend menu is light and delightful, and the wine list at all meals is particularly well considered. Monday nights any bottle of wine over $50 is half off, which, considering that the kitchen will custom prepare a meal to pair with it, is quite a nice deal for a special occasion.

Pig Stand

210-222-2794
1508 Broadway, San Antonio, TX 78215
Open: Daily
Price: Inexpensive
Special Features: Open 24 hours
Additional Location: 210-227-1691, 801
    S. Presa St.

Not one for subtlety, Pig Stand serves meat straight up; try hamburgers, club sandwiches, or its signature Pig Sandwich with mounds of pork BBQ piled high on a bun and smothered with relish and sauce. Shakes, malts, and banana splits take you straight back to the '50s, when ice cream was a fun snack food. The very first Pig Stand opened in Dallas in 1921, and soon

franchises were popping up all over the region. Prolific during this period of growth, the Pig Stand lays claim to inventing the drive thru, onion rings, Texas toast, and the chicken-fried steak sandwich. While the soundness of these claims remains a subject of debate, the Pig Stand is an irrefutable part of regional history in its own right. There are very few Pig Stands remaining, but San Antonio has two. Old photographs, jukeboxes, and pig-themed memorabilia add to the nostalgia of these old-time eateries. Also known for their inexpensive breakfast, the Pig Stands are open 24 hours a day.

Silo Elevated Cuisine

210-864-8686
www.siloelevatedcuisine.com
1133 Austin Hwy., San Antonio, TX
    78209
At the intersection with Mt. Calvary St.
Open: Lunch daily 11–2:30; dinner
    Sun.–Thu. 5:30–10, Fri.–Sat.
    5:30–10:30
Price: Moderate to Expensive

Enter this old farmers' market on the ground floor, now a martini bar, and take the elevator up to the dining room, run by head chef Gus Ortiz. Menu mainstays include chicken-fried oysters served with applewood bacon, sautéed spinach, and apples with a mustard hollandaise sauce, and the Asian-inspired mango-wasabi crab cakes, both of which are crowd pleasers. Dynamic pairings grace the menu: grilled and braised pork shank on whipped cinnamon sweet potatoes; grilled herb marinated jumbo shrimp with roasted corn and tarragon risotto; grilled porcini-rubbed ribeye with bleu cheese potato. Embellishments such as the mint marigold béarnaise, a cognac cream sauce, foie gras port sauce, and a spicy dried cherry sauce bump the dishes up to new heights. While the atmosphere at Silo is usually quite lively and

Tex-Mex in San Antonio

San Antonio is known for its plentiful Mexican and Tex-Mex food. Compared to the established El Mirador, Mi Tierra, and popular Rosario's, the eateries listed below are located somewhat off the beaten tourist path and frequented mostly by locals. From the cloth tablecloths at La Fogata to the paper napkins at Las Brazas, the atmosphere varies widely, but the food is consistently delicious. While every San Antonian has a favorite, the restaurants below always seem to top the list; they are presented here in alphabetical order.

Los Barrios (210-732-6017; 4223 Blanco Rd.) Open: Mon.–Thu. 10–10, Fri.–Sat. 10 AM –11 PM, Sun. 9 AM–10 PM. Price: Inexpensive. Los Barrios does everything so well, from predictably great enchiladas to the more obscure Argentinian CHURRASCO steak with CHIMICHURRI sauce, that they've put it all in a cookbook.

Las Brazas (210-349-6566; 2627 Vance Jackson Rd.) Open: 24 hours. Price: Inexpensive. Not for the faint of heart, Las Brazas is no-frills Mexican food, served up quick, hot, tasty, and super-cheap, both day and night.

La Fogata (210-340-1337; www.lafogata.com; 2427 Vance Jackson Rd.) Open: Mon.–Thu. 11–10, Fri. 11–11, Sat. 10 AM–11 PM, Sun. 10–10. Price: Inexpensive to Moderate. Fresh, homemade northern Mexican cuisine served in a refined tropical setting. The dessert empanadas are delicious.

La Fonda on Main (210-733-0621; www.lafondaonmain.com; 2415 N. Main St. at Woodlawn) Open: Mon.–Thu. 5 –9:30 , Fri.–Sat. 5–10:30, Sun. 11 AM–3 PM. Price: Inexpensive to Moderate. La Fonda has been feeding San Antonio since 1931. Tortilla soup, light and flavorful, with tender chicken, fresh avocado, and crispy tortilla strips, exemplifies the menu. An atmospheric dining room and hacienda-style patio make dinner special.

Guajillo's (210-344-4119; www.guajillos.net; 1001 NW Loop 410 at Blanco Rd.) Open: Mon.–Thu. 11–10, Fri.–Sun. 11–11. Price: Inexpensive. The green MOLE, made with chilies and pumpkin seeds, is a must. A clean, casual, no-nonsense place north of town.

La Hacienda de los Barrios (210-497-8000; www.lhdlb.com; 18747 Redland Rd.) Open: Sun.–Thu. 11–10, Fri.–Sat. 11–11. Price: Moderate. In a residential neighborhood north of Loop 1604, La Hacienda is owned by the enterprising Barrios family (see Los Barrios, above), who bring their well-honed techniques and time-honored recipes to the upscale menu.

Jacala Mexican Restaurant (210-732-5222; 606 West Ave. at Hilderbrand St.) Jacala serves puffy tacos and spinach quesadillas, just as they've done since 1949. Open: Sun.–Thu. 11–9:45, Fri.–Sat. 11–10:45. Price: Inexpensive.

El Jarro de Arturo (210-494-5084; 13421 San Pedro Ave.) Open: Sun.–Thu. 11–10, Fri.–Sat. 11–10:30. Price: Moderate. Outstanding upscale Mexican food made with high-quality ingredients has made El Jarro de Arturo a local favorite for decades.

Martha's (210-690-0066; 5822 Babcock Rd.) Open: Sat.–Thu. 7 AM –9 PM, Fri. 7 AM–11 PM. Price: Inexpensive. A local chain restaurant with several locations in San Antonio, Martha's serves good food fast, making it popular with families.

Picante Grill (210-822-3797; www.picantegrill.com; 3810 Broadway) Open: Sun.–Mon. 11–9, Tue.–Sat. 11–10. Price: Inexpensive. Across the street from the Witte Museum, the Picante Grill makes fabulous fajitas and spicy hot salsa.

Pico de Gallo (210-225-6060; www.picodegallo.com; 111 S. Leona St.) Open: Sun.–Thu. 8 AM–10 PM, Fri.–Sat. 8 AM–midnight. Price: Inexpensive to Moderate. Owned by the same folks who keep Mi Tierra (see "Dining," above) going all night long, this restaurant pleases crowds with its simple breakfasts, traditional Mexican dinners, accomplished mariachi band, and in-house bakery.

Teka Molino (210-735-5471; 2403 N. St. Mary's St.) Open: Mon.–Fri. 7–7. Price: Inexpensive. In business since the 1930s, Teka Molino makes up for in food what it lacks in atmosphere. Order at the counter, pick up your meal when it's ready, and dig into to the sort of Mexican food that makes San Antonio proud.

Tomatillo's (210-824-3005; www.tomatillos.com; 3210 Broadway) Open: Sun.–Thu. 11–10, Fri.–Sat. 11–11. Price: Inexpensive. Hot, hot sauce, meal-sized appetizers, and maragaritas make Tomatillo's a popular happy-hour destination.

---

certainly makes for a lot of fun, the tables are spaced very close together, European-style, which leaves little room for privacy.

Texas Farm to Table Café
210-444-1404
312 Pearl Pkwy., Building 2, Suite 201, San Antonio, TX 78215
Open: Mon. 10:30 AM–2:30 PM, Tue.– Sat. 8–8
Price: Inexpensive

Any local road designated by the letters FM and a number is a "farm to market" road, originally built to facilitate agribusiness by providing a reliable route between rural and urban Texas. Trust Texas Farm to Table Café to deliver fresh, local, seasonal produce straight to your plate. Serving a limited breakfast and lunch, the café's menu changes frequently, but expect to see items along the lines of panini with ham, caramelized onions, and raspberry chipotle sauce and meal-sized salads.

MONTE VISTA AND OLMOS PARK

These two down-to-earth neighborhoods are home to casual, friendly, and folksy restaurants.

Casbeer's

210-732-3511
www.casbeers.com
1719 Blanco Rd., San Antonio, TX 78212
Open: Tue.–Thu. 11–11, Fri. 11–midnight,
    Sat. 5 PM–1 AM
Price: Inexpensive
Special Features: Live music

While Kinky Friedman's fate as a gubernatorial candidate was sealed by the time this book went to press (he lost big), it is worth noting that Casbeer's invented a burger in his honor. The Kinky is a half-pound Texas beef patty with American cheese served on Jewish Rye bread with grilled onions; $1 is—or was—donated to his campaign for every burger sold. This fact illustrates several things about Casbeer's that are important to know before entering the San Antonio favorite; these folks have a sense of humor, lots of community spirit, and a big heart for philanthropy. Take, for instance, the Sunday Gospel Brunch. Once a month a hundred $10 tickets are sold and Casbeer's starts cooking for the massive buffet, which has all the scrambled eggs, chorizo, biscuits, and enchiladas anyone could want. Diners are assigned dining times—these are printed on the tickets—and once everyone has had a chance to fill a plate, Miss Nessie and the Easy Lutherans start playing. The musicians donate their time, Casbeer's donates a portion of proceeds, and a hat is passed, all to benefit the San Antonio Shelter Food Bank. On "regular" days, Casbeer's serves its famous cheese enchiladas, just as it has since 1962, priced at $6.50 for four; these are the most expensive item on the menu, unless you spring the $12.95 for the T-bone. Live music on Friday

and Saturday nights makes this a fun hangout (see Music and Dancing, above); check the Web site for listings.

Chris Madrid's

210-735-3552
www.chrismadrids.com
1900 Blanco Rd., San Antonio, TX 78212
Open: Mon.–Sat. 11–10
Price: Inexpensive

Chris Madrid's is the place to go for burgers in San Antonio, and people do, all day long. Choose from their many topping combinations, which include Porky's Delight with cheddar and bacon and the Flaming Jalapeño with mustard and piles of jalapeños that will clear your sinuses for a week. The Tostada Burger, with mounds of refried beans, chips, onions, and cheddar cheese, despite its dubious description is a crowd pleaser. The freshly made burgers come in two sizes, regular and macho; wolfing down a Macho Burger may give you enough swagger to purchase the "I ate the Macho Burger" bumper sticker and do a little bragging. Casual, no frills atmosphere.

Ciao Lavanderia

210-822-3990
226 E. Olmos Dr. just off McCullough, San Antonio, TX 78212
Open: Lunch Tue.–Fri. 11:30–1:30 and dinner Tue.–Sat. 5:30–9:30
Price: Moderate

Ciao Lavanderia is a less fussy, less expensive spin-off of its popular neighbor, Bistro Vatel (210-828-3141; same hours). With a focus on unpretentious European fare, the menu is neatly divided into three price categories. Start out with spinach salad and gorgonzola cheese, mushroom and goat cheese polenta, or an arrangement of fresh tomatoes and mozzarella. The next tier has pastas, pizzas, seafood, or chicken, while the last grouping is dominated by heartier fare such as creamy seafood risotto or braised duck with olives. Located in a small strip of shops just off the roundabout on McCullough in the Olmos Park neighborhood, Ciao Lavanderia is the sort of restaurant where locals love to meet for lunch or a relaxed dinner. Good food at prices that won't leave you hanging out to dry. Goodbye Laundromat!

ATTRACTIONS, PARKS, AND RECREATION

San Antonio Botanical Garden

210-207-3250
www.sabot.org
555 Funston Place (at N. New Braunfels Ave.), San Antonio, TX 78209
Open: Daily 9–5
Admission: Adults $6, seniors $4, children $3
Special Features: Cash only

The San Antonio Botanical Gardens and Lucille Halsell Conservatory are located north of the city, just a few blocks east of Broadway near the Witte Museum and Brackenridge Park and en route to the McNay Art Museum. The entrance to the 33-acre property is through the stone Daniel Sullivan Carriage House, which was built in town in 1896 and moved, stone by stone, to its present location in 1988. The building also houses a gift shop and a small, casual restaurant offering simple, healthful, and filling dishes, some of which come garnished with fresh, edible flowers (Open Tue.–Sun. 11 AM–2 PM).

Mural on a building in Southtown

Entrance to the San Antonio Zoo

The Botanical Gardens are fascinating for flower enthusiasts, and though the variety and volumes of blooms you see will depend on the time of year you visit, there is something flowering year-round in the warm Texas climate. One of the most fascinating gardens here is the Garden for the Blind, centered on a gurgling fountain and planted with flowers and plants known for their smells and textures, such as the fragrant "root beer plant" and fuzzy lamb's ears, all labeled in braille on metal markers.

A highlight of any trip is bound to be the award-winning Lucille Halsell Conservatory designed by the noted Argentinean architect Emilio Ambasz and opened in 1988. The conservatory is actually a complex of glass structures, each designed to re-create various climates from around the world to grow and display plants in their natural ecosystems. The building regulates the environments through the ingenious use of light and heat, and the results are wonderful to wander through.

San Antonio and Kumamoto, Japan, are sister cities, and gardeners came from Japan to San Antonio to help design the authentic and lovely Kumamoto En Japanese Garden, jam-packed with highly symbolic plants, structures, materials, and gestures. The double granite bridge clearly connotes mutual respect, understanding, and friendship.

Brackenridge Park

The main entrance to Brackenridge Park is in the 2800 block of North Broadway.
Open: Daily 5 AM–11 PM
Admission: Free

Brackenridge Park is a 343-acre urban park 2 miles north of downtown San Antonio beside and behind the Witte Museum on Broadway. The park first opened in 1899, and it has aged since then, gracefully. Home to the popular San Antonio Zoo, the tranquil Japanese Tea Gardens and the neighboring Sunken Garden Theatre, and the Brackenridge Golf Course, the park is also dotted with play structures, picnic tables, and ball fields. The *Brackenridge Eagle*, a replica of an 1863 Central Pacific Huntington steam engine, pulls a miniature train filled with children around a several-mile track (210-735-7455; hours vary seasonally; price: adults $2.75, children $2.25). The San Antonio River, which flows from an artesian spring just north of the park, meanders through, as do shady paved walking paths.

San Antonio Zoo

210-734-7184
www.sazoo-aq.org
3903 N. St. Mary's St., San Antonio, TX 78212
Open: Daily 9–5
Admission: Adults $9, seniors and children $7

The San Antonio Zoo, like many zoos in America, is undergoing major restructuring of both the physical space and the philosophy of keeping animals in captivity. The zoo's master plan, "2020 Vision," will transform it into five zones, each representing a different continent and its respective ecosystems. While the zoo is still enacting this plan, and some of the facility feels old-school by today's standards, the brand-new Africa Live! exhibit is quite dynamic and features animals in their natural habitat, surrounded by native plants and with much more room to roam; its "African Plains" extend around a man-made watering hole, from which various species come and go freely. Additionally, the

Theme Parks

One of the reasons Central Texas is such a popular family getaway is the proliferation of amusement, theme, and water parks just outside San Antonio and easily accessible from both Austin and the Hill Country. By March or April, all are open for the season; most cut back to weekends only after Labor Day. If possible, consider planning your trip early or late in the season, avoiding July and August, for a more manageable visit; in the summer months the parks can be crowded, their sidewalks sizzling hot, and their food, snacks, and cool drinks expensive. Arriving early helps beat both the throngs and the heat, but some park-goers achieve the same result by arriving in the mid-to-late afternoon, once most everyone else has worn themselves out. Arriving early may also help you snag a decent parking spot, but it won't help you avoid the $7–$10 parking fee. All of the parks recommend you wear comfortable shoes and pack sunscreen, a hat, extra towels, and even a change of clothes. For swimming, proper swimsuits are essential; park-goers in anything else may be turned away. In all cases, purchasing tickets on the Internet tends to save both time and money.

Schlitterbahn

830-625-2531

www.schlitterbahn.com

381 E. Austin St., New Braunfels, TX 78130

Open: Last weekend in April to Labor Day weekend, daily from 10 AM to 6–8 PM; check Web site for specifics

Admission: Adults $34.50, children $28.50

Schlitterbahn is located in New Braunfels, an easy drive north from San Antonio, and is the place for soaking-wet, family-style fun; see Attractions, Parks, and Recreation, below, for details.

Sea World San Antonio

210-523-3000 or 1-800-700-7786

www.4adventure.com

10500 Sea World Dr., San Antonio, TX 78251

Open: Daily March–Dec. from 10 AM to 6–10 PM; check Web sites for specifics

Admission: Adults $42, children $33

Part of the larger Busch Garden's group of Sea World parks across the United States, Sea World San Antonio is part amusement park, part water park, and part marine life education center. Smaller than Sea World in either Florida or California, the San Antonio park is more manageable, and tickets are somewhat less expensive. The amusement park includes water rides and roller-coasters, all of which spin, drop, propel, twist, or lurch their riders in the name of fun. The

"Journey to Atlantis," expected to premiere in 2007, promises to combine all these thrills while also leaving you soaking wet. The water park section of Sea World is tamer, with sprinklers, water rides, and wave pools; it's an area easily enjoyed by family members of all ages. Marine life enters the picture, with rare opportunities to interact with the animals, or sit back and watch elaborate shows. The "Shamu-Believe" show is a huge hit with all ages and is awash with visual effects, music, video, and, if you are sitting in the first 14 rows, water. Another popular show, "Viva," features synchronized swimmers, high divers, and Pacific white-sided dolphins and beluga whales engaged in dramatic acrobatics.

Six Flags Fiesta Texas

210-697-5050 or 1-800-473-4378

www.sixflags.com

17000 I-10 West, San Antonio, TX 78257

Open: March–October 10–6, open later in high season; check Web sites for specifics

Admission: Adults $46.99, children under 48 inches $31.99

The name says it all. This is Six Flags Fiesta Texas, not Disney, so expectations should be adjusted accordingly. The park is designed with rides for smaller children scattered in and among those for adults, making it easier for families to stay together and stay sane. Crowd-pleasers include the milelong super-smooth Superman Krypton roller-coaster, and the Texas Tree House, with its cowboy and his ominous 1,000-gallon hat. Award-winning shows and music performances, many of which retain a Texas twang, are fun, as are the holiday-themed events. While it might be nice to have a little less Tweety Bird—who came to stay when Warner Brothers bought the Six Flags group—the park is still a Texas good time.

Splashtown
210-227-1400
www.splashtownusa.com

3600 N. IH-35, San Antonio, TX 78219
Open: April–September with a changing
   schedule; check Web site for specifics
Admission: Adults $24.99, children under
   48 inches tall $18.99

Much more low-key than its high-energy neighbors, Spashtown is a small, fun, easygoing water park just a few minutes north of San Antonio. Perfect for preschool and young children, Spashtown has a wave pool, huge slides, a water bobsled, and the gently flowing Siesta del Rio waterway for tubing.

new barnyard-themed petting zoo is fun for tykes, and the butterfly exhibit, recently rebuilt after a 45-foot-tall red oak tree toppled over and destroyed it in 2005, is of particular local interest. Opened in 2000, Cranes of the World is a verdant environment for all sorts of cranes, including the endangered whooping crane. Wear comfortable shoes for walking, and take a cue from the animals and drink lots of water.

Japanese Tea Gardens
210-821-3120
Open: Daily 8 AM–dusk
Admission: Free

Shady year-round foliage, ponds, bridges, and a 60-foot waterfall have turned this old quarry into a very relaxing respite, the perfect place to rest and recenter on the way to the zoo. The Japanese Tea Gardens were closed for renovations at press time, but since they are simply refurbishing what was already a peaceful spot, I'm confident the gardens will be exquisite when they reopen. Next door, the outdoor Sunken Garden Theatre (see "Performing Arts," above) is known for its Shakespeare productions.

Friedrich Wilderness Park
210-698-1057
www.fofriedrichpark.org
21395 Milsa St., San Antonio, TX 78256
Take I-10 to the Camp Bullis exit and follow the signs
Open: Daily 7:30 AM–sunset
Admission: Free
Special Features: Limited handicapped accessible

Five and a half miles of trails weave throughout this hilly and heavily wooded 232-acre park, which is known as an oasis in otherwise rapidly urbanizing Bexar County. The park is a popular spot for both birders and hikers, and its paths are clearly marked and designated by difficulty levels 1–4. All grade 1 trails are accessible by wheelchairs and strollers. First

Saturday Interpretive Hikes take place on the first Saturday of each month. Two additional natural areas offering trails and fresh air near San Antonio are Medina River Natural Area and Crown Ridge Canyon Natural Area. See www.sanaturalareas.org for more details on all San Antonio natural areas.

Government Canyon State Natural Area
210-688-9055
www.tpwd.state.tx.us
12861 Galm Rd., San Antonio, TX 78254
From the intersection of Loop 1604 and Culebra Road. (FM 471), take Culebra Road. west for 3.5 miles, then Galm Road. north 1.6 miles
Open: Fri.–Mon. 8–6; day use only
Admission: $6 (per person over 13 years old)

Located just outside San Antonio, the Government Canyon State Natural Area was purchased in 1993 and opened to the public for the first time in the fall of 2005. Trails are still being blazed through the park's 8,600 acres, but some are completed and ready for use, as are picnic areas and restrooms.

Mitchell Lake
210-628-1639
www.tx.audubon.org
10750 Pleasanton Rd., San Antonio, TX 78221
Take Loop 410 to exit 46, Moursund Boulevard., and travel south just over a half mile. The gate will be on the left.
Open: Sat.–Sun. 8–4, weekdays by appointment
Admission: $2, tours $5

While you cannot swim in the 600-acre Mitchell Lake, you can spot, if you're lucky, more than 300 species of birds as you hike its protected wetland trails. Managed by the Audubon Society of Texas, the lake is somewhat off the beaten track but worth the trip for birders and nature lovers.

Natural Bridge Caverns
210-651-6101
www.naturalbridgecaverns.com
26495 Natural Bridge Caverns Rd., Natural Bridge Caverns, TX 78266
Open: Daily from 9 AM to 4–7 PM, depending on the week and season; check Web site for details
Admission: Adults $15–$25, children $9–$14.50, Adventure Tour $95

Talk to a native of San Antonio and they'll say that while the amusement parks are fun, this place is really fascinating. A National Natural Landmark, Natural Bridge Caverns will exercise your vocabulary, reminding you that stalactites hang down, stalagmites rise up, and a sluice is "a series of troughs leading from a water-filled tower." The standard North Cavern Tour is an informative 75 minutes that will take you a half mile underground. The Jeramy Room Flashlight Tour is separate and purposefully kept small, as this part of the cavern, opened to the public in 2002, is quite fragile. The very challenging Adventure Tour is open

Torch of Friendship, *created by Mexican artist Sebastian and donated to the people of San Antonio by the people of Mexico in 2002*

to only the physically fit, who will enjoy the challenge of hours climbing, crawling, and rappelling in a room that is otherwise off limits. Kids will love the Watchtower Challenge, a massive outdoor climbing wall with two zip lines, and the chance to pan for treasure.

RECREATION

A tremendous online resource for all outdoor recreation in Texas is www.texasoutside.com.

Bicycling

Bicycling, both road and mountain biking, is big in Central Texas, especially in the Hill Country; helpful Web sites include:

San Antonio Wheelmen (www.sawheelmen.com)

South Texas Off-Road Mountain Bikers (www.storm-web.org)

Texas State Park System (www.tpwd.state.tx.us/exptexas/bike)

Bluestar Bike Tour (210-212-5506; www.bluestarbrewing.com; 1414 S. Alamo St.)

For bicycle rentals and guided tours see "Tours," below.

Bird Watching

San Antonio is a great spot to catch a glimpse of rare, migratory, and native birds. Online, **Texas Parks and Wildlife,** www.tpwd.state.tx.us, and the **Audubon Society of San Antonio,** www.saaudubon.org, both offer a wealth of information. See "Suggested References" in the Information chapter for a selection of bird-watching guides.

Camping

Camping around San Antonio is best accomplished in New Braunfels. See chapter 7, Nearby and In Between.

Fishing

Fishing in Central Texas is excellent, though your best bet is to head west to Medina Lake, north to Canyon Lake or the rivers in New Braunfels, or to a Texas state park where you don't need a license to fish from shore (check www.tpwd.state.tx.us for details). See "Attractions, Parks, and Recreation" and "Texas State Parks" in the Hill Country chapter. Other online resources include www.texasoutside.com, www.txfishing.com, and www.austinkayakfishing.com.

Golf

San Antonio is home to outstanding golf courses (see "Fore!" on facing page). For a complete interactive listing of local courses, visit www.golfsanantonio.org.

Professional Sports

The **Alamodome** (210-207-3663 or 1-800-884-3663; www.sanantonio.gov/dome; 100 Montana St.) hosts the high school Texas Football Classic in September and the Alamo Bowl in December (see "Festivals," above).

Fore!

Though Mark Twain once remarked that golf is just "a good walk spoiled," San Antonians seem to like the walk just fine. The dips and rises of the Hill Country lend themselves perfectly to the game, and some of the courses have been built in old abandoned quarries, a nice reuse of land. With near-constant sunshine and courses ranging from the charming and historic municipal Brackenridge Golf Course to the breathtaking Palmer Course at La Cantera, it is no wonder that San Antonio has become a destination for serious and recreational golfers alike. The courses listed below rank as some of the best; expect to pay $50–$100 and up. For a complete interactive online listing of local courses, visit www.golfsanantonio.org, a nonprofit organization that uses golf to both educate children and enhance charitable giving in San Antonio.

Brackenridge Golf Course (210-226-5612; 2315 Avenue B, Brackenridge Park) With all the great golf to be had in greater San Antonio, one of the charms of this course is that it has that comfortable, well-worn, communal feel of an old-school municipal course. It was designed in 1915 by the fascinating and charismatic A. W. "Tillie" Tillinghast, who was also the mastermind behind what we now consider classic courses across the country—Newport in Rhode Island, Quaker Ridge in Scarsdale, NY, and his triumphant Baltusrol in Springfield, NJ. Golf enthusiasts may enjoy reading about his legacy at www.tillinghast.net.

Canyon Springs Golf Club (210-497-1770 or 1-888-800-1511; www.canyonspringsgc.com; 24405 Wilderness Oak) Canyon Springs is situated on the site of an old homestead, and many of the current buildings are constructed using rocks that were originally part of the 50-mile dry-stack wall encompassing the property. The unique loop design of the course means the scenic views are completely unobstructed.

The Quarry Golf Club (210-824-4500 or 1-800-347-7759; www.quarrygolf.com; 444 E. Basse Rd.) The atmospheric back nine is situated inside an old quarry and surrounded by 100-foot-high walls of rock. Elsewhere there are terrific views of the city, particularly at dusk. From downtown take US 281 out of the city and exit right at Basse Road.

The Westin La Cantera Resort (210-558-6500 or 1-800-937-8461; www.westinlacantera.com; 16641 La Cantera Pkwy.) Built high on a hill on the site of a former limestone quarry—LA CANTERA— this resort is 20 minutes from downtown but in a world all its own. A golfer's fantasy, the resort boasts two championship 18-hole golf courses, which have earned it kudos from national magazines such as GOLF MAGAZINE and Condé Nast TRAVELER.

The AT&T Center (210-444-5000, 210-225-8326 for tickets; www.attcenter.com; One AT&T Center Pkwy.) is host to most sporting events in San Antonio. Texans love their sports; in San Antonio, the sport is basketball, thanks to the three-time NBA champion **San Antonio Spurs** (www.nba.com/spurs) and the **San Antonio Silver Stars** (www.wmba.com/silverstars), the women's basketball team with an enthusiastic following. The **San Antonio Rampage,** the ice hockey team, (www.sarampage.com), keeps things chill.

Swimming
San Pedro Springs Park (210-732-5992; www.sanantonio.gov; 1315 San Pedro Ave.) San Antonio's oldest park, the second-oldest in the nation after Boston Common, San Pedro

Hats for sale in Market Square/El Mercado

Springs Park is popular today primarily for its swimming area, which consists of a natural spring-fed body of cool water, lined with trees and stone walkways.

Tours

Bluestar Bike Tour (210-212-5506; www.bluestarbrewing.com; 1414 S. Alamo St.) Guided bicycle tours of the missions, approximately 12–15 miles long. Price: $20.

SegCity (210-224-0773; www.segcity.com; 124 Lasoya St.) Tours on this self-balancing motorized two-wheel contraption are rumored to be great fun, but be prepared for plenty of stares. Three 3-hour tours daily, departing at 9 AM and 1 and 7 PM. Price: $65, helmet included.

Rio San Antonio Tours (210-244-5700 or 1-800-417-4139; www.riosanantonio.com; 205 N. Presa St., Building B, Suite 201) Narrated cruises lasting 35 to 40 minutes and covering 2.5 miles of Riverwalk. Tickets available online or at ticket booths at the Rivercenter Mall (Commerce St. and Bowie St.), Holiday Inn Riverwalk (St. Mary's and College Sts.), and under the Market Street Bridge at Alamo Street. All ticket booths are near elevators for handicapped access. Rio San Antonio also runs a water taxi (see "Transportation," above). Open: Daily 9–9. Price: Adults $6.50, seniors $4.50, children $1.50.

San Antonio Tours (1-800-804-9486; www.sanantoniotours.net) Bus tours of San Antonio, including an all-day tour of major sights, the IMAX theater, several missions, and a riverboat ride. Also bicycle tours of the city, walking tours of King William District, a "Ghosts and Legends" tour, and bus tours of the Hill Country. Discounted tickets available online. Price: $16–$60.

Texas Trolley Hop (210-212-5395; 217 Alamo Plaza) Two 60-minute tours departing from the Alamo Visitor Center beside the Alamo. With the Hop Pass, visitors are allowed to use the trolley services all day. Price: $9.95, Hop Pass $11.95.

Tubing
Nearby New Braunfels and historic Gruene offer outstanding tubing on the pretty Guadalupe and Comal Rivers. See chapter 7, Nearby and In Between.

Hill Country vista

5

THE HILL COUNTRY

Texas Trails

The Hill Country occupies the eastern portion of the Edwards Plateau and is bounded by the Balcones Fault to the east and the granite domes of the Llano Uplift to the north and west. The green grazing terrain is textured with limestone rocks and boulders and pierced by outcroppings. The region is the perfect habitat for deer, coyote, squirrels, foxes, raccoons, skunks, and armadillo, as well as migrating birds and butterflies, and its many caves and caverns are home to millions of bats. Numerous state parks offer ample opportunity to view nature close-up. You could spend the day or a week in these hills, winding your way from town to town, past wildflowers, vineyards, and fields of lavender, watching the sun move across the enormous Texas sky.

Lodging Price Code

Inexpensive	Up to $100
Moderate	$100 to $150
Expensive	$150 to $250
Very Expensive	Over $250

Dining Price Code

Inexpensive	Up to $12
Moderate	$12 to $25
Expensive	$25 to $40
Very Expensive	$40 or more

Bandera

The self-proclaimed "Cowboy Capital of the World," little Bandera has got some big boots to fill. Located approximately 50 miles northwest of San Antonio on TX 16, Bandera is named for nearby Bandera Pass, the natural V-shaped access point that allowed Native Americans, the Spanish, the United States Army, Texas Rangers, and even cattle during the cattle drives of the 19th century to pass through the rocky ridge separating the Medina and Guadalupe river valleys. Founded in 1852, Bandera was settled by Polish immigrants and was also home to a Mormon colony. Since the 1920s, Bandera and its surrounding countryside have played host to summertime visitors who enjoy the area's ranches, campgrounds,

dance halls, and rodeos. Bandera is known for its dude ranches, twice-weekly rodeos from Memorial Day to Labor Day, summertime water fun in the Medina River and nearby Medina Lake, and scenic trails in the two state natural areas located nearby.

CULTURE

Frontier Times Museum (830-796-3864; www.frontiertimesmuseum.com; 510 13th St., Bandera, TX 78003) Open: Mon.–Sat. 10–4:30. Admission: Adults $5, seniors $3, children $1, children under 6 free. Opened in 1933, the museum today is the result of decades of collecting; its eclectic mix of western memorabilia, artifacts from frontier times, and oddities such as a stuffed two-headed sheep, are sure to intrigue.

Polly's Chapel, a lovely little house of worship with a remarkable history, stands off TX 16, approximately 6 miles southeast of the city near Privilege Creek. Situated on a pretty piece

of land in what feels like the middle of nowhere, the chapel is unexpected, to say the least. It was built entirely by hand by José Policarpo "Polly" Rodriguez more than 120 years ago. Polly was born in Mexico, moved to Texas as a child, became a scout with the U.S. Army, and eventually a Methodist minister. His spiritual awakening prompted Polly's desire to build the chapel, a labor of love he completed in 1882. The doors are usually left unlocked.

Once the sightseeing's done, join the local tradition of live music, mostly country and western and honky-tonk, and dance your boots off. Though hours may vary, there is always a dance hall open Wednesday through Sunday nights, with mellower bring-your-own-guitar jam sessions Sunday afternoons.

Arkey Blue's Silver Dollar Saloon (830-796-8826; 308 Main St., Bandera, TX 78003) Beside the general store and down a flight of stairs, Arkey Blue's Silver Dollar has sawdust floors, a pool table, lots of neon, live music, and cold Shiner longnecks all night long. Quintessential Bandera.

Blue Genes (830-796-7144; www.bluegenesbandera.com; 807 Main St., Bandera, TX 78003) This brand-new, super-friendly dance hall is just waiting for folks to scuff up their dance floor to live country, swing, classic rock, Cajun, and blues. Crease your jeans and get on down.

Cabaret Dance Hall (830-796-8889; www.banderacabaret.com; 801 Main St., Bandera, TX 78003) A fixture on Main Street beginning in 1936, the Cabaret Dance Hall closed its doors after decades of dancing and sat vacant and neglected for years. It was recently reopened by a young, energetic couple, so the beer's flowing again and the music's back on, with live country and western and honky-tonk. The Cabaret is a good old time for singles, couples, or the whole family.

11th Street Cowboy Bar (830-796-4849; www.11thstreetcowboybar.com; 307 11th St., Bandera, TX 78003) A little wooden shack of a bar, the 11th Street Cowboy Bar is a huge, level social playing field with a clientele as varied as the many, many bras which hang from the ceiling. Drink specials, free burgers, and steak nights may lure customers, but it's the fantastic live country and western and country swing music that keeps' em there dancing into the night. The bar runs a "B&B&B" (Beer, Bed, and Breakfast) for those who don't want to leave; call for details.

Rodeos

In Bandera, summertime is rodeo season; the big kickoff event is the **Cowboy Capital PRCA Rodeo** (www.banderarodeo.com), held during Memorial Day weekend in Mansfield Park. Featuring cowboys competing for points to qualify for the National Rodeo Finals, this event always brings out some top-notch riders. Smaller rodeos, such as those at the Twin Elm Guest Ranch (830-796-3628 or 1-888-567-3049; www.twinelmranch.com), are held in various locations Tuesday and Friday evenings until Labor Day. Contact the Bandera Convention and Visitors Bureau (1-800-364-3833; www.banderacowboycapital.com) for more information.

Festivals

Every Saturday from mid-March through October, the Frontier Times Museum's Living History Project sponsors **Cowboys on Main** (1-800-364-3833) featuring storytellers, trick ropers, musicians, and cowboys on horseback. Spice things up in April with the **Annual Silver Sage Corral Benefit Chili Cook-off** hosted by the 11th Street Cowboy Bar, then cool off at the **Riverfest** and its popular **Everything But a Boat River Regatta** held in May.

Boots for sale

Dude Ranches

Out here in Bandera the itch to slide into a pair of jeans, put on cowboy boots, and start wrangling begins to need scratching. Below are some ranches where you can be a cowboy for a day.

Rates are roughly the same, approximately $120 per day per adult and $80 per day per child, plus or minus depending on the season. Limited horseback riding, use of the ranch swimming pool, and participation in ranch-organized events tend to be included, though three meals may not. Often there is a minimum stay of two or three nights. Details vary; check Web sites and don't hesitate to call for clarification. Day visitors are welcome at some of the ranches for horseback riding at rates of approximately $30 an hour; call to inquire.

Dixie Dude Ranch (830-796-7771. 1-800-375-YALL; www.dixieduderanch.com; P.O. Box 548, Bandera, TX 78003)

Mayan Ranch (830-796-3312; www.mayanranch.com; P.O. Box 577, Bandera TX 78003)

Flying L Guest Ranch (830-460-3001 or 1-800-292-5134; www.flyingl.com; 566 Flying L Dr., Bandera, TX 78003)

Hill Country Equestrian Lodge (830-796-7950; www.hillcountryequestlodge.com; 1580 Hay Hollar Rd., Bandera, TX 78003)

Rancho Cortez (830-796-9339 or 1-866-797-9339; www.ranchocortez.com; 872 Hay Hollar Rd., Bandera, TX 78003)

Running R Ranch (830-796-3984; www.rrranch.com; 9059 Bandera Creek Rd., Bandera, TX 78003)

Silver Spur Guest Ranch (830-796-3037; www.silverspur-ranch.com; 9266 Bandera Creek Rd., Bandera, TX 78003)

Twin Elm Guest Ranch (830-796-3628 or 1-888-567-3049; www.twinelmranch.com; P.O. Box 117, Bandera, TX 78003)

DINING

Busbee's BBQ (830-796-3153; 319 Main St., Bandera, TX 78003) Open: Mon., Wed., Thu., Sun. 10:30–8, Fri.–Sat. 10:30–9. Price: Inexpensive. Busbee's smokes up hard-to-resist brisket, sausage, ribs, ham, and chicken, all served on red-checkered tablecloths. The homemade pecan pie and peach cobbler provide the perfect finish.

Fool Moon Café (830-460-8434; 204 Main St./TX 16, Bandera, TX 78003) Open: lunch Tue.–Sat. 11 AM–2 PM, dinner Fri.–Sat. 7–9. Price: Moderate. Bucking Bandera tradition, the Fool Moon Café serves exquisite dishes rooted in classic European tradition, with

Medina

Midway between Bandera and Kerrville, along a picturesque stretch of TX 16, is Medina, a blink-and-you'll-miss-it gem of town. Spend the night at Koyote Ranch, slurp an apple cider slushy at Love Creek Orchards, and savor a little bit of Texas that's off the beaten path.

Love Creek Orchards (830-589-2202 or 1-800-449-0882; www.lovecreekorchards.com; TX 16, Medina, TX) Open: Mon.–Sat. 9–5, Sun. 10–5. Price: Inexpensive. If you aren't hungry when you arrive, the smell of fresh hot apple pie wafting through Love Creek Orchards will have you salivating for a snack in no time. The Patio Café serves big, juicy burgers and sandwiches, with a side of chips and apples, daily 11–3, and the country store sells all things apple, from ciders to jams and ice cream.

Koyote Ranch (830-589-4695 or 1-800-225-0991; www.koyoteranch.com; 23233 TX 16 North, Medina, TX 78055) Price: Inexpensive to Expensive. Koyote Ranch is a collection of new cabins, campsites, and RV sites hugging the lovely green hillside outside Medina. With heated and air-conditioned bathrooms in the campground, a pool, and a camp store complete with a reasonably priced grill and deli, the Koyote Ranch is "roughing it" with family-friendly amenities.

influences from both Mexico and California. The menu is short, ever-changing, and very season-specific; so be prepared to experience the whims of the chef. Diners are encouraged to bring their own wine, and since you won't know the menu until you get there, just bring a favorite.

Old Spanish Trail (OST) (830-796-3836; 305 Main St., Bandera, TX 78003) Open: Mon.–Wed. 6 AM–9 PM, Thu. 6 AM–10 PM, Fri.–Sat. 6 AM–11 PM, Sun. 7 AM–9 PM. Price: Inexpensive. OST takes the cowboy theme to new heights, placing diners high in the saddles that double as lunch-counter stools. Chicken-fried steaks and enchiladas are menu mainstays, the chuckwagon buffets are filling, and even the simple breakfast tacos hit the spot. With spurs on the wall, wagon wheels on the ceiling, and an entire room devoted to John Wayne, you'll never forget you're in the Cowboy Capital of the World.

ATTRACTIONS, PARKS, AND RECREATION

In town, the cypress-lined Medina River is an irresistible spot to cool off, though heavy rainfall can cause it to become temporarily hazardous. Rent tubes and kayaks from the **Medina River Company** (830-796-3248; www.medinarivercompany.com; 2440 TX 16 North, Bandera, TX 78003) for $10–$46 per day, cash only.

To the southeast, **Medina Lake** is a recreational lake with plenty of cabins and cottages for rent; check the Bandera Convention and Visitors Bureau's Web site, www.banderacowboycapital.com, for links to individual properties. The **Oasis at Medina Lake** (830-612-3399; www.medinalake.com; 6600 CR 271, Mico, TX 78056) cooks up moderately priced steaks and seafood served with views of the lake on the side.

Farther south, the 5,500-acre **Hill Country State Natural Area** (see "Texas State Parks," below), makes for terrific hiking and views. Horseback riding events, the Spring Break Trail Ride in March and the Spring Benefit Hill Country Trail Ride in May, are sponsored by the **Hill Country State Natural Area Partners** (830-393-7037; www.hcsnap.net), with all proceeds benefiting the Natural Area. When visiting the Natural Area, remember to bring along your own drinking water. To the west, the **Lost Maples State Natural Area** (see "Texas State Parks," below) is just gorgeous in the fall and has nice hiking all year round. The **Love Creek Orchards** makes a nice lunch stop en route to Kerrville along lovely TX 16.

Blanco

A small ranching and trade town, Blanco got its start in 1858 and almost immediately entered into a power struggle with nearby Johnson City for the title of county seat, a distinction it held until 1890, when Johnson City prevailed. Blanco is typical small-town Hill Country, with a courthouse in the middle, shops all round, and hillside surrounding. Tubing in **Blanco State Park** and pie at the **Blanco Bowling Club** are mainstays, but what really puts Blanco on the map today is the **Blanco Lavender Festival** (www.blancolaven derfestival.com) and the proliferation of lavender farms sprouting up all around (see "Lavender," below).

LODGING

Green Gables (830-833-5931 or 1-888-833-5931; www.greengables-tx.com; 401 Green Gables, Blanco, TX 78606) Price: Moderate. Two little cottages, with pastoral views and a sky-full of stars at night. A retreat for those who really like to get away from it all, located 10 miles southeast of town.

Sleepover

The Hill Country is filled with offbeat places to stay. The really adventurous may enjoy perusing the offerings at **www.backroadstexas.net** for some truly out-of-the-ordinary places to spend the night.

DINING AND FOOD PURVEYORS

Blanco Bowling Club (830-833-4416; 310 Fouth St., Blanco, TX 78606) A very informal and friendly spot where you can just walk on in and plop down at one of the formica tables in the wood-paneled dining room. While the hamburgers, hot roast beef sandwiches, chicken-fried steak, and various Mexican dishes are all certainly worth sampling, be sure to leave room for a slice of the famous meringue pie, an essential part of the dining experience. The glazed doughnuts and cinnamon rolls served hot in the mornings are a perfect pairing for a cup of coffee. And, yes, there is ninepin bowling.

Deutsch Apple Pie Bakery (830-833-2882; www.homemadepies.com; 602 Chandler St., PO Box 835, Blanco, TX 78606) Open Tue.– Fri. 8–5:30 and Sat. 8–4, or until sold out. Hohenroth Farm has an orchard filled with apple, peach, and plum trees, the fruit from which is baked into pies, cobblers, and other treats by the Deutsch Apple Pie Bakery, located on the corner of RR 165 and 163 east of Blanco.

McCall Creek Farms (830-833-0442; www.mccallcreekfarms.com; 4524 US 281, North Blanco, TX 78606) Just north of Blanco on the way the Johnson City, McCall Creek Farms is a small shop that sells only local produce and products including tomato jam, fresh eggs,

Lavender

The Hill Country has several burgeoning lavender farms, thanks to growing conditions tailor-made to the herb and the insight of photographer Robb Kendrick, who noticed, while on a photo shoot in Provence, the similarities of that region and the Hill Country where he lived. Robb solicited advice from French farmers and went home to experiment with the rocky limestone soil around Blanco. He and his wife, Jeannie Ralston, found that Provence lavender grew beautifully, and they started Hill Country Lavender, which sold lavender and offered seminars on lavender farming. At the same time, Richard and Bunny Becker, owners of Becker Vineyard, also returned from a trip to Provence and noticed the very same similarities. The Beckers planted a 3-acre field of the fragrant herb behind their winery. The Hill Country Lavender seminars made an impression on the locals, such as Ganell and Charley Pemberton, who started Lavender Hill, growing both plants and the region's identity as newly anointed "Lavender Capital of Texas." During May, June, and July, the lavender blooming season, the self-guided **Lavender Trails of the Texas Hill Country Trail** (www.lavender-trails-of-the-texas-hill -country.com) is a nice complement to the Texas Hill Country Wine Trail. So many farms participated in the hugely successful first annual Blanco Lavender Festival (www.blancolavenderfestival.com) held in June 2005 that the event is sure to become a Hill Country favorite.

Since new farms seem to be sprouting up yearly, please check the above Web sites for any new-comers. Growing, blooming, and harvesting times vary, as do hours of operation, so call ahead to the farms you hope to visit.

Becker Vineyards (830-644-2681; www.beckervineyards.com; 464 Becker Farms Rd., Stonewall, TX 78671) Behind its main wine-making operation, this lovely vineyard and winery has a 3-acre field of lavender that guests are invited to wander through, drink in hand.

Blanco River Lavender Company (830-833-4494; 4136 Ranch Road 1623, Blanco, TX 78606) On the banks of the Blanco River, approximately 3 miles west of Blanco on RR 1623, this family farm has been a working farm since 1871, though they started lavender production only recently, in 2005.

Heron's Nest Herb Farm (830-833-2627; 1673 River Bend Dr., Blanco, TX 78606) A lovely farm with lavender trails and fields of echinacea. The solar-powered rainwater drip-irrigation system is useful and clever.

Hill Country Lavender (830-833-2294; www.hillcountrylavender.com; 4524 US 281 North, Blanco, TX 78606) The first commercial lavender farm in Texas, Hill Country Lavender has cut-your-own lavender and a store filled with all manner of lavender-themed products, including a cookbook dedicated entirely to cooking with this edible herb.

Hummingbird Farms (830-868-7862; www.hummingbirdlavender.com; 9340 US 290 West, Johnson City, TX 78636) Five lovely acres of organic lavender located 9.5 miles west of Johnson City.

Lavender Hill (830-833-9097; www.lavenderhilltx.com; 1378 River Run, Blanco, TX 78606) On the north side of the Blanco River, near the entrance to Blanco State Park, Lavender Hill is a well-established lavender farm.

LoneStar Lavender Farm (830-833-1317; www.lonestar-lavender.com; 2222 Horton Preiss Rd., Blanco, TX 78606) A newcomer, LoneStar Lavender is a 375-acre working cattle ranch, with a 4.5-acre plot of lavender blooming in the center.

Miller Creek Lavender (512-934-1616; www.millercreeklavender.com; 8453 Miller Creek Loop, Johnson City, TX 78636) Many varieties interspersed with a butterfly garden and a U-pick berry patch.

Rough Creek Lavender (512-847-2888; www.roughcreeklavender.com; 401 Burnet Ranch Rd., Wimberley, TX 78676) Rough Creek Lavender has 5,000 lavender plants, with alighting butterflies, for picking and frolicking among during blooming season. Stop in for a photo op with pumpkins in the fall.

Sweet Dreams Lavender Farm (512-288-7270; www.sweetdreamslavenderfarm.com. 10600 Wagon Rd. West, Austin, TX 78736) This farm is a sweet-smelling escape just 15 minutes west of downtown Austin, a few miles from TX 71/US 290.

Texas Lavender Hills (830-833-9183; www.texaslavenderhills.com; 5110 Kendalia Rd., Blanco, TX 78606) Twenty-seven acres of hillside blanketed with lavender and tended by a tenacious young family whose great-grandfather originally owned the land.

Triple L Farms (830-990-4195, 830-456-6049; www.lllfarms.com; 9229 Old San Antonio Rd., Fredericksburg, TX 78624) Four and a half acres of lavender thrives on this farm near tiny Grapetown on the outskirts of Fredericksburg.

Villa Texas (830-997-1068; www.villatexas.com; 4273 Morris Ranch Rd., Fredericksburg, TX 78624) The farm, located between Fredericksburg and Kerrville, is seasonal, but the shop in town is open all year. Shop: 234 W. Main St., Fredericksburg, TX 78628.

Wimberley Lavender Company (830-833-1595; www.wimberleylavender.com; 11300 FM 2325, Wimberley, TX 78676) On a bucolic hilltop between Wimberley and Blanco, Wimberley Lavender Company has 3000 lavender plants, a lavender labyrinth, and lavender lemonade.

and artisan goat cheeses made by a very industrious local teenager. All baked goods made in their bakery, the Kitchen, are made from scratch, and the vanilla, chocolate, and peach custard ice creams are churned daily. Hill Country Lavender (see "Lavender") is located in the fields behind the farm.

ATTRACTIONS, PARKS, AND RECREATION

Blanco State Park (830-833-4333; www.tpwd.state.tx.us; P.O. Box 493, Blanco, TX 78606) Open: Daily. Admission: $3. One of the oldest parks in the state, Blanco State Park was opened in 1934 and is located just four blocks from the town square on Park Road 23, surrounded by Hill Country scenery. While the park offers camping and picnicking, the biggest draw here is tubing on the Blanco River. Tube rentals available; call for details.

Boerne

Located in the San Antonio metropolitan area approximately 30 miles north of downtown, Boerne (pronounced BURN-ee) was settled in 1849 as a small agricultural community and maintains a small-town atmosphere with distinctly German roots. Its population fluctuated until the 1960s, when the completion of I-10 made it a bedroom community for growing San Antonio. Located on the banks of Cibolo Creek, Boerne makes a nice day trip from San Antonio or a jumping-off point into the Hill Country.

LODGING

Ye Kendall Inn
830-249-2138 or 1-800-364-2138
www.yekendallinn.com
128 W. Blanco St., Boerne, TX 78006

Once a stagecoach stop, Ye Kendall Inn is now a destination and a Texas historic landmark. Built in 1859, the solid limestone inn has a charmed atmosphere, with details such as a galvanized metal tub in the Texas Suite and rustic primitive decor in the Waco Cabin, a structure dating from the mid-1800s. Each of the inn's 34 very individualized guest rooms and cabins are well documented on its Web site, which is worth perusing before making your reservations. The on-site Coffee Café (Open: Daily 7–5; Price: Inexpensive) is ready and willing to meet caffeine needs.

CULTURE

German-themed festivals such as the **Berges Fest** (www.bergesfest.com), held on Father's Day weekend and featuring watermelon-eating contests and dachshund races, **Oktoberfest-Wurstbraten** in October, and **Weihnachts (Christmas) Fest Parade Weekend** in December celebrate the town's heritage, while **Cowboy Christmas** festivities exemplify the region's distinctly Texas twang.

DINING AND FOOD PURVEYORS

Bear Moon Bakery (830-816-2327; 401 S. Main St., Boerne, TX 78006) Price: lunch Inexpensive, dinner Moderate. Open: Tue.–Thu. 6–6, Fri.–Sat. 6 AM–9 PM, Sun. 8–4. Leave room to sample the sweet treats at this outstanding bakery, which also offers daily soups and sandwiches and a bistro dinner menu Friday and Saturday nights.

The Creek Restaurant (830-816-2005, 119 Staffel St., Boerne, TX 78006) Open: Tue.–Sat. 11–3 and 5–9, Sun. 11–3. Price: Moderate. Housed in three buildings, each with individual charms, the Creek has an ambience that is well suited to its menu. From the German venison schnitzel to the traditional pecan pie, the food is hearty, warm, and comforting.

The Dodging Duck Brewhaus (830-248-3825; www.dodgingduck.com; 402 River Rd., Boerne, TX 78006) Open: Sun.–Thu. 11–9, Fri.–Sat. 11–10. Price: Inexpensive. With a nice view of Cibolo Creek and plenty of home-brewed beer on tap, this is a popular place to unwind.

Limestone Grill (830-249-2138 or 1-800-364-2138; www.yekendallinn.com; 128 W. Blanco St., Boerne, TX 78006) Open: lunch Mon.–Sat. 11–2:30; dinner Tue.–Thu. 5:30–9, Fri. –Sat. 5–9. Price: Moderate. Located in Ye Kendall Inn, the Limestone Grill offers a sophisticated menu including a soup sampler, Gulf Coast seafood, and a prime rib special every Wednesday night.

Po-Po Family Restaurant (830-537-4194; www.popofamilyrestaurant.com; 829 FR 289, Boerne, TX) Open: Sun.–Thu. 11–9, Fri.–Sat. 11–10. Price: Inexpensive to Moderate. A

Gift shops in Boerne

roadside classic since 1929, Po-Po Family Restaurant is widely known for its crispy yet juicy fried chicken, catfish, and shrimp. Order from the standard menu or choose the all-you-can-eat specials available Monday through Thursday from 4 PM onward. You haven't seen a big group of souvenir plates until you've seen the display at Po-Po's. Located 6 miles north of Boerne off exit 533/Welfare. Reservations recommended.

Welfare General Store and Café (830-537-3700; www.welfaretexas.com; 223 Waring-Welfare Rd., Boerne, TX 78006) Open: Wed.–Fri. 5 PM–9 PM, Sat. 5 PM–10 PM, Sun. 11–9. Price: Moderate to Expensive. Reservations recommended. Though technically in Boerne, the Welfare General Store is located approximately 10 miles north of town, on the Waring-Welfare Road (SR 1621), just off I-10/US 87. Irresistible gourmet food served in an irresistibly charming 1920s general store and post office. While the *Kartoffelpfannekuchen*—potato pancakes served with apple sauce or sour cream—and a half dozen versions of schnitzel are clear references to the region's German heritage, the *pad thai* knows no cultural bounds, and the steaks are pure Texas.

ATTRACTIONS, PARKS, AND RECREATION

While the aboveground geography of the Hill Country is fascinating, the eerie subterranean landscapes of the region's caves and caverns can be an interesting and fun diversion. The natural area in and around Boerne offers both.

Cascade Caverns (830-755-8080; www.cascadecaverns.com; 226 Cascade Caverns Rd., Fair Oaks Ranch, TX 78015. Located approximately 3 miles south of Boerne; take exit 543 off I-10) Home to the endangered albino Cascades Cavern salamander, Cascade Caverns is 140 feet deep and a half mile long. The highlight of the 45-minute tour is a peek at the 100-foot waterfall for which the cavern is named. Open: Memorial Day to Labor Day 10–5, Labor Day to Memorial Day daily 10–4. Admission: Adults $11, children $7.

Cave Without a Name (830-537-4212 or 1-888-839-2283; www.cavewithoutaname.com; 325 Kreutzberg Rd., Boerne, TX 78006. Take FM 474 northeast for approximately 5 miles, then a right onto Kreutzberg Road) In 1939, when a contest was held to name this cave, a boy remarked that it was "too pretty to name," and it is. Open: Memorial Day to Labor Day 9–6, Labor Day to Memorial Day 10–5. Admission: Adults $12, children $6, children under 5 free.

Cibolo Nature Center (830-249-4616; www.cibolo.org; P.O. Box 9, Boerne, TX 78006. From town, travel east on TX 46 for 1 mile to City Park Rd., turn right, and follow to the nature center) The four distinct ecosystems represented in the center's 100 acres make its pedestrian-only trails interesting and educational. Picnic tables and outdoor concerts invite visitors to stay the day, and the center's Mostly Native Plant Sale in April draws gardeners from near and far. Open: Trails daily 8–dark; Visitors Center Mon.–Fri. 9–5, Sat. 9–1.

Nearby

From Boerne, travel north along FM 1376 approximately 13 miles to Sisterdale, stop in at Sister Creek Vineyards (see "Hill Country Vineyards," below) for a wine tasting, then head on to Comfort. Or head east on TX 46, then north on US 281 to Guadalupe River State Park (see "Texas State Parks," below). Alternatively, take TX 46 westward to pretty TX 16 and head north to Bandera and Kerrville, or, from TX 16 take CR 337 farther west to Lost Maples State Natural Area (see "Texas State Parks," below).

Comfort

Located near the intersection of TX 27, US 87, and I-10, Comfort is a lovely Hill Country hamlet nestled along the banks of gentle Cypress Creek. Settled by educated, free-thinking Germans, who arrived via New Braunfels in 1852, Comfort has always marched to its own drummer. Opposed to slavery, the town was sympathetic to the Union in the Civil War, and it lost many men to the cause at the battle of Nueces in 1862. To commemorate their bravery, the *Treue der Union* ("True to the Union") Monument stands on High Steet between Third and Fourth Streets. Averse to central authority, the settlers organized a communal form of self-governance and didn't get around to building a church until 1892. Comfort has many examples of traditional *fachwerk* (half-timber construction) and Victorian buildings, and much of the town is listed on the National Register of Historic Places. Comfort has weathered its share of tragedy. In 1978 a flood destroyed many historic buildings in town, and in 2006 a fire leveled the beloved Ingenhuett Store (834 High St.), a general store owned and operated by the same local family since 1867 and very much the anchor of town. Despite these losses, tiny Comfort is sweet comfort indeed.

The business part of town is only a few blocks long and takes in several restaurants, cafés, and antiques shops. See the town Web site, www.shopcomfort.com.

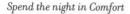

Spend the night in Comfort

High's on High Street in Comfort

LODGING

Comfort Common (830-995-3030; www.comfortcommon.com; 717 High St., P.O. Box 539, Comfort, TX 78013) Price: Inexpensive to Moderate. Right in the center of town, this historic inn has four atmospheric suites to let, each with American country decor and details, including a two-story log cabin with a working fireplace and a Victorian cottage done all in whites.

Meyer Bed and Breakfast (830-995-2304 or 1-888-995-6100; www.meyerbedandbreak fast.com; 845 High St., Comfort, TX 78013) Price: Inexpensive to Moderate. Farther along High Street, this congenial B&B is a complex of buildings dating from the 1800s to the early 1900s, each with clean and comfortably worn rooms. A lovely common breakfast area is lined with windows overlooking Cypress Creek.

Riven Rock Ranch (830-995-4045; www.rivenrockranch.com; 390 Hermann Sons Rd., Comfort, TX 78013) Price: Expensive to Very Expensive. Perched high on a hilltop overlooking the fertile pastures and land that has been farmed for over a century, Riven Rock Ranch is surrounded by cows, sheep, and plenty of solitude. Brand-new cottages—generally the size of an average house—are skillfully decorated with warm earth tones, rich textures, and original artwork. Fully equipped kitchens allow for self-sufficiency. The Guadalupe River runs through the property, offering opportunities for fishing and canoeing.

DINING AND FOOD PURVEYORS

814 A Texas Bistro (830-995-4990; 713 High St., Comfort, TX 78013) Open: lunch Wed.–Sun. 11:30–2:30, dinner Thu.–Sat. 6–9. This cozy bistro with quilts hanging on the exposed brick walls turns out fresh salads and sandwiches for lunch and pricier gourmet meals for dinner. BYOB.

High's on High Street (830-995-4995; 726 High St., Comfort, TX 78013) Open: Mon., Tue., and Thu.–Sat. 8:30–4:30, Sun. 11–4.) High's offers fantastic coffee, muffins, sandwiches, salads, soups, and a refreshing homemade key lime tart with a graham cracker crust that is perfect on a summer day. The friendliness of High's lovely owners has quickly turned this Comfort newcomer into the nexus of town.

Comfort Cellars Winery (830-995-3274; 723 Front St., Comfort, TX 78013) Open: Daily noon–6. This winery pours free sips in its tasting room in town. For more area vineyards, see below.

Nearby

The outstanding meals at the Welfare General Store and Café (see "Boerne"), a 15-minute drive south, are worth every mile, and the road to Sister Creek Vineyards is a treat unto itself.

Fredericksburg

Fredericksburg, named for Prince Frederick of Prussia, was founded in 1846 by John O. Meusebach and a group of 120 German immigrants who came to the area from New Braunfels as participants in the Adelsverein, the planned German settlement of Texas. At the time, as was the case in most of the Pedernales Valley, the area that would become

Hill Country Vineyards

The similarities between Texas and Tuscany are striking. Sure, you have to look past the cowboy hats and longhorn cattle to really see it, but the distinct qualities of the limestone outcroppings, the berries growing wild along the roadsides, and the hot, hot sunshine shared by the regions are notable. And those similarities are not lost on Texas winemakers, who toil year-round to create a little bit of Italy in the Lone Star State. The region's rich alluvial soil is mixed with limestone, flint, and shale chips from rivers past and provides ideal conditions for growing grapes. For the past 40 years vintners have coaxed their vineyards to take root in the Hill Country, and consumers and connoisseurs are now drinking the fruits of their labor.

All wineries offers tastings; some are complimentary and others charge a small fee, usually between $1 and $5. Those new to the experience of wine tasting will enjoy any of the wineries listed below, as they all have their individual strengths, charms, and personalities. Those with a more discerning palate might enjoy perusing the vineyards' comprehensive Web sites for specific labels or vintages before planning their trip. **Texas Hill Country Wineries** (1-866-621-9463; www.texaswine trail.com) comprises the 20 member wineries listed alphabetically below. For up-to-the-minute information regarding festivals, special events, and the Wine and Wildflower Trail, a coordinated effort of all the vineyards, please check the Web site.

Alamosa Wine Cellars
325-628-3313
www.alamosawinecellars.com
P.O. Box 212, Bend, TX 76824
3 miles west of Bend, on CR 580 at the intersection of CR 430
Open: Fri.–Sat. 10–5, Sun. noon–5
Tasting Fee: Complimentary

Perched at an elevation of 1,200 feet, Alamosa Wine Cellars overlooks San Saba County.

Becker Vineyards
830-644-2681
www.beckervineyards.com
464 Becker Farms Rd., Stonewall, TX 78671
11 miles east of Fredericksburg, 3 miles west of Stonewall, off US 290. Exit Jenschke Lane and turn right at 464 Becker Farms Road
Open: Mon.–Thu. 10–5, Fri–Sat. 10–6, Sun. noon–6
Tasting Fee: Complimentary

Becker Vineyards has acres of grapes, fields of lavender, and a small B&B (830-997-5612).

Chisholm Trail Winery
830-990-2675 or 1-877-990-2675

www.chisholmtrailwinery.com
2367 Usener Rd., Fredericksburg, TX 78624
Usener Road is 9 miles west of Fredericksburg off US 290
Open: Thu.–Mon. noon–6
Tasting Fee: $1–$2

A low-key winery in the hills west of Fredericksburg

Comfort Cellars
830-995-3274
723 Front St., Comfort, TX 78013
Open: Daily noon–6
Tasting Fee: $2

Whether you are coming or going from Comfort, the scenic drive along CR 473 to Sisterdale offers great views of the Guadalupe River Valley.

Driftwood Vineyards
512-858-9667
www.driftwoodvineyards.com
4001 Elder Hill Rd. (CR 170), Driftwood, TX 78619
Follow RR 12 halfway between Dripping Springs and Wimberley, then CR 170 to the east.
Open: Daily 10–6

Tasting Fee: $5
Special Features: Tours Sat. and Sun. at 2

This small family-run vineyard debuted its first wine in 2003.

Dry Comal Creek Vineyard
830-885-4121
www.drycomalcreek.com
1741 Herbelin Rd., New Braunfels, TX 78132

Near TX 46 just northwest of New Braunfels
Open: Daily noon–5
Tasting Fee: $3–$6
Special Features: Tours $3

The rooster you see on the roof is also featured on their labels.

continued on following page

Hill Country Vineyards continued

Fall Creek Vineyards
325-379-5361
www.fcv.com
1820 CR 222, Tow, TX 78672
From Llano take TX 29 east to RR 2241 north, through Tow and 2.2 miles past post office.
Open: Mon.–Fri. 11–4, Sat. 11–5, Sun. noon–4
Tasting Fee: Complimentary

Started in 1975, Fall Creek Vineyards is known for its signature Meritus wine, which is a blend of cabernet sauvignon, merlot, and petit verdot.

Flat Creek Estate
512-267-6310
www.flatcreekestate.com
24912 Singleton Bend East Rd., Marble Falls, TX 78654
20 miles east of Marble Falls and 6 miles west of Lago Vista off FM 1431
Open: Tue.–Fri. noon–5, Sat. 10–5, Sun. noon–5
Tasting Fee: $5

Located on former pastureland just west of Austin, Flat Creek Estate is a sophisticated yet casual 80-acre vineyard with endless views.

Fredericksburg Winery
830-990-8747
www.fbgwinery.com
247 W. Main St., Fredericksburg, TX 78624
Open: Mon.–Thu. 10–5:30, Fri.–Sat. 10–7:30, Sun. noon–5:30
Tasting Fee: Complimentary

A winery right on Main Street in Fredericksburg.

Grape Creek Vineyards
830-644-2710
www.grapecreek.com
US 290, Stonewall, TX 78671
Open: Mon.–Sat. 10–5, Sun. noon–5
Tasting fee: Complimentary

This vineyard changed owners in 2006; call or check Web site for possible changes.

Lost Creek Vineyard
325-338-3753, 830-798-4034
www.lostcreekvineyard.com
1129 RR 2233, Sunrise Beach, TX 78643
Take TX 71 to RR 2233.
Open: Sun.–Fri. noon–5, Sat. 10–5
Tasting Fee: $2

A casual vineyard near the north shore of Lake LBJ.

Mandola Estate Winery
512-858-1470
www.mandolawines.com
13308 FM 150 W., Driftwood, TX 78619
Open: Mon.–Sat. 10–6, Sun. noon–5
Tasting Fee: Complimentary

The impressive winery of Damian Mandola, Houston restaurateur and host of the PBS cooking show Cucina Amore, gives tasters a peek at the wine-making process.

McReynolds Wines
830-825-3544
www.mcreynoldswines.com
706 Shovel Mountain Rd., Cypress Mill, TX 78633
From Johnson City take US 281 north and turn east onto RM 962, then left onto Shovel Mountain Road
Open: Fri.–Sat. 10–6, Sun. noon–6
Tasting Fee: Complimentary

A very informal family-run winery located between Johnson City and Spicewood.

Pillar Bluff Vineyards
512-556-4078
www.pillarbluff.com
300 Burnet CR 111, Lampasas, TX 76550
From Lampasas, take FM 1478 west for 3 miles; turn left onto CR 111.
Open: Fri.–Sat. 10–5, Sun. 12:30–5
Tasting Fee: $2–$5

Pillar Bluff specializes in French varietals.

Sister Creek Vineyards

830-324-6704

www.sistercreekvineyards.com

1142 Sisterdale Rd., Sisterdale, TX 78006

12 miles north of Boerne on FM 1376

Open: Mon.–Sat. 11–5:30, Sun. noon–5:30

Tasting Fee: Complimentary

These friendly folks make European-style wines aged in oak barrels.

Spicewood Vineyards

830-693-5328

www.spicewoodvineyards.com

1419 Burnet CR 409, Spicewood, TX 78669

From Austin take TX 71 west to Spicewood; turn left on Burnet CR 408.

Open: Wed.–Sat. 10–5, Sun. noon–5

Tasting Fee: $2

Spicewood Vineyards hosts a variety of dinner, dessert, and live music events.

Stone House Vineyard

512-264-3630

www.stonehousevineyard.com

24650 Haynie Flat Rd., Spicewood, TX 78869

From Austin take TX 71 west to Paleface Ranch Rd. and right onto Haynie Flat Road

Open: Fri.–Sun. noon–5

Tasting Fee: $2–$5

Befitting its name, Stone House Vineyard occupies a lovely white limestone winery on Lake Travis.

Texas Hills Vineyard

830-868-2321

www.texashillsvineyard.com

P.O. Box 1480, Johnson City, TX 78636

Located at 878 RR 2776 a mile east of Johnson City en route to Pedernales Falls State Park

Open: Mon.–Sat. 10–5, Sun. noon–5

Tasting Fee: Complimentary

Texas Hills Vineyard built a rammed-earth tasting room to protect their wine and their environment—a creative solution, with charming results.

Torre di Pietra

830-644-2829

www.texashillcountrywine.com

10915 E. US 290, Fredericksburg, TX 78624

10 miles east of Fredericksburg

Open: Sun.–Thu. 10–6, Fri.–Sat. 10–7

Tasting Fee: $5

Patios, live music, and wine-filled chocolates only enhance the tasting experience.

Woodrose Winery

830-644-2539

www.woodrosewinery.com

662 Woodrose Lane, Stonewall, TX 78671

Located just off US 290 between Stonewall and Fredericksburg

Open: Fri.–Sun. noon–6

Tasting Fee: Complimentary

A wonderful winery with big plans to add B&B-style cottages and a restaurant in the near future.

Fredericksburg was inhabited by Native Americans, in this case the Comanche. In 1847, Meusebach and the Native Americans hammered out the details of the Meusebach-Comanche Treaty, establishing peace in their shared valley—a remarkable feat given the times and circumstances.

The town, patterned after villages in Germany, was laid out with one long, wide road, Main Street, running parallel to Town Creek, and residents set about building the *fachwerk* homes that are now synonymous with Hill Country architecture. The Vereins Kirche, a multipurpose building, served as school, church, fortress, and gathering place. Crops were planted, stores opened, and the town prospered.

The Civil War challenged the immigrants to square their communal beliefs with those of their new home country. Many were opposed to slavery and secession, with most supporting the Union, but all endured the hardships of Confederate martial law in 1862. The experience galvanized the German sense of self-determination; many residents spoke only German for decades afterward in an effort to distance and insulate themselves from national issues.

At the turn of the century, Fredericksburg was a manufacturing center, with various factories, quarries, and plants, but in the 1930s the town's reputation as a resort area began to grow. Today, Fredericksburg is known as a weekend getaway spot, with restful B&Bs, gourmet dining, and historical sites, surrounded by parks, wineries, and wildflowers. At times it can feel a little kitschy, but head off the beaten path and there's plenty of genuine Hill Country to be enjoyed.

LODGING

The locus of Fredericksburg is Main Street, and the nearby neighborhoods are just teeming with B&Bs, guesthouses, and boutique hotels. Alternatively, the usual roster of chain hotels can be found along US 290 on the outskirts of the city. Fredericksburg is such a popular weekend destination that it's essential to book a room in advance, particularly during festivals.

Most of the establishments listed below are independently owned and operated by the very folks you'll meet when you call or visit. Another useful way to book a room is to use the following reservation services, which handle a wide variety of B&Bs and guesthouses: **Gastehaus Schmidt** (1-866-427-8374; www.fbglodging.com; 231 W. Main St., Fredericksburg, TX 78624); **Main Street Reservations Service** (830-997-0153 or 1-888-559-8555; www.travelmainstreet.com; 337 E. Main St., Fredericksburg, TX 78624).

Ab Butler's Dogtrot at Triple Creek
877-262-4366
www.abbutler.net
801 Triple Creek Rd., Fredericksburg, TX 78624
Price: Expensive

Ab Butler's Dogtrot is a two-story cabin, built in Kentucky in the 1800s and moved to Texas in 1997. There are two suites, each with a wood-burning fireplace in the living room downstairs and a secluded bedroom and bathroom with Jacuzzi tub upstairs under the eaves. Rocking on the front porch under the shady oak trees, it's easy to feel like a pioneer—until a hot breakfast delivered to your room gently interrupts the fantasy.

Das Garten Haus
830-990-840
www.dasgartenhaus.com
604 S. Washington St., Fredericksburg, TX 78624
Price: Moderate to Expensive
Special Features: Free WiFi

Kevin and Lynn operate a spotlessly clean and very functional B&B with three private suites, each with a kitchen or kitchenette, and perks such as fresh flowers, homemade cookies, and popcorn. The delicious breakfasts, sometimes made with produce from the owners' gardens, are delicate and delicious, yet healthy and filling. Spend a minute poking around the lovely gardens, planned and nurtured by Kevin, a professional horticulturalist.

Hangar Hotel

www.hangarhotel.com
830-997-9990
155 Airport Rd., Fredericksburg, TX 78624
Price: Moderate to Expensive
Special Features: Children welcome; free
    WiFi; handicapped access

Adjacent to the small Gillespie County
Airport, the Hangar Hotel isn't just for avi-
ation buffs. The appealing decor is reminiscent of the 1940s South Pacific, a theme
that is carried through in the mahogany and
rattan furniture, the armchairs covered in
bomber-jacket leather, the hexagonal white
floor tile in the bathrooms, and music playing in the common areas. The on-site
Officers' Club (Open: Thu. 5 PM–11 PM,
Fri.–Sat. 5 PM–midnight) serves drinks,
while the Airport Diner (Open: Wed.–Fri.
11 AM–2 PM, Sat. 8–4, Sun. 8–2) has the
classic curved ceiling and cozy booths, with
a menu of burgers, malts, and onion rings
to match.

Hoffman Haus

830-997-6739 or 1-800-899-1672
www.hoffmanhaus.com
608 E. Creek St., Fredericksburg, TX
    78624
Price: Moderate to Expensive
Special Features: Children welcome; free
    WiFi; limited handicapped access

The individualized rooms, each with wood
floors, high ceilings, luxurious linens, and
several well-chosen pieces of antique or
reproduction furniture, are both rustic and
sophisticated. Rough-hewn beams, chink-
ing, whitewash, and simple window treatments give the rooms a historical feel. Have
breakfast in bed, then stroll the spacious
gardens or rock in the rockers on the porch.

The Hog Stop Inn

830-997-6166 or 1-888-251-2137
www.hogstopinn.com
10207 US 290, Fredericksburg, TX 78624
9 miles east of Fredericksburg
Price: Inexpensive to Moderate

The Hog Stop Inn, as the management suc-
cinctly states, is "the only B&B in Texas
catering exclusively to the motorcycle community." The inn consists of six small,
neatly kept modern cabins, each with a
microwave, refrigerator, and coffeemaker.
Groups are welcome, and everyone likes to
hang out at the neighboring Ice Haus and
Wine Bar (830-990-9499) in the evening,
laughing, drinking, and talking shop.
Didn't bring your bike? The Hog Stop Inn
can hook you up with a local late model
Harley-Davidson rental outfit, and they are
keen to suggest scenic rides. Check-in is at
Der Peach Garten (see "Dining," below)
where you can also pick up some local
peach preserves.

Fredericksburg Inn and Suites

830-997-0202
www.fredericksburg-inn.com
210 S. Washington St., Fredericksburg, TX
    78624
Price: Moderate
Special Features: Children welcome; free
    WiFi; pool

The Fredericksburg Inn is a very casual
spot, located just blocks from Main Street,
that some guests try once and others return
to again and again. The inn has very basic,
though very clean, rooms; an outdoor
recreation area including a hot tub, two
pools, and fireplace; free beverages; and a
family-friendly atmosphere. By the same
token, lots of children and adolescents,
under various levels of supervision, can
sometimes mean things are a little noisy,
but if you go prepared for an environment
that closely resembles summer camp,
you won't be surprised. A good-natured
good time at a great price makes the
Fredericksburg Inn a solid value.

Inn on the Creek

1-888-559-8555
www.inn-on-the-creek.com
337 E. Main St., Fredericksburg, TX 78624
Price: Inexpensive to Moderate
Special Features: Limited handicapped
  access

As close as you can get to Main Street, the Inn on the Creek is only 40 feet away, but on a large, shaded lot with gardens that feels quite removed from the bustle. Four-poster beds, canopy beds, and sleigh beds, each topped with colorful coverlets and down pillows, are the centerpiece of the rooms in the 19th-century B&B. The price makes this a great choice for the value-minded.

Settlers Crossing

830-997-2722 or 1-800-874-1020
www.settlerscrossing.com
104 Settlers Crossing Rd., Fredericksburg,
  TX 78624
Take US 290 east to FR 1379.
Price: Expensive
Special Feature: Children welcome

Located just off RR 1376 on the way to Luckenbach, this 35-acre spread includes seven 19th-century cabins, some relocated from Indiana, Missouri, and Pennsylvania.

The country antiques, wood-burning fireplaces, and period touches throughout breathe life into these historic gems. Most have fully equipped kitchens, some have Jacuzzi tubs, and all have outdoor grills. Far more than just spending the night, staying at Settlers Crossing is like living in pioneer times, albeit much, much more luxuriously.

Two Wee Cottages

830-990-8340 or 1-877-437-7739
www.2weecottages.com
108 E. Morse St., Fredericksburg, TX 78624
Price: Moderate to Expensive

The two little cottages, Granny Hein House and My Little House, are tucked in a little garden behind the host's home on Morse Street, eight blocks north of Main Street. The cottages have their own individuality; the Granny Hein House feels a tad more formal, with dark wood and an adorable old-fashioned kitchen, while My Little House is light and cheerful. Both cottages have hot tubs on private screened-in porches, hammocks large enough for two, and breakfast fixings in the fridge. The fresh-baked goods make a lasting impression. Skip and Kate, the on-site hosts, are happy to offer recommendations for dining and entertainment.

Sunday Houses

Devoutly religious, German settlers on farms and ranches outside Fredericksburg were determined to journey to town for church services, but the long distances, road conditions, and weather made this difficult. The solution was to build "Sunday houses." These tiny houses were built on small parcels in town and used by families coming to town for shopping on Saturday and church on Sunday. The houses were frame construction, with steeply pitched roofs and decorative millwork, with a lean-to kitchen tacked on the back and sometimes a staircase on the outside to a second floor, designed to save precious space indoors. Sunday houses were wildly popular between 1890 and 1910 and the ones that survive today are sprinkled throughout Fredericksburg and the Hill Country, and many are used as B&Bs. In Fredericksburg, small groups of Sunday houses can be seen on West San Antonio Street, near St. Mary's Church, on West Main Street, and South Milam Street.

Fourth of July Parade in Fredericksburg

CULTURE

Fort Martin Scott (830-997-9895; www.fortmartinscott.com; 1606 E. Main St., Fredericksburg, TX 78624) Open: Tue.–Sun. 10–5. Admission: Free; donations accepted. An old U.S. Army frontier outpost, Fort Martin Scott was used between 1848 and 1853, though various groups, the Texas Rangers among them, have been cycling in and out ever since.

The **Gillespie County Historical Society** (830-997-2835; www.pioneermuseum.com; 312 W. San Antonio St., Fredericksburg, TX 78624) The guardian of the county's history, the society looks after the following three museums.

The **Pioneer Museum** (830-990-8441; www.pioneermuseum.org; 309 W. Main St., Fredericksburg, TX 78624) Open: Mon.–Sat., 10–5. Admission: Adults and children over 11 $4. The homestead of one Henry Kammlah, as well as six other buildings, open for those interested in taking a look at pioneer life in the mid-1800s.

Vereins Kirche Museum (830-997-7832; www.pioneermuseum.org; 100 W. Main St., Fredericksburg, TX 78624) Open: Mon.–Sat. 10–4, Sun. 1–4. Admission: $1. This replica of Fredericksburg's first social building is home to a permanent historical display and a gallery with changing photography exhibits.

The National Museum of the Pacific War
830-997-4379
www.nimitz-museum.org
340 E. Main St., Fredericksburg, TX 78624
Open: Daily 9–5
Admission: Adults $6, seniors and military $5, children $4, children under 6 free

This state-run museum complex is spread over 9 acres and includes the George Bush Gallery, Admiral Nimitz Museum, Plaza of Presidents, Veterans' Walk of Honor, Japanese Garden of Peace, Pacific Combat Zone, and the Center for Pacific War Studies. The National Museum of the Pacific War leads visitors through both the chronology and the emotions of Word War II in the Pacific, through restored artifacts such as a South Pacific PT boat, Avenger dive-bombers, and pieces of battleships, photographs, and personal effects. From the scary sounds of mortar fire to the distressing reports of casualties, the only respite seems to be in the reverence of the commemorative Veterans' Walk of Honor, or the calm of the Japanese Garden of Peace. Honoring Admiral Chester Nimitz, the war icon and native of Fredericksburg, the museum that bears his name is located in the old Nimitz Hotel, once his family's business. A must for military history buffs.

Festivals

Fredericksburg loves its festivals, and the city seems to be in a perpetual state of celebration. The biggest is **Oktoberfest** (830-997-4810; www.oktoberfestinfbg.com. Admission: Adults $6, children $1, 2/3-day pass $10/$15), a weekend extravaganza of German food, music, and beer held at the beginning of October. At the end of the month, a great way to sample area cuisine is the **Fredericksburg Food and Wine Festival** (830-997-8515; www.fbgfoodandwinefest.com. Admission: Adults $20–$75, children $5). The first weekend in December, the **Weihnachten,** or Christmas festival and market, ushers in the holiday season. The **Easter Fires Pageant,** held the Saturday evening before Easter, commemorates the Meusebach-Comanche Treaty. As the story goes, during the tense moments before the treaty was announced, a pioneer mother told her anxious children that the fires they saw in the hills—the fires belonging to Comanche families awaiting news—were those of the Easter Bunny boiling eggs for Easter. To this day, Easter fires are lit Easter eve, the story is retold, and peace cherished. Throughout the spring and summer, festivals of peaches, lavender, wildflowers, and wines abound; details online at www.fredericksburg texas.com.

DINING AND FOOD PURVEYORS

As in many "tourist towns," eating establishments in Fredericksburg cater to their captive—and hungry—audience with little impetus to alter the menu or force a direct correlation between quality and price. You can get a burger anywhere, pay more than you'd like, and walk away full; but if you know where to look, there are plenty of really special and memorable meals to be had in Fredericksburg. I've also included recommendations for treats, snacks, and samplings. Many restaurants are closed Monday, and some cafés serve just breakfast and lunch, then close for the day at 2 or 2:30; hours of operation have been noted below.

Clear River Pecan Company
830-997-8490
www.icecreamandfun.com
138 E. Main St., Fredericksburg, TX 78624
Open: Sun.–Thu. 8–8, Fri.–Sat. 8–8
Price: Inexpensive

Clear River has ice cream, shakes, malts, coffee, and a ridiculous number of baked treats fresh from the oven; a great place for families to unwind over sugar.

Cottage Café
830-990-1037
www.cottagecafe.net
232 W. Main St., Fredericksburg, TX 78624
Open: Mon.–Sat. at 5 PM
Price: Moderate to Expensive
Special Features: Reservations recom-
    mended

Whether you are dining in the diminutive cottage or alfresco on their lovely covered patio, the indoor-meets-outdoor dining atmosphere at the Cottage Café can't be beat, except perhaps by the food. Hill Country wines are paired with seafood, quail, duck, buffalo, and a nightly venison special. The dessert medley, a taste of all the café's desserts on one plate, is brilliant.

Cuvée
830-990-1600
www.cuveewine.net
342 W. Main St., Fredericksburg, TX 78624
Open: Tue.–Sat. at 4 PM
Price: Expensive to Very Expensive
Special Features: Reservations recom-
    mended

Part restaurant, part food purveyor, and part wine merchant and tasting room, Cuvée is a must for diners who love fantastic food. The dining areas are decorated with rich woods and leathers set against exposed limestone walls for a rustic yet sophisticated Hill Country look. The menu is entirely deter-mined by the creativity and whim of Chef

Jaime, who is known for using only the freshest ingredients in his very inspired dishes. The market (Open: Tue.– Sat. at 11) sells artisanal breads, gourmet meats and cheeses, and local produce paired with wine, which makes a nice European-style picnic.

Der Peach Garten
830-997-6166 or 1-888-251-2137
www.derpeachgarten.com
10207 US 290, Fredericksburg, TX 78624
9 miles east of Fredericksburg

This gift shop specializes in all things peachy: jalapeño peach, amaretto peach, strawberry peach, or just plain peach pre-serves, peach cobbler, peach salsa, and peach cider. The owners also operate the Hog Stop Inn, a B&B for bikers (see "Lodging," above).

Dietz Bakery
830-997-3250
218 E. Main St., Fredericksburg, TX 78624
Open: Tue.–Sat. till everything's gone

Old-time German pastries, cookies, treats, and oven-fresh breads, sold at old-fash-ioned prices. They sell out fast; the early bird gets the sticky bun.

Fredericksburg Brewing Co.
830-997-1646
www.yourbrewery.com
245 Main St., Fredericksburg, TX 78624
Open: Mon.–Thu. 11:30–9, Sat.–Sun.
    11:30–10, Sun. 11:30–7
Price: Inexpensive to Moderate

In a restored 1890s building in the middle of the action on Main Street, the Freder-icksburg Brewing Co. is known for its microbrews, pub food, and Biergarten, as well as its B&B—"Bed and Brew"—upstairs, where a four-beer sampler comes with your night's stay (830-997-9990; www.your brewery.com. Price: Moderate. Special Features: Handicapped access).

Enjoy memorable homemade meals at the Hill Top Café.

Fredericksburg Herb Farm
830-997-8615 or 1-800-259-4372
www.fredericksburgherbfarm.com
407 Whitney St., Fredericksburg, TX 78624
Open: Mon.–Thu. 9:30–5:30, Fri.–Sat.
9:30–9, Sun. noon–4
Restaurant open lunch Mon.–Thu. 11:30–3,
Fri.–Sat. 11:30–2:30, Sun. noon–3; dinner Fri.–Sat. 6–9
Price: Inexpensive to Moderate

Certainly a farm, but also a B&B (Price:
Moderate to Expensive), a restaurant, a
day spa, and a shop stocked with soaps,
lotions, spritzers, colognes, tea and coffee,
honey, and gourmet herb-infused oils and
vinegars.

Fredericksburg Pie Company
830-990-6992
www.fredericksburgpiecompany.com
509 W. Main St., Fredericksburg, TX 78624

Price: Inexpensive
Open: Tue.–Sat. 10–7

One bite of the bourbon orange pecan pie
and you'll immediately know why it's a
best-seller: Sweet, but not cloying, easy on
the bourbon, with bright notes of orange,
this pie is exemplary. The fruit pies, especially the peach made from the local har-
vest, are also wonderful. The bakery opens
at 10 and has been known to sell out of the
daily special by 11, so plan on having your
pie mid-morning or you'll surely miss out.

Hill Top Café
830-997-8922
www.hilltopcafe.com
10661 US 87, Fredericksburg, TX 78624
10 miles north of Fredericksburg
Open: Wed., Thu., Sun. 11–9, Fri.–Sat.
11–10
Price: Inexpensive
Special Features: Reservations recommended; live music

Sitting on a hilltop overlooking the scrubby
countryside, the Hill Top Café has the look
and feel of a well-worn honky tonk—creaky
wooden floors, and walls jammed with old
signs, license plates, posters, and memorabilia to which there seems very little rhyme
or reason. The same could be said of the
menu, where *kefalotiri saganaki* (an appetizer of flaming Greek cheese), Cajun spiced
frog legs, and pan-seared quail are all on
offer. Though the atmosphere seems scattered, the Hill Top is very focused when it
comes to service and hospitality. From the
breadbasket of warm crusty homemade
sourdough bread that greets you at your
table to the "Come back and see us again"
that ushers you out the door, the Hill Top
Café is a pure delight. The menu description of the fried oysters could be used to
describe this entire enterprise—"cornmeal-
breaded and fried with love."

Then there's the live music. Bluesman,
musician, and transplanted Rhode

Islander, owner Johnny Nicholas hosts live blues, jazz, and boogie-woogie at his joint when he's not on the road performing with his band, Johnny Nicholas and the Texas All Stars. See the Web site for details.

The Nest

803-990-8383
www.thenestrestaurant.com
607 S. Washington St., Fredericksburg, TX 78624
Open: Thu.–Mon. 5:30 PM–close
Price: Moderate to Expensive
Special Features: Reservations recommended

One mile south of Main Street, far from the crowds, The Nest strikes the perfect balance between relaxed and sophisticated. Housed in an old bungalow, the restaurant has homey wood floors and window trim, soothing wall color, and simple decor. The refined menu features items such as rack of lamb with a pecan pesto, or quail stuffed with bacon, spinach, goat cheese, and sun-dried tomatoes. The Nest is a popular place for celebrating special occasions or a romantic night out.

Peach Tree Tea Room

830-997-9527
www.peach-tree.com
210 S. Adams St., Fredericksburg, TX 78624
Open: Mon.–Fri. 11 AM–2:30 PM,
Sat. 11 AM–3 PM, Sun. 11 AM–2 PM
Price: Inexpensive
Special Features: Gift shop; reservations recommended

With over 30 years of service and several cookbooks under its belt, the Peach Tree Tea Room is now run by the children of the couple who founded it. Savory quiches, soups, and inventive sandwiches such as ham and Swiss on raisin pecan bread or the fried green tomato BLT make the Peach Tree a terrific option for lunch. Several child-friendly items and a relaxed atmos-phere make this an enjoyable rest stop for families.

Rather Sweet Bakery and Café

830-990-0498
www.rathersweet.com
249 E. Main St., Fredericksburg, TX 78624
Tucked behind the Main Street storefronts, the café is somewhat easier to reach from S. Lincoln Street
Price: Inexpensive
Open: Mon.–Sat. 8–5

Imagine a world where bakers don't shy away from butter and sugar and enter the wonderful melt-in-your-mouth universe of Rather Sweet Bakery and Café. Pastry chef Rebecca Rather, author of *The Pastry Queen*, fashions pastries, cookies, and cakes that are just spectacular. For example, the key lime tart pairs a crisp buttery crust with a tangy, sweet, and creamy key lime confection, dollops of whipped cream, and fresh limes. The bakery and café also serves lunch featuring burgers, homemade soups, salads, and sandwiches, such as homemade egg salad on a slightly sweet and airy focaccia bread. Eat in the garden, on the second story porch, or in the bright, colorful upstairs dining room. Rather sweet indeed!

Rustlin' Rob's

830-990-4750
www.rustlinrobs.com
121 E. Main St., Fredericksburg, TX 78624
Open: Mon.–Fri. 10–5:30, Sat. 10–6

Hankering for pickled quail eggs? Jalapeño peanut butter? Chowchow relish? Rob's rustled a huge variety of Texas-made sauce, salsas, jams, jellies, and preserves and put them up for sale in this condiment emporium. It's Rob's policy to provide a multitude of tasting opportunities, and samples are provided throughout the store. If you're looking for hot sauce that'll make you cry or honey butter that's pure love, head to Rob's and go home happy!

ATTRACTIONS, PARKS, AND RECREATION

Wildseed Farms
830-990-1393 or 1-800-848-0078
www.wildseedfarms.com
425 Wildflower Hills, Fredericksburg, TX 78624
7 miles east of Fredericksburg on US 290
Open: Daily 9:30–6

Wildflowers

Springtime in Central Texas is lovely. The sun is out, the birds are singing, and the humidity has yet to arrive. Also making an appearance are the millions upon millions of wildflowers that dot pastures and highway medians, line fences and riverbanks, and rise up with their colorful blooms turned sunward. By April, sometimes as early as March, these little native flowers—bluebonnets, Indian paintbrushes, and Mexican hats—seem to appear out of nowhere. In May, this first magical spray disappears and other, less well-known, though equally exquisite, native flowers bloom in their place. And so it goes, through summer, fall, and even a mild winter. In fact, in Texas the careful observer can find something in bloom all year long.

In Austin, the **Lady Bird Johnson Wildflower Center** is both beautiful and informative. If you are in the Hill Country, stop in at **Wildseed Farms** (see "Attractions, Parks, and Recreation," above) in Fredericksburg for a closer look, or drive the **Bluebonnet Trail**, a self-guided tour winding through Burnet (the Bluebonnet Capital of Texas), Marble Falls, and Llano and continuing on alongside the Highland Lakes (see individual listings below for all these places). Maps are available online at www.burnetchamber.org /bluebonnetmap.

Other scenic routes include the **Willow City Loop** outside Fredericksburg, **TX 16 South** between Kerrville and Medina, and along the **Devil's Backbone** in Wimberley. Or call the local wildflower hotlines for advice; the Lady Bird Johnson Wildflower Center (512-832-4037) and the Texas Department of Transportation (1-800-452-9292; www .dot.state.tx.us) both have frequently updated recordings describing particularly colorful routes.

A word of warning, however. Before you pull off the highway and plop your children down for a photo amid the petals, please watch your step; wildflowers and fire ants seek the same habitat, a sunny, dry, hot field.

Admission: Butterfly Haus: Adults $5, children and seniors $3; the Meadows: Adults $5, seniors and children $3

Though it is a commercial nursery, Wildseed Farms feels like an education center, botanical garden, or nature preserve with its winding paths through fields exploding with color. This is a must-stop wildflowers photo op. Wildseed Farms has seeds of both native and nonnative plants, workshops, tips for growing and identifying native plants, and a Butterfly Haus filled with butterflies. While there is a fee to stroll "The Meadows," the distant view is free, and you are welcome to meander through the rows and rows of plants for sale to your heart's content. A small café serves refreshments.

Nearby
Located at the western edge of the Hill Country, Fredericksburg is a great home base for exploring the surrounding area. From Fredericksburg, TX 16 heads north to Enchanted Rock State Natural Area or south to Kerrville, US 87 travels a particularly scenic stretch on its way south to Comfort, and a short trip east along US 290 takes in both Stonewall and Johnson City, deep in historic LBJ country, and the legendary Luckenbach. Both the Wine Trail and Lavender Trail swing past Fredericksburg, and wildflower lovers might enjoy driving the picturesque Willow City Loop—take US 16 north for 13 miles, turn right on FM 1323, follow it to Willow City and turn left, staying on FM 1323, to begin the loop.

Johnson City

Johnson City was established in 1876 and named for James Polk Johnson, an ancestor of the town's most famous native son, President Lyndon Baines Johnson. A rural ranching center and county seat, Johnson City did not have modern utilities as late as the 1930s. When President Franklin D. Roosevelt established the Rural Electrification Administration in 1935, a 28-year-old Lyndon Johnson, by then a congressman, lobbied hard for services in the sparsely populated Hill Country, succeeding in 1938.

Located at the intersection of US 281 and US 290, Johnson City makes a convenient stopover and is also the destination of LBJ devotees who come to visit his childhood home in town and the family's ranch in nearby Stonewall. Johnson City is also the site of the Blanco County Fair and Rodeo (830-868-7684; www.lbjcountry.com; Blanco County Fairgrounds, US 281, Johnson City, TX 78636), held at the end of August, and showcasing livestock, arts and crafts, food, and country music.

LODGING

While the usual chain hotels, including the particularly practical Best Western Johnson City Inn (830-868-4044, 107 US 281/290, Johnson City, TX 78636. Price: Inexpensive to Moderate), are well represented in Johnson City, some of the best lodging is out of town. **A Room with a View B&B** (1-888-588-8439; www.hillcountryroomwithaview.com; 103 Ridgeview Dr., Johnson City, TX 78636. Take US 281 South to CR 290 East to RR 3232) Several miles out of town, this appropriately named B&B offers panoramic views of sunsets and wildflowers from the porch. Two airy rooms with honey-colored wood floors and simple decor coupled with baked goods in the morning add to the air of calm.

CULTURE

LBJ National Historical Park is in Johnson City, and the **LBJ State Park and Historic Site** is in nearby Stonewall; taken together, they offer insight into both LBJ the man who was president and LBJ the little boy who grew up in rural Texas, an upbringing that affected and informed his domestic policies. See "LBJ's Texas," below.

DINING

Hill Country Cupboard

830-868-4625
www.hillcountrycupboard.com
101 US 281 South, Johnson City, TX 78636
Open: Sat.–Thu. 6 AM–9 PM, Fri. 6 AM–midnight
Price: Inexpensive

There's nothing fancy about the Hill Country Cupboard. The tables are covered with disposable checkered tablecloths, and iced tea is served in battered plastic tumblers. Then again, there's no need for niceties when your specialty is chicken-fried steaks the size of dinner plates. Just as the sign out front proclaims, this place makes some of the best steaks around and serves them up with the requisite sides of coleslaw, rice, black-eyed peas, fried okra, and cornbread muffins. There is also BBQ, catfish, chicken, sandwiches, and several wines from nearby Texas Hills Vineyard.

Silver K Café

830-868-2911
www.silverkcafe.com
209 E. Main St., the Old Lumber Yard Complex, Johnson City, TX 78636
Open: Mon.–Sat. breakfast 7–10:30, lunch 11–3, Sun. buffet 11–3; Sun.–Wed. homestyle
   dinner 5–8, Thu.–Sat. 5–9
Special Features: Live music
Price: Inexpensive to Moderate

The atmosphere at the Silver K is bold and wonderfully eclectic, with deep red walls decorated with backlit bronze stars and chandeliers shaped like cacti. The offerings at breakfast and lunch range from overflowing omelets to pimiento cheese sandwiches. Though the dinner menu changes, it tends to include delicious regional dishes such as honey pecan fried chicken and corn-fed, dry-aged beef sirloin and tenderloin; and a nice selection of Texas wines are available. The more modestly priced Frito pie, crispy fried catfish and Parmesan-crusted meat loaf sandwiches on the homestyle dinner menu served Sunday through Wednesday are a great deal. The Silver K is also a music venue, featuring Texas music played by local singer-songwriters; see the Web site for listings.

Nearby

Leaving Johnson City and heading east on RR 2766, you can stop in for a glass of wine at Texas Hills Vineyard (830-868-2321; www.texashillsvineyard.com; 878 RR 2766, Johnson City, TX 78636) before continuing on to Pedernales Falls State Park.

LBJ's Texas

Johnson City and nearby Stonewall are each home to significant sites from the life of President Lyndon Baines Johnson. There is no entrance fee for the parks, though donations are accepted and there is a charge for the 90-minute bus tour of the LBJ Ranch.

In Johnson City, the **National Park Service Visitors Center** is located in the former Pedernales Hospital (830-868-7128; www.nps.gov/lyjo; located on the corner of Ladybird Lane and Avenue G, Johnson City, TX 78636. Open: Daily 8:45–5). It displays exhibits, photographs, and videos pertaining to President Johnson's life and times. Behind the center, visitors can take a free guided tour of **Johnson's boyhood home** (Open: Daily 9–11:30 and 1–4:30), which has been restored to the look and feel of the 1920s. To the west, a short 10-minute walk away, the Johnson Settlement includes original buildings built by President Johnson's ancestor James Polk Johnson. The barn, windmill, water tank, and cooler house help to illustrate the pioneer ranching life of the 1800s.

Located on US 290 14 miles west of Johnson City near Stonewall is the **LBJ State Park and Historic Site Visitors Center** (830-644-2252; www.tpwd.state.tx.us; P.O. Box 238, Stonewall, TX 78671. Open: Daily 8–5). The state park is a recreational area, and the visitors center is the launching point for the **National Park Bus Tour of the LBJ Ranch** (830-868-7128; www.nps.gov/lyjo. Tours: Daily 10–4. Admission: Adults $6, children and seniors $3, children under 6 free). The tours are the only way to see the ranch, as private vehicles are not permitted.

LBJ spent so much time at his beloved ranch during his administration that it became known as the Texas White House. These days it remains a working ranch, with an operating Head Start preschool started during Johnson's administration. It is the final resting place of the president, who was buried here in the family's cemetery on January 25, 1973.

The pace slows down in the Hill Country. Ali Blum

Kerrville

Established in the early 1850s, Kerrville has always depended on water for its success and prosperity. In 1857 a German miller and millwright built a large gristmill and sawmill here that transformed the town into a regional economic center and supplier of lumber and other goods to growing San Antonio, 62 miles to the southeast.

Water is still important here, with the clean, cool Guadalupe River running right through town and the surrounding parks. A quiet county seat, Kerrville is the largest town in the area and perhaps best known these days for its highly acclaimed music marathon, the Kerrville Folk Festival (see below).

CULTURE

Thirteen galleries and museums in Kerrville have organized the Second Saturday Art Trail, hosting afternoon receptions in their respective establishments from 3–6 on the second Saturday of every month.

Hill Country Museum

830-896-8633
www.kerrdowntown.com/hillcountrymuseum
226 Earl Garrett St., Kerrville, TX 78028
Open: Mon.–Sat. 10–4:30
Admission: Adults $5, children $2

The Hill Country Museum housed in Captain Schreiner's home, a massive native-stone structure built between 1879 and 1896, might instead be called "the Schreiner Museum." A native Frenchman, Schreiner moved to San Antonio with his family in 1852 and joined the Texas Rangers in 1854 at the age of 16. Schreiner fought in the Civil War, opened a mercantile establishment, excelled in banking, ranching, and marketing wool and mohair, and, in 1880, purchased the Y.O. Ranch. As Schreiner's wealth grew, so did his philanthropic interests, and he established the Schreiner Institute, now Schreiner University, in 1917. This museum, with its creaky hardwood floors, period furnishings, and quirky details, such as the trapdoor leading to a tunnel the captain used to safeguard money, tells the story of his bygone era and his lasting effect on Kerrville.

Kerr Arts and Cultural Center

830-895-2911
www.kacckerrville.com
228 Earl Garrett St., Kerrville, TX 78029
Open: Tue.–Sat. 10–4, Sun. 1–4

Housed in the town's historic former post office, this cultural center exhibits works from photography to quilting, basketry to ceramics, created by the center's 600 member artists.

Museum of Western Art

www.americanwesternart.org
830-896-2553

1550 Bandera Hwy., Kerrville, TX 78029
Open: Tue.–Sat. 9–5, Sun. 1–5

In a limestone building designed by Texan architect O'Neil Ford, this museum pays homage to the West and its inhabitants. The artwork depicts western life from a wide range of perspectives, with images of the hardworking cowboy, Native Americans, and pioneer women figuring prominently. The interior of the museum is a juxtaposition of elements—mesquite wood floors and Saltillo tiles, crisp white display walls and bronze statues—with as much rough-hewn gracefulness as the artwork adorning it.

Festivals

Kerrville Folk Festival
830-257-3600, tickets 1-800-435-8429
www.kerrvillefolkfestival.com
PO Box 291446, Kerrville, TX 78029
Quiet Valley Ranch, 9 miles south of Kerrville on TX 16

This nationally acclaimed folk festival is held on an outdoor stage at the Quiet Valley Ranch RV Park and Campgrounds (www.qvranch.com) in the peaceful Hill Country. When the festival began in 1972, it was centered on folk music, but it has grown to include acoustic rock, bluegrass, blues, country, and jazz. Many major-label artists played "Kerrville" on their way up, and some frequently return. The event takes place in May, starting the Thursday before Memorial Day, and lasts for 18 days.

OTHER FESTIVALS
Kerrville celebrates Easter weekend with an event that includes lots and lots of food and exercise, the **Annual Kerrville Easter Festival and Chili Classic** (830-792-8387). With a 5K Easter Run, egg hunts, children's games, washer pitching (akin to the game of horseshoes), armadillo races, and copious amounts of chili, this one's fun. At the same time, the Easter Hill Country Bike Tour draws cyclists from throughout the region to the back roads of the Hill Country.

In May, on Memorial Day weekend, the **Texas State Arts and Crafts Fair** (803-896-5711 or 1-888-335-1455; www.tacef.com) is a family-friendly good time with close to 200 artists, music, and activities for children.

In September, the **Kerrville Wine and Music Festival** is four days of mellow singer-songwriter music and regional wine tasting. Organized by the folks at the Kerrville Folk Festival, the **Wine and Music Festival** is held over the Labor Day weekend at the Quiet Valley Ranch and is a very popular Hill Country festival, drawing crowds from near and far.

At the end of September, the Texas Heritage Music Foundation hosts the **Texas Heritage Living History Weekend** (830-792-1945; www.texasheritagemusic.org), a three-day event devoted entirely to Texas music and heritage. An impressive and eclectic lineup of talent includes gospel choirs, storytellers, trick ropers, *vaqueros* (cowboys), square dancers, and cloggers, all performing on the Schreiner University campus.

The Kerr County Fair (830-2576833; www.kerrcountyfair.com) in October features a parade, carnival, 4H livestock exhibits, chili and BBQ cook-offs, dancing, and music.

Kerr County Market Days are held at the Kerr County Courthouse Square on the second and fourth Saturday of each month, April through December, except August.

Dining

Café Riverstone (830-895-9878; www.caferiverstone.com; 1521 Junction Hwy., Kerrville, TX 78208) Hours: Mon.–Thu. 11–9, Fri.–Sat. 11–10. Price: Moderate. Café Riverstone's appetizers such as fried green tomatoes or goat cheese fondue give diners just a taste of gourmet cowboy comfort foods. The pecan-encrusted antelope with maple butter, tequila pasta, and salmon roasted on mountain cedar are all fresh and inventive. Dine inside or outside on the deck overlooking the water. Adjacent, the **Backporch Cantina** has a more casual atmosphere and menu and live music Saturday 9 PM–midnight.

Cowboy Steak House (830-896-5688; www.cowboysteakhouse.com; 416 Main St., Kerrville, TX 78028) Open: Mon.–Sat. 5 PM–10 PM. Bar opens at 4. Price: Inexpensive to Moderate. Not surprisingly, the menu is almost exclusively meat, but the variety is a bit unexpected. Stick with a porterhouse or try some quail. Sample shish kebab sirloin chunks or branch out into buffalo steak. Choose between rack of lamb, chicken breast, and whole catfish. While any entrée is served with soup or a salad, other vegetables are available only "on request."

Francisco's (830-257-2995; 201 Earl Garrett St., Kerrville, TX 78028) Open: Mon.–Sat. 11–3, Thu.–Sat. 5:30 PM–9 PM. Price: Moderate. For fine Mexican dining in Kerrville, folks head to Francisco's, where the tortilla soup and *chile rellenos* are tops.

Hill Country Café (830-257-6665; 806 Main St., Kerrville, 78028) Open: Mon.–Fri. 6 AM–2 PM, Sat. 6 AM–11 AM. Price: Inexpensive. The Hill Country Café has been around forever, serving eggs, toast, bacon, and hot coffee to Kerrville's early risers. Cash only.

Joe's Jefferson Street Café (830-257-2929; 1001 Jefferson St., Kerrville, TX) Open: Mon.–Fri. 11–2 and 5–9, Sat. 5 PM–9 PM. Price: Moderate. Down-home cooking, melt-in-your-mouth steaks, hot rolls and cornbread, seasonal veggies, and a changing list of dessert choices.

The Lakehouse (830-895-3188; www.thelakehouse.com; 1655 Junction Hwy., Kerrville, TX 78028) Open: Mon.–Thu. 11–8:30, Fri.–Sat. 11–9, Sun. 11–3. Price: Inexpensive. Residents flock to the Lakehouse for, among other things, the all-you-can-eat fried catfish filets and bite-size shrimp served with pinto beans, coleslaw, french fries, and hush puppies. A comfortable, no-nonsense place right on the water.

Attractions, Parks, and Recreation

Kerrville-Schreiner State Park
830-257-5392
www.tpwd.state.tx.us or www.kerrville.org
2385 Bandera Hwy., Kerrville TX 78028
Open: Daily 8–5
Admission: $3 a person

This 500-acre park on the banks of the Guadalupe River 3 miles southeast of Kerrville offers picnicking, boating, and camping. There is tent camping along the water, two dozen air-conditioned cabins, and one large cabin that sleeps six. This stretch of the river is known for its fishing, and swimming is allowed, though there aren't lifeguards on duty.

Riverside Nature Center
830-257-4837
www.riversidenaturecenter.org
150 Francisco Lemos St., Kerrville, TX 78028
Open: Mon.–Fri. 9–4, Sat.–Sun. 10–3. Arboretum dawn–dusk
Admission: Free
Special Features: Handicapped access

The Riverside Nature Center began to take shape in 1992 when a parcel of land was purchased and its native plants and habitat restored through great community effort and volunteerism. The center opened in 1999, and its trails, which meander past native trees, wildflowers, birds, and butterflies, are as educational as they are relaxing.

LODGING

It is essential to book a room in advance, particularly during festivals. Reservations may be made directly or through the following reservation services (the reservation services in Fredericksburg book rooms in Kerrville as well): **Main Street Reservations Service** (830-997-0153 or 1-888-559-8555; www.travelmainstreet.com; 337 E. Main St., Fredericksburg, TX 78624); **Gastehaus Schmidt** (1-866-427-8374; www.fbglodging.com; 231 W. Main St., Fredericksburg, TX 78624).

Inn of the Hills Resort & Conference Center
830-895-5000 or 1-800-292-5690
www.innofthehills.com
1001 Junction Hwy., Kerrville, TX 78028
Price: Inexpensive to Expensive
Special Features: Limited handicapped access

Over 40 years old, this resort and conference center has stood up to hundreds of family reunions, business conferences, and the stampede of children's feet racing through the courtyard to the tree-shaded, Olympic-size pool. While the rooms can feel somewhat dated, they are all clean and serviceable, with native-stone walls and ironwork details; ask for one of the pleasant poolside rooms on the ground floor. Annemarie's Alpine Lodge, the on-site restaurant, is known for its buffets, especially Sunday brunch, with its prime rib and abundant desserts. The Inn Pub features drinks and country and western music for dancing.

Mo-Ranch Conference Center
1-800-460-4401
www.moranch.com
2229 FM 1340, Hunt, TX 78024
On the North Fork of the Guadalupe River, 10 miles west of Hunt

Price: Moderate to Expensive
Special Features: Limited handicapped access

The Presbyterian-affiliated Mo Ranch is known for hosting conferences, youth groups, and Elderhostels, but there is also plenty of room for individuals and families who would like to come enjoy swimming, horseback riding, a ropes course, and other recreational activities. Accommodations range from simply furnished two-bedroom apartments to tent camping sites, with hotel rooms and cabins in between. Since Mo Ranch is in a remote, rural area, all guests are required to purchase the modestly priced meal plan served in the communal dining hall.

River Run Bed & Breakfast
830-896-8353 or 1-800-460-7170
www.riverrunbb.com
120 Francisco Lemos St., Kerrville, TX 78028
Price: Moderate

The native-stone exterior and tin roof give this downtown Kerrville B&B a traditional Hill Country feel. The rooms, each named for a notable Texas personality, are refreshingly simple, with country details like quilts on the beds and throw rugs on the honey-colored hardwood floors. Mornings bring a filling breakfast served in the dining room.

Y.O. Ranch Resort and Conference Center
830-257-4440 or 1-877-967-3767
www.yoresort.com
2033 Sidney Baker St., Kerrville, TX 78028
Price: Inexpensive to Expensive
Special Features: Limited handicapped access

With its western decor, ranch-themed carpets, and memorabilia-filled lobby, the Y.O. Ranch Resort is definitely a little bit o' Texas. Spacious rooms, two-room suites with bunk beds, a children's playground, swimming pool, and tennis, basketball, and volleyball courts, coupled with fairly reasonable rates and convenient location near town, have made this resort a family favorite for years. Of course, this has also meant years of gentle wear and tear, but while it could use some updating or a fresh coat of paint, the Y.O. Ranch currently has a comfortable, well-worn feel that is right at home in the Hill Country. The weekday lunch buffet at the Branding Iron, their on-site restaurant, is very popular with locals.

Luckenbach

If you really want to slow down, grind to a halt in Luckenbach, where the only movement is tapping feet and guitar picking in the shade of surrounding oak trees. A tiny cluster of rustic wooden buildings, including the multipurpose General Store, make up this little community, which is worth a trip for the music and dancing alone.

Immortalized in Waylon Jennings' song "Luckenbach, Texas (Back to the Basics of Love)," little Luckenbach came into being in the 1840s and 1850s when several German-

Statue of John Russell "Hondo" Crouch, former "mayor" of Luckenbach

speaking families decided to settle along the banks of Grape Creek. The population fluctuated from 150 in 1896 to 492 in 1902, but by the 1960s it had leveled off to 25. In 1971, John Russell (Hondo) Crouch purchased the settlement, declared himself mayor, and set its spirit free. Live music on holidays brings out the locals, visitors, and Harley riders, who queue up for pulled-pork sandwiches and beer. Offbeat and good-natured events, such as the annual Hug-In held in February, capture the character of the hamlet beautifully. As the town slogan goes, "Everybody is somebody in Luckenbach." And if you're lucky enough to go, you will be too.

The General Store (830-997-3224 or 1-888-311-8990; www.luckenbachtexas.com; 412 Luckenbach Town Loop, Fredericksburg, TX 78624; Open: Daily 10–9). Open for business since 1849, the store is old and creaky, with a sloping front porch, a bar in the back, and spaces in between the floorboards that let in the draft. Folks here just love it to death. With live music every night at 7 and plenty of Hondo-style cowboy hats for sale, what's not to love? The store's sleek Web site has all the details.

LODGING

Full Moon Inn (830-997-2205 or 1-800-997-1124; www.fullmooninn.com; 3234 Luckenbach Rd., Fredericksburg, TX 78624) Price: Moderate to Expensive. There aren't many options for lodging in Luckenbach, but fortunately there is the Full Moon Inn. A log cabin from the 1800s, an old smokehouse, and a replicated Sunday house (see p. 196) form a little compound of accommodations on 12 grassy acres with a creek. Soft sheets, Jacuzzi tubs, and sweet potato pancakes more than make up for the lack of television.

Go Texan

As part of a marketing campaign of the Texas Department of Agriculture, when you travel in Texas you may see the GO TEXAN sticker or stamp on agricultural products such as food, wine, and beef that indicates the item was grown or processed in Texas. Nonagricultural products—art and jewelry, for example—are also sometimes designated. The Department of Agriculture provides education and encourages various practices such as gardening with native plants. For a list of statewide produce stands and farmers' markets, organized by county, or even recipes using state-grown produce, visit www.picktexas.com and support Texas businesses; check www.gotexan.org for more information.

Marble Falls

Marble Falls, so named for the marble outcroppings over which the nearby Colorado River flows, was founded in 1887. Located just north of town on RM 1431, Granite Mountain was once a huge dome of pink and red granite; it was quarried in the 1880s to construct the Texas Capitol in Austin. These days, there is not much granite to see; a plaque at the picnic area across the road tells the story. Located on US 281 between Johnson City and Burnet and within striking distance of many of the Highland Lakes, Marble Falls is a good place to stop for a bite to eat. The town comes alive in April when the **Bluebonnet Blues and Fine Arts Festival** (www.bluebonnetblues.com) brings in some of the best blues performers in Texas for a long weekend of music.

DINING

Bluebonnet Café
830-693-2344
www.bluebonnetcafe.net
211 US 281, Marble Falls, TX 78654
Open: Mon.–Thu. 6 AM–8 PM, Fri.–Sat.
6 AM–9 PM, Sun. 6 AM–1:45 PM
Price: Inexpensive
Special Features: Cash only

Chocolate cream pie and coffee at the Bluebonnet Café

The Bluebonnet Café is not much to look at. In fact, you just might miss its red and white sign when rounding the curve over the bridge in Marble Falls. One thing you're sure to notice is the line of people snaking out the front door, particularly on weekends. Constantly crowded, this very casual diner just keeps reelin' 'em in with pot roasts, chicken-fried steaks, fried okra, catfish, and an all-day breakfast menu. Morning, noon, or night, you'd be wise to follow the advice of the sign on the wall and "Try some pie." Double-crust pies, cream pies, and pies with meringue a mile high—the Bluebonnet Café makes great pie. Ask your waitress which she likes best.

Brothers Bakery
830-798-8278
www.brothersbakery.com
519 US 281 North, Marble Falls, TX 78654
Open: Mon.–Fri. 6:30–4, Sat. 7:30–3
Price: Inexpensive

A great spot for lunch, Brothers serves crisp, healthy salads and a variety of sandwiches made on just-baked breads. The tuna salad with walnuts, apples, and olives is particularly popular. Plenty of pastries, cookies, and treats go well with a midday cup of coffee.

Café 909
830-693-2126
www.cafe909.com
909 Second St., Marble Falls, TX 78654
Two blocks west of US 281 in downtown Marble Falls
Open: Mon.–Sat. 5:30 PM–close; bar opens at 5
Price: Expensive

A modern eatery, decorated with punches of color, Café 909 serves a menu that is worth a detour. The prime 14-ounce ribeye steak with poblano chili *sofrito* coupled with pickled red onions is sure to awaken your taste buds, while something as simple as a wedge of iceberg lettuce with capers, dried corn, and a buttermilk ranch dressing reveals that great food doesn't have to be fussy. For dessert, the coconut-green tea crème brûlée with Hawaiian sugar macaroons is imaginative and delicious.

Nearby
From Marble Falls, you can easily visit the Highland Lakes, Spicewood Vineyards (see Hill Country Vineyards, above), and Sweet Berry Farm (830-798-1462; www.sweetberryfarm .com; 1801 FM 1980, Marble Falls, TX 78654) with its mazes, hayrides, picnic tables, and U-pick fruits and vegetables: strawberries and blackberries in the spring, tomatoes in the summer, and pumpkins in the fall.

Stonewall

On the Pedernales River some 13 miles east of Fredericksburg on US 290, tiny Stonewall is best known as the birthplace of Lyndon B. Johnson and the site of the **Lyndon B. Johnson State Historical Park** and the **LBJ Ranch** (see "LBJ's Texas, p. 205). Stonewall is also known for agriculture, as its extraordinary soil sustains some of the best peach orchards and vineyards in the Hill Country. The Annual Peach Jamboree and Rodeo in mid-June is always a sweet success (see www.stonewalltexas.com for details).

LODGING

Rose Hill Manor
830-644-5541 or 1-877-767-3445
www.rose-hill.com
2614 Upper Albert Rd., Stonewall, TX 78671
Price: Expensive

Though reminiscent of a Charleston-style plantation home, the wide porches and large windows of the Rose Hill Inn seem well-suited to the Hill Country. Each of the four rooms in the main house are thoughtfully decorated with a restrained use of floral prints and appointed with queen-size beds, sunporches, sitting areas, or access to the veranda. The cozy cottages have king-size beds, simple white bead-board walls, vaulted ceilings, warm wood floors, and small front porches for lounging. A full gourmet breakfast is served each morning and is included in the price.

The **Hog Stop Inn**, while technically in Fredericksburg (see "Lodging"), is just a short drive west of Stonewall. So, ride your Harley into the sunset.

DINING

Austin's
877-767-3445
Open: Wed.–Sun. 6 PM–close
Price: Expensive
Special Features: Reservations required

Large windows filled with views of the Hill Country, crisp table linens, candles, and flowers all contribute to the ambience at the Rose Hill Manor's lovely on-site restaurant. The fundamentally French menu in the large dining room is a five-course prix fixe ($39.95) that changes with the seasons, while the small dining room features à la carte dining, with soup, salad, desserts priced at $9.95 and entrées between $25 and $35. The wine list is impressive, as are the desserts, expertly made by pastry chef Chad, who is also in charge of breakfast for lucky overnight guests.

Texas Peaches
Gillespie County, which includes both Fredericksburg and Stonewall, produces 40 percent of Texas's peach crop annually, making it the largest peach-producing county in Texas. Though the crop is susceptible to variable weather conditions—and a late frost or spring hail can wreak havoc—when the conditions are right, the peaches are perfect, sun-ripened to a golden juicy sweetness.

To find a farm stand or an orchard that allows you to pick your own peaches, this 35-mile route is suggested: From Fredericksburg head east along US 290; in approximately 13 miles turn left onto Gellerman Lane, the site of the largest concentration of peach trees in Texas; continue to FM 2721, where you turn west back toward Fredericksburg. Continue to FM 1631 and follow it the 7 miles back to Main Street. Allow 45 minutes for the drive. Check www.texaspeaches.com for ripening dates, which fall anywhere between early May and late July, and orchards.

Stop by a farm stand for a taste of homegrown Texas.

Highland Lakes

The Colorado River passes through the northern part of the Hill Country, picking up the spring-fed Pedernales, Llano, San Saba, and Concho Rivers as tributaries before flowing through the city of Austin. The river then continues over the flat, alluvial land of the Coastal Plain and into the Gulf of Mexico. During the early 1800s, the Colorado was prone to impassable logjams and periodic flooding that threatened riverside settlements. The need for irrigation, a reliable water source, and flood control prompted the Lower Colorado River Authority (LCRA) to construct six dams along the river between 1935 and 1951, creating a chain of six lakes known as the Highland Lakes. The Highland Lakes and their 25 waterside parks are favorite spots for boating, fishing, camping, and ecotourism. The lakes and their shoreline also provide habitat for rare, endangered, and migratory birds, including the American bald eagle, and support a large variety of wildlife.

Area Web sites—www.highlandlakes.com, www.lakesandhills.com, www.lcra.org, and www.texas outside.com—provide details of the region's lodging, dining, and recreation.

Lake Buchanan

Lake Buchanan, some 31 miles long, is the largest, oldest, and northernmost of the Highland Lakes; it is located approximately 75 miles north of Austin. The eastern shoreline is rocky, with granite cliffs, waterfalls, and deep cold water, while the western shore has beaches for swimming. The majestic American bald eagle nests in the area surrounding the lake during the winter and early spring. The closest large towns are Burnet to the east and Llano to the west.

Burnet

Designated as the Bluebonnet Capital of Texas, Burnet stages the Bluebonnet Festival (www.burnet chamber.org) the second weekend in April, complete with a parade, carnival, food, and music.

Austin Steam Train (512-477-8468; www.austinsteamtrain.org) Price: Adults $27, seniors $24, children $17. Open: Saturday; March–May Sat. and Sun. The Hill Country Flyer travels south from downtown Burnet and loops back again. While the train does not have air conditioning, it makes up for it with plenty of vintage details such as wood window moldings, upholstered seating, and an old-time concession stand.

Canyon of the Eagles Lodge and Nature Park (512-756-8787; www.canyonoftheeagles.com; 16942 RR 2341, Burnet, TX 78611) This lodge, complete with fairly basic accommodations (Price: Moderate to Expensive), cabins, campground, restaurant (Inexpensive to Moderate), and tiny swimming pool, is located within the confines of an LCRA-owned 940-acre public park, most of which is a nature preserve. There are 14 miles of hiking trails (maps available at the main lodge) and an educational nature center.

Lake Buchanan Adventures (512-756-9911; www.lakebuchananadventures.com; 16942 RR 2341, Burnet, TX 78611) Boat rentals and tours.

Vanishing Texas River Cruise (512-756-6986 or 1-800-474-8374; www.vtrc.com; 443 Waterway Lane, Burnet, TX 78611) Price: Adults $20, seniors $12.50, children $12.75. The boat leaves from the Canyon of the Eagles Lodge and Nature Park for ecological cruises on Lake Buchanan; vineyard tours and wildflower and dinner cruises are also offered.

Eagle Eye Observatory (www.austinastro.org; Austin Astronomical Society) This observatory houses a 16-inch Ealing Educator Telescope and hosts monthly stargazing parties; see Web site for details.

LLANO

Cooper's Old Time Pit Barbeque (325-247-5713; www.coopersbbq.com; 505 W. Dallas St., Llano, TX 78643) Open: Sun.–Thu. 10:30–8, Fri.–Sat. 10:30–9. The absolute best BBQ this side of Lockhart. Pick your meat at the pit, watch the pit master submerge it in sauce, and proceed inside to pick out your sides.

TOW

Fall Creek Vineyards (see "Hill Country Vineyards," above) Situated at the northwest end of the lake, Fall Creek Vineyards makes a good destination for wine lovers.

INKS LAKE

Inks Lake State Park (512-793-2223; www.tpwd.state.tx.us; 3630 Park Road 4 West, Burnet, TX 78611) Open: Daily. Admission: $5 a person 13 and older. Formerly ranchland, Inks Lake State Park is now a recreational facility on the eastern shores of Inks Lake, whose water levels remain constant throughout the year, regardless of drought, making it a reliable spot for swimming (unsupervised beach), fishing, and boating. Tent camping ($12–$18 a night) and primitive backpack camping ($8) are available. Brand-new limited-use cabins ($45) are equipped with two bunk beds, air conditioning, electricity, outdoor grill, and water spigot. Two of the cabins are handicapped accessible. Canoes and paddleboats are also available for rent, as are golf clubs and carts for the waterfront nine-hole golf course.

Nearby **Longhorn Cavern State Park** (see "Texas State Parks," below) is a geological wonder.

LAKE LBJ

The shoreline of Lake LBJ is very developed, with large homes along the resort town of Horseshoe Bay and particularly Applehead Island. A popular spot for boating, the lake can get crowded on weekends. Nearby, Longhorn Cavern State Park makes an easy side trip. The closest large town is Marble Falls, to the east. Part of the **Texas Wine Trail** winds through the region, with **Lost Creek Vineyard** near Sunrise Beach on the western shore of Lake LBJ and **Spicewood Vineyards** just a short drive south along TX 71. For boaters, **Sunrise Beach Marina and Lodge** (325-388-9393; www.sunrise beachmarina.com) rents watercraft.

LAKE MARBLE FALLS

The smallest of the Highland Lakes, this narrow, almost riverlike lake is surrounded by mostly steep, rocky, and privately owned land, though there are three modest city parks on the north shore of the lake just west of US 281. In August, the **Marble Falls LakeFest** (www.marblefallslakefest.com) brings ear-splitting speedboat drag racing to the lake. The nearby town of Marble Falls offers several tasty restaurants, all of which are local favorites.

LAKE TRAVIS

A party lake, Lake Travis is often swarming with motorized watercraft on weekends. Numerous parks allow day-trippers to get a little closer to nature on the outskirts of Austin, and a variety of eateries make this Highland Lake a sophisticated stopover for drinks or a meal.

continued on following page

Highland Lakes continued

Parks

Hippie Hollow (512-266-1644; www.hippiehollow.com; 7000 Comanche Trail, Austin, TX 78732)
Admission: $10. A favorite spot along the rocky shores of Lake Travis for Texans who like to swim
and sunbathe in the buff. From MoPac (Loop 1), Capital of Texas Hwy. (Loop 360), or I-35, take
2222 west to Hwy. 620 and follow signs.

Boat Rentals

Daybreak Boat Rentals (512-266-2176; www.daybreakboatrentals.com)

Just for Fun (512-266-9710; www.jff.net)

Dining

For wild game, try **Hudson's on the Bend** (see "Dining" in Austin section).

The Oasis (512-266-2442; www.oasis-austin.com; 6550 Comanche Trail, Austin, TX 78732)
Open: Mon.–Thu. 11:30–10, Fri. 11:30–11, Sat. 11–11, Sun. 11–10. Price: Inexpensive to Moderate.
With multiple levels of decks jutting over Lake Travis, each dotted with dozens of colorful umbrel-
las, the Oasis has a very congenial, come-as-you-are atmosphere; just the sort of place to relax
and unwind over food, drinks, and live music. Splendid views of Lake Travis and the stunning
Central Texas sunsets.

LAKE AUSTIN

Located within the city limits, Lake Austin is an aquatic playground of parks, boats, cruises, plenty of
casual, family-friendly spots to grab food and drinks, and lots of live music.

Parks

Emma Long Metropolitan Park (512-346-1831; www.ci.austin.tx.us/parks/emmalong; 1600 City
Park Rd., Austin, TX 78730) Open: Daily 7 AM–10 PM. Admission: Mon.–Thu. $5 per vehicle,
Fri.–Sun. $8. Biking, camping ($6 without utilities, $15 with utilities), hiking, swimming.

Boat Rental

Sun & Fun Watercraft Rentals (512-306-1820; www.sunfunrental.com; 1600 Scenic Dr., Austin, TX
78703) Rents Jet Skis and pontoon and ski boats.

Cruises

Lake Austin Riverboats (512-345-5220; www.austinriverboats.com; 3700 Lake Austin Blvd., Austin,
TX 78703)

Austin Duck Adventures (512-477-5274; www.austinducks.com) Price: Adults $21.95, seniors
$19.95, children $13, plus tax. Drive around Austin in an amphibious British Alvis Stalwart before
splashing into Lake Austin.

Lodging

Lake Austin Spa (see "Lodging" in Austin section)

Dining

County Line BBQ (512-346-3664; www.countyline.com; 5204 RR 2222, just before Loop 360,
Austin, TX 78731) Open: Sun.–Mon. 11:30–9, Tue.–Wed. 11:30–9:30, Thu.–Fri. 11:30–10, Sun.
noon–10. Price: Inexpensive. The place to go for great BBQ with a great view.

Hula Hut (512-476-4852; www.hulahut.com; 3826 Lake Austin Blvd., Austin, TX 78703. Open:
Sun.–Thu. 11–10, Fri.–Sat. 11–11.) A favorite spot for drinks, Hula Hut specializes in Mexico-meets-
Polynesia cuisine with guacamole salads served beside pupu platters. Owned by the creators of the

local Tex-Mex chain restaurant Chuy's (www.chuys.com) and the Shady Grove, who also own
Lucy's Boatyard (512-651-0505; www.lucysboatyard.com; 3825 Lake Austin Blvd., Austin, TX
78703. Open: Sun.–Thu. 11–10, Fri.–Sat. 11–11), which is known for its seafood. Both Lake Austin
eateries have seating overlooking the water and a fun, breezy vibe.

Mozart's Coffee Roasters (512-477-2900; www.mozartscoffee.com; 3825 Lake Austin Blvd.,
Austin, TX 78703) Open: Mon.–Thu. 7 AM–midnight, Fri. 7 AM–1 AM, Sat. 8 AM–1 AM, Sun. 8
AM–midnight. Price: Inexpensive. On the banks of Lake Austin a few minutes' drive from downtown
Austin, Mozart's seems worlds away. Sleek and sophisticated, Mozart's can do things with coffee,
chocolate, and cheesecake that defy restraint and define indulgence. Stellar views of Lake Austin,
outdoor seating on a spacious deck and nightly live jazz, folk, or classical guitar music add romance
to the euphoria of caffeine and sugar.

The Pier (512-327-4562; pierlakeaustin.com; 1703 River Hills Rd., Austin, TX 78733) Open:
Mon.–Fri. 11 AM–midnight, Sat.–Sun. 7 AM–midnight. Price: Inexpensive. Burgers, Tex-Mex, live
music, and sand volleyball.

Ski Shores Waterfront Café (512-346-5915; www.skishores.com; 2905 Pearce Rd., Austin, TX
78730) Open: Mon.–Thu. 11:30–8, Fri. 11:30–9, Sat. noon–9, Sun. noon–9. Price: Inexpensive.
Super-casual place for a fantastic burger right on the water. Laughing children, folks in flip-flops,
live music, and weekend movie nights.

Wimberley

Along the banks of Cypress Creek, just 30 minutes south of Austin or 15 minutes west of
San Marcos along RR 12, Wimberley is a small but thriving town of artists and other folks
who just like living "not in Austin." Its creek lined with bald cypress and pecan trees, the
town is beautifully scenic. The dramatic Devil's Backbone (see "Attractions, Parks, and
Recreation" below) is visible from certain lookout points.

Founded in 1856, when a Mr. Winters built a small gristmill along the creek, the tiny
settlement was first known as Winter's Creek. The Cude family then bought the mill,
and the community became known as Cude's Mill. In 1874 Pleasant Wimberley took over
the mill and the town's moniker changed again, this time to Wimberley's Mill. In 1880,
on a petition for a post office, the town was referred to as Wimberleyville. The name stuck
and was shortened over time to simply Wimberley. The mill continued operating, as a
lumber mill, gristmill, flour mill, molasses mill, and cotton gin before being razed in 1934.
The community that had built up around the mill remained, and starting in the 1930s
Wimberley became a tourist destination. Market Days, held the first Saturday of each
month from April through December, are a big draw. Wimberley has a culture, community,
and charm all its own and is enjoyable as a day trip or as an overnight retreat.

LODGING

Blair House Inn
887-549-5450
www.blairhouseinn.com

100 Spoke Hill Rd., Wimberley, TX 78676
Price: Expensive to Very Expensive

With deluxe cottages, a cooking school, an art gallery, and a restaurant, pool, and spa here, once you arrive at Blair House you'll have no reason to leave. The themed rooms revolve around Texas and the Southwest, with three archangels thrown in. The Fort Worth Room, for example, has a rich leather sofa and chair, tan walls, a dark wood sleigh bed, crimson details, and a few requisite stars on the walls, just enough to capture the feel but not overly drawn out. A pool, spa services, and stunning views round out the luxurious offerings.

Creekhaven Inn
512-847-9344 or 1-800-827-1913
www.creekhaveninn.com
400 Mill Race Ln., Wimberley, TX 78676
Price: Expensive
Special Features: Limited handicapped access

The inn itself may be relatively new, but it shares the banks of Cypress Creek with several towering cypress trees that are as old as anybody's guess. The 13 rooms are as unique and colorful as the wildflowers they're named for.

Red Corral Ranch
1-866-833-4801
www.redcorralranch.com
505 Red Corral Ranch Rd. (CR 113), Wimberley, TX 78676
Price: Moderate to Expensive

Between Wimberley and Blanco, the Red Corral Ranch is a large facility that frequently hosts weddings, corporate functions, reunions, and spiritual retreats but also rents several freestanding guesthouses to individuals and small groups. Each guesthouse has a full kitchen, grill, and hot tub, and a continental breakfast is included in the price. What makes Red Corral Ranch really stand out are its grounds: over a thousand acres of hike-and-bike trails, along with a walking labyrinth, a cool, crystal-clear, aquifer-fed swimming pool, an organic garden, pecan groves, stands of wildflowers, dozens of white peacocks, and multitudes of deer, butterflies, and birds.

Southwind Bed and Breakfast
512-847-5277 or 1-800-508-5277
www.southwindbedandbreak.com
2701 FM 3237, Wimberley, TX 78676
Price: Inexpensive
Special Features: Children welcome in cabins; limited handicapped access

The property has three guest rooms in its main building, as well as three spacious cabins equipped with full kitchens, two of which are wheelchair accessible; all three accommodate well-behaved children and pets. The rooms in the inn have a formal feel, with wood floors and pretty wallpaper, while the cabins are rustic, with exposed beams crossing the vaulted ceilings.

CULTURE

An enclave of artists, Wimberley has some galleries and cultural events of particular note and a full calendar of festivals. The Cypress Creek Café (see below) hosts two annual festivals that have become local favorites. The **Crawfish Festival**, usually the last Saturday in April, has live music and an enormous catch of crawfish boiled up for partygoers. If hundreds and hundreds of crawfish aren't enough to get you in the mood, perhaps a variety of gumbo, étouffée, red beans and rice, andouille sausage, key lime pie, or bread pudding eaten elbow to elbow might just do the trick. Also hosted by the Cypress Creek Café, the **Wimberley Winter Jazz Festival** brings together jazz musicians from Texas and beyond to play a series of intimate concerts in February.

EmilyAnn Theatre (512-847-6969; www.emilyann.org; P.O. Box 801, Wimberley, TX 78676) The EmilyAnn is an outdoor community theater that stages, among other productions, a summerlong Shakespeare under the Stars, performed entirely by children and young adults no older than high school seniors (the only accredited high school Shakespearean theater in the United States). The theater also hosts a number of family-friendly events such as a holiday tree lighting in December and a Butterfly Festival in April.

Meek Studio (512-847-6768; www.meekstudio.com; 15520 RR 12, Wimberley, TX 78676) Open: Call for hours. The Meek Studio displays new artwork and retrospectives of various well-known Texas artists, but it is mostly known for glimpses it offers of the process and product of Bill Meek, a local glass sculptor. Located a mile and a half north of Wimberley Square.

Wimberley Glass Works (1-800-929-6686; www.wgw.com; 6469 RR 12, San Marcos, TX 78666) Open: Mon.–Sat. 10–5, Sun. noon–5. Glassblowing Mon. and Wed.–Sat. 10:15–12:30 and 1:30–4:30. Opened by Tim de Jong in 1992, the Wimberley Glass Works rose quickly to become one of the region's foremost art glass studios and galleries. While the gallery space here is filled with exquisite handblown glass in every imaginable shape, size, and color, the best part of the Wimberley Glass Works is the live demonstrations where you can see artists coaxing vases, pitchers, stemware, and art out of molten glass. After many years in Wimberley, the Glass Works has a new space on RR 12 halfway between Wimberley and San Marcos, and a new San Marcos address.

DINING

Cypress Creek Café (512-847-2515; www.cypresscreekcafe.com; on the Square, Wimberley, TX 78676) Open: Tue.–Sat. 7:30 AM–8 PM (or 10 PM, depending on the season—call ahead), Sun.–Mon. 7:30 AM–3 PM. While there are many good places to eat in Wimberley, the Cypress Creek Café has been serving up homemade breakfasts, lunches, and dinners for over 25 years now, and they've gotten quite good at it. The lightly breaded Home Style Steak is "griddle fried" and covered with a ladleful of cream gravy and seems much lighter than its cousin, the deep-fried chicken-fried steak. The chicken scampi strikes a delicious balance, with grilled chicken and sautéed mushrooms served over penne with a lemon garlic sauce. You can have a classic BLT or an old-fashioned half-pound hamburger, and then again you could sink your teeth into the hot pesto portabella mushroom sandwich; vegetarians will enjoy the café. Live music almost every night; check the Web site for details.

Picnic in a state park

Texas State Parks

Texas's state parks preserve the natural icons of Texas, the sunsets that stretch for miles, the spring-time fields of bluebonnets, the earnest roadrunners, and pokey armadillos. In the Hill Country, the limestone ravines, extensive caverns, wooded trails, and gurgling streams showcase the diversity of the region's plant life and wildlife. The Hill Country is home to the gray fox, white-tailed deer, armadillo, coyote, opossum, raccoon, bobcat, rock squirrel, and javelina, as well as rarer species, such as the golden-cheeked warbler, who is partial to nesting in the region's Ashe junipers, the Cagle's map turtle, the Guadalupe bass, the Texas salamander, and the Honey Creek Cave salamander.

Given that over 96 percent of the land in Texas is privately owned, the state park system really is a gift to the public. The parks of the Hill Country are a popular recreation destination, particularly for those making day trips from Austin and San Antonio for hiking, biking, climbing, birding, or fishing. Since the parks are so popular, many have capacity limits in an effort to reduce wear and tear on the environment, and it is not unusual for those parks to close because that number has been reached. Scheduling a visit for early morning, after 5 PM, or weekdays is a good way to beat the crowds.

Unfortunately, Texas's state parks, like many around the country, are experiencing serious financial troubles. Belts are so tight that many have scaled back hours, cut unnecessary services, and even closed, rather than repaired, amenities such as restrooms. To avoid disappointment, consider calling your destination in advance of your visit. Despite cutbacks, the staff and rangers remain as helpful, informative, and energized as ever and more than happy to chat about the wonders of their respective parks; visit them in person or online at www.tpwd.state.tx.us. Help support America's natural heritage, get your boots dirty in a Texas state park. Listed alphabetically:

Blanco State Park
(see "Attractions Parks, and Recreation," under
Blanco, above)

Enchanted Rock State Natural Area
325-247-3903
www.tpwd.state.tx.us
16710 RR 965, Fredericksburg TX 78624
The park is 18 miles north of Fredericksburg on
   RR 965.
Open: Daily
Admission: $6. Camping $12, primitive
   camping $8

It is easy to imagine how Enchanted Rock might
have gotten its name. Amid the scrubby woods
of oak, cedar, and mesquite and prairielike grass-
lands, the enormous pink granite dome gleams in
the sun and emits mysterious creaking and groan-
ing sounds that have astounded human visitors
for thousands of years. The Tonkawa Indians
attributed the noises to ghosts, but scientists
now say they are due to the expansion and con-
traction of the rock in the heat of the day and
cool night air. The rock itself, covering 640
acres, is a batholith, an underground rock formation that has been partially exposed by erosion.
The surrounding area is home to abundant
wildlife and birds; a bird checklist is available at
the office. Hiking, primitive camping, and rock
climbing are all options, though campers will
need reservations and climbers must check in at
headquarters. A much-loved natural Hill Country
wonder, Enchanted Rock is on the National
Register of Historic Places and tops many locals'
lists of rural day-trip destinations and sights to
show visitors. Due to the fragility of its environment, the park limits the number of visitors per
day and must close when it reaches capacity. It is
best to arrive early in the morning or after 5 PM;
in both cases consider calling ahead.

Guadalupe River State Park
830-438-2656
www.tpwd.state.tx.us
3350 Park Road 31, Spring Branch, TX 78070
From the intersection of US 281 and TX 46
   (north of San Antonio and west of New
   Braunfels) take TX 46 west, then a right onto
   Park Road 31.

continued on following page

Enchanted Rock State Park

Texas State Parks continued

Open: Daily

Admission: $6. Overnight camping $12–$19 per night, depending on hookups

Hugging an idyllic 9-mile stretch of the river, Guadalupe River State Park is a favorite nature retreat for day-trippers from San Antonio, 30 miles to the south, and a popular place for camping, picnicking, and hiking. Depending on the time of year and rainfall, the river can be placid or powerful, making tubing, swimming, and fishing along the bald-cypress-lined river an adventure. This park is also a favorite of canoeists. The 5-mile equestrian trail (you'll need to bring your own horse!) is also open to mountain bikers. Nature enthusiasts may enjoy the adjacent Honey Creek State Natural Area (www.honeycreekfriends.com), which is open only for guided interpretive tours offered Saturday at 9 AM; call Guadalupe River State Park to confirm.

Hill Country State Natural Area

830-796-4413

www.tpwd.state.tx.us

10600 Bandera Creek Rd., Bandera TX 78003
From Bandera take TX 173 south, across the Medina River to CR 1077, and turn right. Follow the paved road for 10 miles, continuing along the unpaved road and following signs to the park.

Open: Daily Feb.–Nov., weekends Dec.–Jan.

Admission: Day use $6; primitive camping $3

This 5,300-acre park is minimally developed, making it a good choice for more experienced hikers, backpackers, and campers who enjoy primitive sites. The 40 miles of trails are terrific for horseback riding and mountain biking. The water in the park is not potable, so be sure to bring your own.

Inks Lake State Park

(See "Highland Lakes," above)

Goin' fishin'

Longhorn Cavern State Park
830-598-2283; 1-877-441-2283
www.tpwd.state.tx.us
P.O. Box 732, Burnet, TX 78611
Located on Park Road 4, approximately
  6 miles west and 6 miles south of Burnet, off
  US 281
Open: Daily
Admission: Adults $10.95, children $5.95 for
  guided tour of the cavern
Special Features: The park offers 90-minute
  tours, covering 1.25 miles of trail; call ahead
  or see Web site for details.

A natural landmark, Longhorn Cavern is an
amazing formation with a history to match. Years
ago, a drop in underground water levels dissolved, bit by tiny bit, the solid limestone rock,
slowly carving a subterranean streambed and
cavern with soft undulating curves. The
Comanche used the cavern for shelter, and with
the temperature inside a constant 68 degrees, it
is easy to speculate why. Legends surround the
cavern—for instance, there has been talk of Sam
Bass's hidden treasure of $2 million in stolen
bills—but the big draw is its beauty.

Lost Maples State Natural Area
830-966-3413
www.tpwd.state.tx.us
37221 FM 187, Vanderpool, TX 78885
5 miles north of Vanderpool on FM 187
Open: Daily
Admission: Day use $5; $6 Oct.–Nov.; primitive
  camping $3

Lost Maples State Natural Area covers more than
2,000 acres of craggy limestone canyons, with
the clear-running Sabinal River, grassy plateaus,
and one very dramatic and lovely stand of unusual
Uvalde bigtooth maples, whose fall color is by far
the brightest in the area. During the last two
weeks of October and the first two weeks of
November, visitors descend on the park to catch a
glimpse of the glowing red and yellow leaves. The

bigtooth maple can stand 50 feet tall, is drought
tolerant, prefers the local limestone and igneous
soil, and has a fragile root system that is easily
damaged by foot traffic— visitors are urged to
remain on the 11 miles of marked trails. It is possible to drive the one mile into the park to a scenic
viewing location, a particularly helpful option for
those with limited mobility. Lost Maples is home
to many birds, including the rare green kingfisher
and the endangered golden-cheeked warbler,
making the park a boon for birders.

**Lyndon B. Johnson State Park
and Historic Site**
830-644-2252
www.tpwd.state.tx.us
1048 State Park Road 49, Stonewall, TX 78671
The park is located on US 290, 14 miles west of
  Johnson City and 2 miles east of Stonewall.
Open: Daily 8–5 Admission: Free

Dedicated to President Lyndon B. Johnson, the
state park and historic site are located across
from the LBJ Ranch. The park offers fishing,
swimming, and picnicking, and, in spring, its
many, many acres are dotted with wildflowers.
Visitors have a chance to see the buffalo, longhorn cattle, wild turkey, and white-tailed deer
that roam in grassy enclosures. The visitors center contains exhibits of memorabilia from
President Johnson's time in office, and informa-
tional bus tours of the LBJ Ranch are available
(see "LBJ's Texas," above). The Sauer-Beckmann
Living History Farm, just east of the visitor center, brings to life daily existence on a Texas farm
in the early 1900s.

Old Tunnel Wildlife Management Area
1-866-978-2287
www.tpwd.state.tx.us
Texas Parks and Wildlife Department, 102 E.
  San Antonio St., Suite B, Fredericksburg,
  TX 78624

continued on following page

Texas State Parks continued

Despite its Fredericksburg mailing address, the area is located along Old San Antonio Rd. approximately 11 miles south of Fredericksburg and 13 miles north of Comfort.

Open: Daily, sunrise to sunset; May–Oct. bat viewing nightly

Admission: Free. Guided tours: adults $5, seniors $3, children $2, children 5 and under free.

The Old Tunnel Wildlife Management Area occupies a snug 16 acres, but up to three million Mexican free-tailed bats (TADARIDA BRASILIENSIS) and 3,000 cave myotis bats (MYOTIS VELIFER) call this old and abandoned railroad tunnel home from April to October. As the story goes, when the railroad moved out in 1942, the bats moved in and have been here ever since. They emerge from their tunnels each night in a spectacular vortex of flapping wings, heading toward either the Guadalupe or Pedernales River in search of food—moths and insects—and return to the tunnel sometime after midnight. Bat viewing is possible from either the upper viewing areas, which are open daily and free of charge, or from the lower viewing area, which is part of a guided tour (open Thu.–Sun. during bat season).

Pedernales Falls State Park

830-868-7304

www.tpwd.state.tx.us

2585 Park Road 6026, Johnson City, TX 78636

From Johnson City take FM 2766 east for 9 miles. From Austin take US 290 west 32 miles, then north on FM 3232 for 6 miles.

Open: Daily

Admission: Day use $5, camping $20, primitive camping $10

The Pedernales River runs through this 5,000-acre park, at one point gently tumbling down a series of stepped layers of limestone known as the Pedernales Falls, the park's main attraction. Depending on the time of year and amount of rainfall, the current can be brisk, slight, or even nonexistent. Those unfamiliar with the Hill Country's rivers and streams should always be on alert for any change in water level, which may indicate an imminent, and quite possibly immediate, flooding, even in pleasant weather. The park features opportunities for camping, picnicking, swimming, and tubing. Additionally, there are close to 20 miles of hiking and mountain-biking trails. For birders, this park has an enclosed watching station, which is wheelchair accessible, with feeders providing lots of close-ups of the area's many birds.

ATTRACTIONS, PARKS, AND RECREATION

Natural attractions in Wimberley include **Blue Hole** (www.friendsofbluehole.org), a renowned natural swimming hole where folks come to splash and swing among the cypress trees, just a short walk from the center of town. Stunning scenery is visible from **Devil's Backbone**, a steep scenic ridge that offers stunning views; drive out RR 12 to RR 32 and turn west. **Bella Vista Ranch** (512-847-6514; www.texasoliveoil.com or www.bvranch.com; 3101 Mt. Sharp Rd., Wimberley, TX 78676) opened a *frantoio*, or olive pressing facility, in 2001, and it offers samples of the oils fresh off the press as well as wines made from grapes and berries grown on the ranch. Open: Mon. and Thu.–Sat. 10–5, Sun. noon–4. Tours at 10, 1, and 3.

RECREATION IN THE HILL COUNTRY

A tremendous online resource for all outdoor recreation in Texas is www.texasoutside.com.

Bicycling

Bicycling, both road and mountain biking, is big in Central Texas, especially in Austin and the Hill Country. Rentals are available through **Hill Country Bicycle Works** (830-990-2609, www.hillcountrybicycle.com; 702B E. Main St., Fredericksburg, TX 78624. Additional location: 830-896-6864; 141 W. Water St., Kerrville, TX 78028).
Helpful Web sites include:

Cycle Texas (www.cycletexas.com)

Bicycle Texas (www.bicycletexas.com)

Hill Country Bicycle Touring Club (www.hcbtc.org)

Texas State Park System (www.tpwd.state.tx.us/exptexas/bike)

Bird Watching

The Hill Country is a great spot to catch a glimpse of rare, migratory, and native birds. Online, **Texas Parks and Wildlife**, www.tpwd.state.tx.us, and the **Travis County Audubon Society**, www.travisaudubon.org, both offer a wealth of information. See "Suggested References" in the Information chapter for a selection of bird-watching guides.

Boating, Canoeing, and Kayaking

Boat rentals are available at the Highland Lakes and in Kerrville.

Camping

The state parks dotting the Hill Country offer a variety of camping opportunities. There is a state park with camping on Inks Lake in the Highland Lakes and another in Blanco (see "Texas State Parks," p. 222). Kerrville's city park has camping. A terrific online source for all camping in the region—private or public, tent or RV—is **www.texasoutside.com**.

Climbing

Cypress Valley Canopy Tours (512-264-8880; www.cypressvalleycanopytours.com; 1223 Paleface Ranch Rd., Spicewood, TX 78669) Tour participants use steel zip lines to travel between treetop platforms among old-growth cypresses. In the Hill Country 30 minutes west of Austin. Price: $60–$125.

Mountain Madness Rock Climbing School (512-329-0309; www.mtmadness.com; P.O. Box 162643, Austin, TX 78716) Weekend classes held at Enchanted Rock State Natural Area near Fredericksburg. Price: $100 for one day, $160 for two.

Fishing

There is plenty of fishing in the Highland Lakes and state parks; you don't need a license to fish from shore in a Texas State Park. See www.tpwd.state.tx.us for details. Other online resources include www.texasoutside.com and www.txfishing.com.

Golf

Lady Bird Johnson Municipal Golf Course (830-997-4010 or 1-800-950-8147; www.golffredericksburg.com; 341 Golfers Loop, Fredericksburg, TX 78624)

Scott Schreiner Municipal Golf Course (877-660-7200; 1 Country Club Dr., Kerrville, TX 78028)

Swimming

Swimming is available at the beaches of the Highland Lakes and several of the state parks (see separate listings).

Tours

The **Bluebonnet Trail**, **Texas Lavender Trail**, and **Texas Wine Trail** are self-guided. The **Austin Steam Train** (512-477-8468; www.austinsteamtrain.org.) runs vintage trains through the Hill Country, and boat cruises are available on the **Highland Lakes.** (See separate listings on all the above.) **Texpert Tours** (512-383-8989; www.texperttours.com) offers a variety of tours throughout Austin and the Hill Country.

Tubing

Probably the best spot to tube in the Hill Country is Blanco State Park (see "Attractions, Parks, and Recreation" under Blanco).

6

Nearby and In Between

En Route

Interstate 35, which connects Austin and San Antonio, also passes Georgetown, New Braunfels, and San Marcos, all of them great places to pull in for a meal, a day, or even a weekend. Thirty miles north of Austin, historic Georgetown is a remarkably well-preserved town with a restored courthouse at its center, antiques shops surroundings its square, and a lovely hike-and-bike trail. Thirty miles south of Austin, San Marcos has become known for its outlet malls, though nature enthusiasts will enjoy a trip to the educational Aquarena Center for a ride down the river on a glass-bottom boat. Another 20 miles south, New Braunfels has a reputation for some of the best river tubing in the area and as home to lovely historic Gruene.

Lodging Price Code

Inexpensive	Up to $100
Moderate	$100 to $150
Expensive	$150 to $250
Very Expensive	Over $250

Cypress trees along the Guadalupe

Dining Price Code

Inexpensive	Up to $12
Moderate	$12 to $25
Expensive	$25 to $40
Very Expensive	$40 or more

Georgetown

Straddling I-35, Georgetown is located at the spot where the fertile plains of East Texas start to give way to the jagged wooded ravines and sloping hills of the Hill Country. On a former settlement area of the Tonkawa Indians, Georgetown was founded in 1848, its free-flowing San Gabriel River and abundant timber and farmland drawing immigrants first from the mountain regions of the American South, then Scandinavia and Eastern and Western Europe.

Georgetown is home to Southwestern University. A Methodist school chartered in 1875, Southwestern is often cited at the state's oldest university. Southwestern's relationship with Georgetown is one of quiet intermingling. The university's studious student body of 1,200 seems more focused on community service projects than partying, and the town remains quiet, peaceful, and oddly devoid of the bars, burger joints, and rundown student housing commonly associated with college towns. The school's contribution to the town is certainly felt in other ways as well. Concerts, gallery shows, and theatrical productions are offered throughout the school year and are open to the public; details at www
.southwestern.edu.

Georgetown has successfully preserved its historic downtown, which comprises dozens of detail-rich buildings and homes dating to the 1880s gathered around a traditional Texas square, with a courthouse in its center. The seat of Williamson County, Georgetown has become a popular commuter town for families and, with recent construction of age-restricted developments, a home for retirees who come for the area's livability, climate, and access to Austin. Rapid growth has Georgetown focused on maintaining the small-town atmosphere that makes it such an enjoyable destination.

LODGING

Harper-Chesser Historic Inn
512-864-1887
www.harperchesserinn.com
1309 College St., Georgetown, TX 78626
Price: Moderate
Special Features: Limited handicapped access

Peachy-pink walls, green accents, and delicate hand-painted, nature-themed murals set the tone for this four-bedroom B&B near Southwestern University. The rooms have tall ceilings and windows, giving them an airy spaciousness, and pretty window treatments that don't feel too fussy. The main house, built in 1890 by a local judge, was an addition to the original limestone abode constructed 30 years prior by a local doctor. The inn is on the

Browse the antiques shops in Georgetown

National Register of Historic Places. Owners Ruth and R.C. whip up a gourmet breakfast each morning, making this inn more than just a place to stay the night.

San Gabriel Motor Court

512-819-9374
www.sangabrielmotel.com
103 N. Austin Ave., Georgetown, TX 78626
Price: Inexpensive
Special Features: Limited Handicapped Access

The core units of the San Gabriel Motor Court were built in the 1930s, when such single-story lodging units were standard. Built along the San Gabriel River and the city's hike-and-bike path, near downtown Georgetown, the San Gabriel Motor Court has expanded its facilities with the addition of two new wings. Some of the individually decorated rooms are enhanced by one-of-a-kind furniture and decorations handcrafted from cedar, mesquite, and iron by local artisan Paul Burkle. These items are for sale, and custom orders are welcome. A variety of bed configurations, the surrounding wide-open lawns, and the imaginative southwestern or rustic, early-Texas-themed rooms make the San Gabriel Motor Court a nice alternative to the hotels lining the highway, especially for families or anyone who enjoys the comfortable, lived-in feel of vintage Americana.

CULTURE

Georgetown Palace Theatre (512-869-7469; www.thegeorgetownpalace.org; 810 S. Austin Ave., Georgetown, TX 78627) Built in 1925, the Palace Theatre was originally a silent movie house. "Talkies" arrived in 1929, and the building was given its present art deco facade in 1936. A respite from the hard times during the Great Depression, World War II, and droughts in the 1950s, the Palace was the town's cultural and creative center. In 1989, the building was put up for sale; three hundred concerned citizens bonded together to purchase, improve, and convert the Palace from a cinema to a theater. A true community endeavor, the now-thriving Palace stages some nine spirited shows a season, offering up both enjoyable theater and a slice of small-town Texas.

Georgetown's historic small-town ambience makes a scenic backdrop for a variety of festivals and special events. In April, Georgetown, the "Red Poppy Capital of Texas," hosts the **Red Poppy Festival** (www.redpoppyfestival.com) and several events for the region-wide **Saveur Texas Hill Country Wine and Food Festival** (512-249-6300; www.texas wineandfood.org). In June, the Georgetown Symphony Society (www.georgetowntexas symphony.org) produces **Festival of the Arts,** a weekend of live classical music performances and a juried art show. **Market Days** (www.downtowngeorgetownassociation.org/ MarketDays) are held from 10 until 5 on the second Saturday of each month between March and December. And the **Georgetown Farmers' Market** (512-281-3699; www.gtfma .com) presents locally grown produce and homemade products between May and November. The town's particularly comprehensive Web site, www.visitgeorgetown.com, lists all upcoming events.

DINING

Dos Salsas
512-930-2343
www.dossalsas.com
1104 S. Main St., Georgetown, TX 78628
Open: Mon.–Thu. 7 AM–9 PM, Fri.–Sat. 7 AM–10 PM, Sun. 7 AM– 3 PM
Price: Inexpensive

The minute you arrive at your table, expect hot tortilla chips and the two kinds of salsa, one spicy and one less so, that give Dos Salsas its name. The food is fresh and tasty and comes in numerous combinations for diners who like a lot of variety. Tacos, enchiladas, tostadas, and tamales come stuffed with chicken, beef, brisket, pork, or *carne guisada* (slow-cooked beef tips with gravy), paired with rice, beans, or guacamole salad. For dessert, the *tres leches* cake is delicate and sweet. This family-run restaurant is a local favorite and, consequently, frequently packed.

Monument Café
512-930-9586
www.themonumentcafe.com
1953 S. Austin Ave., Georgetown, TX 78627

Open: Sun.–Thu. 7 AM–9 PM, Fri.–Sat. 7 AM–10 PM
Price: Inexpensive to Moderate

Open since 1995, the Monument has quickly become an institution in Georgetown; trying to get a seat in its '40s-style dining room or lunch counter at meal time can take some patience. Diners flock here for the fried whole catfish, the Kobe steaks, and the fried chicken with cream gravy, all served with generous side portions of comfort foods. The Monument makes old-time favorites, but they are very food-forward, serving as many organic vegetables and dairy products, free-range eggs, and fresh-squeezed juices as possible. If you need a reason to save room for dessert, you'll find it at the Monument. From the thick, nutty crust made of toasted pecans, through its silky rich chocolate mousse filling, and the homemade whipped cream slathered on top, the Monument's signature chocolate pie is the real thing.

Wildfire
512-869-3473
www.thewildfire.com
812 S. Austin Ave., Georgetown, TX 78626
Open: Mon.–Fri. 11–9, Sat. 11–10, Sun. 9–9
Price: Inexpensive to Moderate

Just off the main square, a block from the Palace Theatre, Wildfire is Georgetown's "date night" restaurant. The oak-fired grill serves as the inspiration for the inventive menu featuring southwestern fare. A casual yet sophisticated adult-friendly ambience pairs nicely with expertly prepared dishes such as ostrich medallions drizzled with a cilantro-citrus demi-glace and agave honey-glazed carrots, oak-grilled Jamaican jerk pork loin with habanero apple chutney, or *pepita*-encrusted American bison strip loin. For dessert, bananas are soaked in brandy and brown sugar, grilled, and topped with vanilla ice cream, chocolate sauce, and a sprinkling of Texas pecans. The Sunday champagne brunch is especially enjoyable.

ATTRACTIONS

Georgetown has earned kudos for its preservation of land for public use and recreation; much of this land adjoins the San Gabriel River, which runs through town. The North and South Forks of the San Gabriel merge in San Gabriel Park, the city's main park and the starting point of miles of hike-and-bike trails, which are dotted with playgrounds and benches and include a lighted walkway to Blue Hole Park, a popular natural swimming hole. Georgetown Parks and Recreation (512-930-3595; www.georgetownparks.org) has all the details. Lake Georgetown is a popular recreation area located 3.5 miles northwest of town. The Army Corps of Engineers operates several parks along the lake, each with picnicking, camping, boating, fishing, and swimming; details online at www.swf-wc.usace.army.mil/georgetown.

Inner Space Cavern
512-931-2283
www.innerspace.com

Georgetown, TX 78627
Off I-35, exit 259
Hours: Memorial Day to Labor Day daily 9–6, Labor Day to Memorial Day Mon.–Fri. 9–4,
Sat.–Sun. 10–5. Closed mid-December to Jan. 2.
Admission: Adventure Tour, adults $14.95, children 4–12 $8.95, children 3 and under free

Inner Space Cavern is located directly below busy I-35; it was discovered in 1963 during drilling to determine the stability of the ground prior to highway construction. As the holes were bored, the bit being used abruptly dropped dozens of feet, indicating the presence of a cavity beneath 40 feet of solid limestone. An adventurous highway worker rode a drill bit underground to take the first peek. Today, Inner Space Cavern is one of the more accessible caves in the region, with a unique cable car, paved trails, and a year-round temperature of 72 degrees. The standard Adventure Tour lasts 1 hour and 15 minutes and covers three-quarters of a mile; longer and more detailed tours are available.

The Candle Factory
512-863-6025 or 1-800-955-6973
www.thecandlefactory.com
4411 S. I-35, Georgetown, TX 78628
Hours: Mon.–Sat. 9–5:30, Sun. 10–5:30

If you've been looking for candles in the shape of hot peppers, penguins, pilgrims, or the state of Texas, then look no further than the Candle Factory, which has hundreds of shapes, sizes, and scents to choose from. The Candle Factory is one of the last places in the country to make its tapers entirely by hand, dipping them 17 times in a blended wax, guaranteeing that each is unique.

New Braunfels and Gruene

New Braunfels, located right off I-35 approximately 45 miles south of Austin and 30 miles north of San Antonio, was established under the auspices of the *Verein zum Schutze deutscher Einwanderer* in Texas, the "Society for the Protection of German Immigrants in Texas," or, simply, the *Adelsverein*.

As immigration to Texas picked up in the early 1800s, word of the region's potential reached a group of 21 enterprising noblemen near Mainz, Germany, who started making plans for a mass immigration and sent two men to investigate the possibilities. In May 1842, Count Joseph Boos-Waldeck and Count Victor August of Leiningen-Westerburg-Alt-Leiningen arrived and approached Sam Houston, who offered them acreage in the hostile frontier west of Austin, which they politely declined.

In 1845, after much discussion and many failed attempts, the first wagon train of German immigrants staggered into Central Texas. The group founded New Braunfels, named for Prince Carl of Solms-Braunfels, and immediately began readying the parcel of land on the banks of the Comal River to receive more Germans, who would number between 300 and 400 by the following summer. Soon, the operation was handed over to John I. Meusebach, who, confident he could deal diplomatically with the Native Americans in the Hill Country to the west, went on to phase two of *Adelsverein* and founded Fredericksburg in 1846.

Soda fountain, Gruene

Kick up your heels on the creaky wooden dance floor in Gruene Hall.

New Braunfels quickly established itself as a commercial and manufacturing center in the region, feeding, clothing, and fixing the wagons of pioneers headed to the frontier. These days, visitors make the trip to New Braunfels for several reasons. One is Schlitterbahn (see below), the slippery, soaking wet, family magnet of a water park that draws visitors from near and far. Another is the Guadalupe and Comal Rivers, whose lazy courses are perfect for that beloved Central Texas pastime of "tubing," floating slowly with the current on large inflatable inner tubes for hours and hours on end. And then there is Gruene.

In the 1850s, the tiny settlement of Gruene (pronounced "green") was founded by German farmers who built a thriving economy based on cotton growing and processing. By the 1870s a busy cotton gin was up and running, as were a mercantile store and dance hall. When the railroad passed through in the 1880s, commercial development grew and the town prospered. When the boll weevil blight of the 1920s decimated the cotton crops, however, and the Great Depression of the 1930s hit, many residents abandoned the town. In the 1970s interest in preserving the town grew, and it was placed on the National Register of Historic Places. These days, the restored town is a favorite of visitors who come for the restaurants and the music at the historic Gruene Hall (see below). Located just 3 miles north of downtown New Braunfels, Gruene is considered a historic district within that city's limits.

LODGING

In warm weather, water enthusiasts are drawn to New Braunfels like flies to honey. The city is an easy day trip from San Antonio or Austin, but if you plan to spend the night, it is necessary to book a room in advance. Options include chain hotels near the highway and

B&Bs, though if you plan on staying longer a cottage rental might prove a good choice; most accommodations are particularly family friendly.

Comal Inn

830-629-6060
www.comalinn.com
424 Comal Ave, New Braunfels, TX 78130
Price: Moderate

Wood floors, down comforters, and contemporary colors make the Comal Inn a relaxing, modern-feeling place to stay. Spacious individual rooms can sleep four, perfect for couples and those traveling with children. Two cottages, each with two bedrooms and two full baths, can easily accommodate larger groups. The Comal Inn serves an abbreviated continental breakfast.

Comfort Suites

830-643-1100 or 1-877-424-6423
www.choicehotels.com
1489 I-35 North, New Braunfels, TX 78130
Price: Moderate

A decent option close to the highway, towns, and tubing. Outdoor entrances mean no elevator in this two-story complex, but the pool, breakfast, and clean rooms still make it a solid value.

Gruene Homestead Inn

830-606-0216 or 1-800-238-5534
www.gruenehomesteadinn.com
832 Gruene Rd., New Braunfels, TX 78130
Price: Moderate

A collection of seven historic homes, dating from the 1850s to 1900s, was moved to this location, renovated, and readied to receive guests. The Tavern on the Gruene (Open: Mon.–Fri. 3–midnight, Sat. noon–1 AM, Sun. noon–midnight) shares the 8-acre spread.

Gruene Mansion Inn B&B

830-629-2641
www.gruenemansioninn.com
1275 Gruene Rd., New Braunfels, TX
    78130
Price: Expensive

Located beside Gruene Hall, the Gruene Mansion is within easy walking distance to anything in town, including the river.

An inviting bench in front of the general store in Gruene

Converted stables, barns, corncrib, and carriage house are now home to 30 individually decorated rooms, each with its own porch for lounging.

Kuebler Waldrip Haus and Danville Schoolhouse B&B

830-625-8300 or 1-800-299-8372
www.kueblerwaldrip.com
1620 Hueco Springs Loop Rd., New Braunfels, TX, 78132
Price: Moderate

Three buildings, two dating from the mid-1800s, house the 11 rooms of this B&B, which is set on 43 rural acres teeming with deer. It's a particularly family-friendly place, and the size and configuration of the rooms is conducive to groups.

Camping

The region is also known for its camping, and opportunities are ample. Strap the bikes on the car, pack s'more fixings, slide on your flip-flops, and bring the family for that damp-swimsuit, dirty-feet, sticky-face, stay-up-too-late-playing-cards kind of vacation that memories are made of. Prices for overnight camping average about $10 a person, tube and raft rentals are approximately $15–$25, and fishing advice is free.

Gardo's (979-204-3500; www.gardos.us; 4440 River Dr., New Braunfels, TX 78132) A tent and RV campsite along the Guadalupe River opposite a dramatic 600-foot cliff, Gardo's is just good old-time fun. There are two rooms to rent in a lakeside cottage for large families or reunions. No dogs.

KL Ranch Camp (830-625-3038; www.klranchcamp.com; 5300 River Rd., New Braunfels, TX 78132) KL Ranch Camp, on the Guadalupe River, has tent and RV camping. Hot showers are $1. Kids yes, pets no.

Mountain Breeze Camp (830-964-2484; www.mountainbreezecamp.com; 201 Mountain Breeze Camp Rd., New Braunfels, TX 78132) Offers tent camping near the river, tiny cabins lined up in a row in a sunny field, each with air conditioning and a bed, and some RV sites. Family-owned since 1951, Mountain Breeze has a lot of experience with summertime fun. No pets.

CULTURE

The Gruene Historic District (www.gruenetexas.com) is easily identifiable by its gray water tower, which is visible for miles. The town motto is "gently resisting change," and the pace of life flows along as slowly as the nearby river. Packed with shops and restaurants, Gruene is perhaps best known as home of **Gruene Hall** (830-606-1281; www.gruenehall.com; 1281 Gruene Rd., New Braunfels, TX 78130), the oldest dance hall in Texas, with a reputation for fantastic music from the likes of Willie Nelson, Lyle Lovett, and George Strait. Folks come to kick up their heels and throw back a cool one, and the place is packed most weekends.

McKenna Children's Museum (830-620-0939; www.nbchildren.org; 801 W. San Antonio St., New Braunfels, TX 78130) Open: Mon.–Sat. 10–5, Sun. noon–5. Closed Mon. from Labor Day to Memorial Day. Admission: $7.50, Labor Day to Memorial Day $5.50. A bright,

Tables in Gruene Hall, the oldest dance hall in Texas

cheerful, and educational museum for families looking to meet some friends or pass a rainy day.

Museum of Art and Music (830-625-5636; www.nbmuseum.org; 1259 Gruene Rd., New Braunfels, TX 78130) Open: May–August Mon.–Thu. 10–6, Fri.–Sat. 10–8, Sun. noon–8. August–May Mon.–Sat. 10–6, Sun. noon–6. Admission: Adults $4.50, seniors $3, children $1. Located in Gruene, this museum makes for an interesting side trip for Texas music fans. Past exhibits have included in-depth looks at Texas icons, Texas music photographers, and Texas poets.

Museum of Texas Handmade Furniture (830-629-6504; www.nbheritagevillage.com; 1370 Church Hill Dr., New Braunfels, TX 78130) Open: 1–4, Feb.–Nov. Closed Dec.–Jan. and major holidays. Admission: Adults $5, seniors $4, children $1. Located in Heritage Village, this museum displays fine examples of Texas Biedermeier furniture, 1845–80.

Festivals

In April, the **New Braunfels Wine and Saengerfest** (830-608-2100, ext. 252; www.ci.new -braunfels.tx.us) celebrates area music and wine making with dancing, food, and a "Grape Stomp." The tasty **Gruene Music and Wine Fest** (www.gruenehall.com) ushers in October, and the cooler weather of November brings the **Wurstfest** (www.wurstfest.com), New Braunfels's annual 10-day sausage festival, toward the start of the month. Between February and November, the Gospel Brunch in Gruene Hall (www.gruenehall.com) elevates the second Sunday of the month, while the Old Gruene Market Days (830-832-1721; www.gruenemarketdays.com) occupy the third weekend of the month.

Dining and Food Purveyors

Clear Springs Café
830-629-3775
www.clearspringscafe.com
1692 TX 46 South, New Braunfels, TX 78132
Open: Sun.–Thu. 11–9, Fri.–Sat. 11–10. In summertime, they stay open a half hour later.
Price: Inexpensive

After you've spent a day tubing, seafood sure hits the spot, and the Clear Springs Café is a local favorite. The pan-seared tilapia, served with a Dijon peppercorn crawfish sauce, is popular, as are the blackened catfish filets topped with crawfish étouffée; both are served with a scoop of garlic mashed potatoes and steamed vegetables. Even simpler fare like fried catfish, seafood po-boys, fish tacos, or thick-cut steaks keeps the crowds satisfied. The "Texas" in the Texas onion rings must refer to size; a "small" is enormous, as are the portions of just about everything else served at the Clear Springs Café. While this is the original eatery, located in a building that dates back to 1869, the Clear Springs Café also operates restaurants in San Antonio, Midland, Tyler, and Nacogdoches, Texas.

Dry Comal Creek Vineyards
830-885-4121
www.drycomalcreek.com.
1741 Herbelin Rd., New Braunfels, TX 78132
Open: Daily noon–5
Tasting Fee: $3–$6, $3 tours

Don't be fooled by Dry Comal Creek Vineyards' whimsical labels, laid-back operation, and fanciful tasting room—they are serious about their wine. In a secluded valley west of New Braunfels, Dry Comal Creek Vineyards have coaxed native grapes into very dry, dark red wines, such as the 2004 Black Spanish, which was just declared the Texas Grand Star Winner at the 2006 Lone Star International Competition.

For wine tasting in Gruene, stop in the Grapevine (830-606-0093; www.grapevinein gruene.com; 1612 Hunter Rd., New Braunfels, TX 78130).

The Gristmill River Restaurant and Bar
830-625-0684
www.gristmillrestaurant.com
1287 Gruene Rd., New Braunfels, TX 78130
Open: Sun.–Thu. 11–10, Fri.–Sat. 11–11
Price: Inexpensive to Moderate

Located in the shell of an old cotton-gin mill, the Gristmill Restaurant is situated behind Gruene Hall in historic Gruene. Seating is at well-worn wooden tables inside the rough-hewn mill, in the shady river grove, or on the decks overlooking the river.

The menu offers chicken-fried steaks, Polish Wedding Sausage with BBQ sauce, meal-sized salads topped with grilled meats, and whatever fish is the catch of the day, served blackened or grilled. You can kick up the flavor of any sandwich or burger order with the addition of one of the Gristmill's homemade sauces, Spicy Queso, Garlicky Hot Sauce,

Tomatillo Verde, or Gringo Pico de Gallo.
The Gristmill can get crowded, so consider
stopping in early for mealtimes.

Gruene River Grill

830-624-2300
www.gruenerivergrill.com
1259 Gruene Rd., New Braunfels, TX 78130
Open: Sun.–Thu. 11–9, Fri.–Sat. 11–10
Price: Inexpensive

The Gruene River Grill in Gruene is owned
by the same folks as the Clear Springs Café
(see above); in fact, they've included the
popular pan-seared tilapia from Clear
Springs on the menu. The offerings are
mostly comfort foods—a few, such as the
spicy southwestern meat loaf, with a kick.
There are more adventurous signature
items such as the Shrimp Won Ton appetizer in which jumbo shrimp mixed with
cheese, bacon, and serrano peppers are
fried in wonton wrappers and served with
a cherry mustard sauce. The Chipolte
Chicken Diablo, a mix of chicken, mushrooms, tomatoes, and garlic served over
fettuccine and doused with a spicy chipotle

Cold drinks for sale on a hot Texas day

cream sauce, and a grilled salmon entrée with a sweet-chili glaze both pack some heat. The
patios and porches overlooking the river are a fantastic spot for a drink or dessert. To
accommodate demand, the homemade strawberry shortcake, which is really a sour cream
pound cake smothered with sweet strawberries and fluffy whipped cream, comes in two
sizes, for one person or two.

Huisache Grill and Wine Bar

830-620-9001
www.huisache.com
303 W. San Antonio St., New Braunfels, TX 78130
Open: Daily 11–10
Price: Moderate to Expensive
Special Features: Reservations not accepted, but you can call ahead for a spot on the wait-
    ing list

With wood floors and a soaring ceiling, Huisache has panache. The restaurant started out
in a rundown building with a sketchy past, which the owners set about renovating. They
went on to restore adjacent buildings, eventually completing an entire commercial center,
the Grassmarket, now populated by merchants and eateries. This tenacity and dedication is
equally evident in Huisache's culinary endeavors. The sophisticated menu includes
reworked southern staples like an angus beef chicken-fried steak or pecan-encrusted pork

chops served with a Jack Daniel's butter sauce. The Hot and Crunchy Rainbow Trout with a sesame almond breading and jalapeño tartar sauce is decidedly different, while the hot ham and Gouda cheese sandwich with caramelized onions tastes familiar and homey. If you're not tempted yet, the enormous and impressive wine list and homemade desserts are reason enough to stop in at Huisache.

Naegelin's Bakery
877-788-2895
www.naegelins.com
129 S. Seguin, New Braunfels, TX 78130
Open: Mon.–Sat. 6:30 AM–5:30 PM

German strudels and cookies such as *springele*, *pfefernuesse*, and *lebkuchen* have been baked here since 1868. With apricot *kolaches*, bear claws, and ten different kinds of bread pulled fresh from the oven, you really could follow your nose to Naegelin's.

Naegelin's Bakery, "the oldest bakery in Texas"

ATTRACTIONS, PARKS, AND RECREATION

Schlitterbahn
830-625-2531
www.schlitterbahn.com
381 E. Austin St., New Braunfels, TX 78130
Open: Last weekend in April to Labor Day weekend, daily 10 until 6–8 PM; check Web site for specifics
Admission: Adults $34.50, children $28.50

German for "slippery road," Schlitterbahn is the place for soaking wet, family-style fun.

The park is consistently voted one of the best water parks in the country, and there are some obvious reasons why. The park is expansive, built on two different locations along the Comal River, with shuttle service in between. There are numerous chutes (some spring-fed from the river), beaches, slides, pools, tubs, and playgrounds, all very well designed for a variety of age-appropriate thrills. Adventurers may wait over an hour to ride the Master Blaster, a jet-propelled water roller-coaster, while others are perfectly content to float along in tubes on the low waves and currents of The Torrent. While there are plenty of food and drinks for sale inside the park, you are actually allowed to bring your own (no alcohol or glass, however) into the park, where picnic tables are thoughtfully provided. Schlitterbahn has on-site lodging, which, while modest and well-used, is certainly serviceable, with kitchens and BBQ areas for do-it-yourself meals; see Web site for details.

The Rivers

People come from far and wide to spend the afternoon just floating down the rivers in New Braunfels, an activity that can be wonderfully relaxing or invigorating. The gentle little Comal River, the shortest river in the world, begins at Comal Springs in Lanada Park (see below) and travels 2.5 miles to meet the swifter and choppier Guadalupe River in downtown New Braunfels.

The Spanish discovered Comal Springs in 1691, stumbling upon the Native Americans who were living here. Early written references describe the springs and their almost unimaginable amounts of pure cool water surrounded by lovely groves; even today the springs gush 8 million gallons of water per hour, water that is both consistently clear and a refreshing 72 degrees.

The Comal is favored by families, while the Guadalupe has been known for its revelry, an image the city is working to shake. Local authorities are in no-nonsense mode after pressure from the public and politicians to keep the river clean and safe. While alcohol is legal on the rivers, there are restrictions, and authorities issue stiff fines for infractions.

Smack in the middle of town, just north of the Main Plaza, **Lanada Park** (www.nbpard .org) is a terrific place for recreation. Fun for the whole family, the park has miniature golf ($2) and a miniature train ($2), as well as the gentle 1.6-mile Panther Canyon Nature Trail (trail map available in the Parks Department Office). Adjacent **Prince Solms Park** (830-608-2165; www.nbpard.org) is home to the Chute, a section of the Comal River channeled by concrete that provides a smooth, swift ride for tubers. Admission, parking, and tube rental are $5 apiece. Fishing is another popular pastime in area parks; anglers enjoy the Guadalupe River for its rainbow and brown trout, though largemouth, smallmouth, striped, and Guadalupe bass, as well as sunfish, also swim the river.

Tube Rental

There are dozens of tube rental places up and down the rivers, and all tend to follow the same general rules, routines, and pricing. Each outfit allows guests to park their car at the rental location, to which a free shuttle service downstream will provide a lift back. Generally, rental fees run $10–$15, and life jackets are free. Consider paying a few dollars extra for the tube with a bottom in order to avoid scraping yours. The Web sites below post handy checklists of what to bring and expect, and many have coupons you can print and bring with you for discounts.

Texas Tubes (830-626-9900; www.texastubes.com; 250 Meusebach St., New Braunfels, TX 78130)

Gruene River Company (830-625-2800 or 1-888-705-2800; www.toobing.com; 1404 Gruene Rd., New Braunfels, TX 78130)

Rockin 'R' River Rides (1-800-55FLOAT; www.rockinr.com; 193 S. Liberty St. for the Comal River and on Gruene St. for the Guadalupe River, New Braunfels, TX 78130)

Nearby

For more water recreation, Canyon Lake (830-964-3341; www.swf-wc.usace.army.mil or www.canyonlakechamber.com), located 20 miles north of New Braunfels, has eight public parks around its 80 miles of shoreline. These seasonal parks, managed by the Army Corps of Engineers, offer plenty of opportunities for fishing, swimming, camping, boating, and picnicking. Thirty-seven miles west of New Braunfels, Guadalupe River State Park (see "Texas State Parks," above) is a nice natural retreat with lots of swimming, tubing, and hiking trails.

San Marcos

San Marcos is located on I-35 at the eastern edge of the Hill Country, 30 miles south of Austin, 49 miles north of San Antonio, making it an easy day trip from either city. Home to a state university, two huge outlet shopping areas, and plenty of recreation, San Marcos makes an agreeable side trip.

Established in 1846, San Marcos has always been a crossroads. The site of several failed missions in the 1700s, it was an important stopping point for travelers on the Old San Antonio Road, the route from northern Mexico to Nacogdoches in East Texas, used by Native Americans and the Spanish crisscrossing Texas. It was on the Chisholm Trail, used for the cattle drives between 1864 and 1884. Southwest Texas State Normal School, later Southwest Texas State University, and now Texas State University–San Marcos, was chartered in 1899. The San Marcos Baptist Academy followed in 1907, establishing the city as an education center and diversifying its economy.

With lovely natural resources, San Marcos has long been a regional recreation destination. Aquarena Springs flows at a rate of 150 million gallons of crystal-clear water a day, feeding the San Marcos River, which runs through the city. By the 1960s a resort had grown up around Aquarena Springs, Wonder World was opened as an attraction, and the tourist industry became a reliable and growing source of income. At the same time, population growth, increasing water demands, and the constant threat of drought have been a cause for concern for the spring's future. Both the San Marcos River Foundation (www.sanmarcosriver.org) and Aquarena Center (see below) work to educate the public about the importance of their river, a fragile ecosystem that is home to several endangered species.

These days, San Marcos has the comfortable, lived-in feel of a college town, with an old-fashioned town square lined with casual eateries and shops, and is rapidly becoming a residence for commuters to Austin. Just minutes from Wimberley, San Marcos is also a good jumping-off point into the Hill Country.

LODGING

Crystal River Inn
1-888-396-3739
www.crystalriverinn.com
326 W. Hopkins St., San Marcos, TX 78666
Price: Moderate
Special Features: Limited free WiFi

The Crystal River Inn is a group of several 19th-century buildings conveniently located near downtown San Marcos, with a wide variety of accommodations. The decor in the rooms of the Victorian-style Main House and the Young House, the town's first apartment

Statue of Texas Ranger Jack C. Hays in front of the courthouse in San Marcos

building, ranges from ranch to Victorian to English country garden, but modern amenities keep the rooms from seeming dated. The Rock House, a bungalow from the 1930s, has two suites and two additional rooms, and two fully furnished apartments are available for longer stays. Reserve early for the popular Murder Mystery series; the fun begins in August and runs until January.

Eastwood Hill
512-805-0200
www.eastwoodhill.com
200 Eastwood Lane, San Marcos, TX 78666
Price: Moderate

For a more rural setting, consider the 25 Hill Country acres west of San Marcos that are home to Eastwood Hill. The original four-room cottage was built in 1850, the columns and two-story wraparound porches added in 1900; the overall effect is simple, rustic charm. The four guest rooms at Eastwood Hill are simply decorated with richly painted walls offset by iron beds dressed with crisp linens and understated artwork. The lovely complimentary breakfast is continental on weekdays and sit-down on weekends.

Hampton Inn and Suites–San Marcos
512-754-7707
www.hamptoninn.com
106 I-35 North, San Marcos, TX 78666

Despite its highway-side location, the Hampton is remarkably quiet. The building feels newer than some of its neighbors, with a spacious lobby, pool, complimentary breakfast buffet, and microwave popcorn in each room. A basic hotel near the outlet malls that is reliably neat and clean.

CULTURE

Museums
It may be a little hard to locate, but the **Wittliff Gallery of Southwestern and Mexican Photography** (512-245-2313; 7th floor of the Albert B. Alkek Library, Texas State University–San Marcos, TX 78666. Open: Mon., Tue., Fri. 8–5, Wed.–Thu. 8–7, Sat. 9–5, Sun. 2–6) curates provocative, insightful, and educational exhibits that appeal to both art aficionados and history buffs.

Festivals
San Marcos festivals make a good day trip from either Austin or San Antonio. In May, the city of San Marcos celebrates the **Texas Natural/Western Swing Festival** (www.ci.san -marcos.tx.us), with a weekend of Texas history, traditions, and music in Courthouse Square, featuring a "Texas Grown" farmers' market. Also in May, the **Viva Cinco de Mayo** (512-353-8482; www.vivacincodemayo.org; Hays County Civic Center, San Marcos, TX 78666) and state championship **Menudo Cook-Off** are held together and add up to great

fun. In October, the **San Marcos River Fall Fest** (512-353-1103) fills San Marcos Plaza with music, games, food, arts and crafts, and kiddie rides. December brings the **Sights and Sounds of Christmas** (512-393-5900; www.sights-n-sounds.org), a festival of lights, food, and music along San Marcos Plaza and San Marcos City Park.

DINING

Café on the Square
512-369-9999
126 S. LBJ Drive, San Marcos, TX 78666
Open: Daily 6 AM–11 PM
Price: Inexpensive
Special Features: Live music Wed. nights

This casual spot on the square is popular with locals and students who come for the good food, friendly service, and preread copies of the newspaper. Simple Mexican-inspired breakfasts, burgers, soups, and sandwiches for lunch, and a more elaborate and adventurous dinner menu.

Centerpoint Station
512-392-1103
www.centerpointstation.com
3946 IH-35 South (exit 200), San Marcos, TX 78666
Open: Mon.–Wed. 10–8, Thu.–Sat. 10–9, Sun. 11–6. Bakery opens Mon.–Sat. 8 AM, Sun. 9.
Price: Inexpensive

A welcome change from the usual highway-side offerings and the meager outlet mall pickin's across the way, Centerpoint Station is a very casual roadside restaurant that also sells gifts, gags, and fudge. While the Centerpoint is not as old as it seems, its baked goods, hamburgers, and milkshakes hark back to a time when food was truly homemade. Try the warm cinnamon roll, a fruit *kolache*, or some "San Marcos River Mud," a frosted slice of chocolate Texas sheet cake warmed and topped with Texas-made Blue Bell ice cream. It beats drive-thru hands down.

Hill Country Grill and Martini Bar
512-396-6100
www.hillcountrygrill.com
100 W. Hopkins St., on the Square, San Marcos, TX 78666
Open: Mon.–Thu. 11–9, Fri.–Sat. 11–10
Price: Inexpensive to Moderate

Located in a historic building on the square, the Hill Country Grill has tall windows and ceilings, and vaults that hint at its former role as a bank. The grill features American bistro food. The lunch menu, which combines favorites from the dinner menu with a large selection of sandwiches and burgers, is a good value.

'Cue

If you're coming to Texas, chances are you're expecting to sample some drip-down-your-chin juicy BBQ. Before you settle in with a dozen paper napkins and a pack of saltines, you might like to know the provenance of the tradition of which you are about to partake. Though the earliest details are somewhat murky, we know that folks around the world have been cooking outdoors since the dawn of time. At some point, these chefs began to dig pits to cook in, concentrating heat, smoke, and flavor and rendering even tough, stringy, and sinewy slabs of meat edible, moist, and tender. From clambakes to pig roasts, each culture has its version. The origins of the name—barbecue—are even more elusive, but theories abound. It may derive from BARBACOA, the Spanish version of the name that the Taino Indians of the Caribbean give to the process they had perfected of slow-cooking and smoking large pieces of meat over a pit fire.

In the United States, the style and flavor of BBQ depend on the region. In the Southeast, folks love to drown their pork BBQ in a sweet tomato sauce with a vinegary twang, while the Southwest favors its meat dry-rubbed without any sauce at all. Chicago BBQ is heavy on both the sauce and the pepper. Generally speaking, the farther north you go, the greater the chance that if you order BBQ, you'll get chicken. In Texas, BBQ has always meant beef above all. Typically, the meat is dry-rubbed, smoked, and sauced with various signature concoctions that run the gamut from sweet and smoky to hot and spicy. Many BBQ aficionados in Texas will insist that until you've made the trip to Lockhart 30 miles south of Austin and stuffed yourself silly, you don't even know what BBQ is. In Lockhart you'll find Kreuz Market, the highest evolution of BBQ in Central Texas, by most accounts.

Kreuz Market (512-398-2361; www.kreuzmarket.com; 619 N. Colorado St., Lockhart, TX 78644) Kreuz (pronounced "krites") Market will serve you a huge hunk of hot-from-the-pit beef, pork, or sausage, wrapped in butcher paper, a meal you will likely remember for years to come. No sauce and no utensils come with your order—the custom for over 100 years—you get just meat, some saltines, a huge pickle, and half an onion and off you go to one of the communal tables to dig in. Many customers come for the brisket alone, but the prime rib and clod (shoulder) have garnered raves, and although it is very un-Texan, the pork chop is fabulous. When Kreuz moved from more modest digs down the street to this newer, larger space in 1999, they updated their menu by adding German potato salad, sauerkraut, and beans. Other than that, happily, they haven't changed a thing. Open: Mon.–Sat. 10:30–8.

Palmer's Restaurant Bar and Courtyard

512-353-3500
www.palmerstexas.com
218 Moore St., San Marcos, TX 78666
Open: Sun.–Thu. 11–10, Fri.–Sat. 11–11
Price: Inexpensive to Moderate

Located in historic west San Marcos near the university, Palmer's has an extensive menu of steaks, pastas, poultry, and seafood, served with such sides as southern fried corn fritters with honey. Vegetarians and the health-conscious will find a wide selection. Diners have the pleasant option of eating outdoors beside the gurgling fountain or inside near the crackling fireplace.

The three other BBQ restaurants in Lockhart are all worthy contenders, each ranking high on locals' lists of regional favorites, and all of them open on Sunday, when Kreuz is closed.

Black's BBQ (512-398-2712; www.blacksbbq.com; 215 N. Main St., Lockhart, TX 78644) Open: Sun.–Thu. 10–8, Fri.–Sat. 10–8:30.

Chisolm Trail Lockhart Bar-B-Q & Hot Sausage (512-398-6027; 1323 S. Colorado St., Lockhart, TX 78644) Open: Daily 9–8:30.

Smitty's Market (512-398-9344; 208 S. Commerce St., Lockhart, TX 78644) Mon.–Fri. 7–6, Sat. 7–6:30, Sun. 9–3.

In Central Texas, BBQ is often served with a side of sausage—a smoky beef bratwurst—and the region's gold standard is Elgin sausage, made in Elgin, TX. The three listed here are legendary.

Crosstown BBQ (512-281-5594; 202 S. Avenue C, Elgin, TX 78621) Founded in 1882 and run by the same family since 1968. While there's not much to the decor at Crosstown, the luscious sausage, ribs, and brisket pack a punch that more than makes up the difference. Open: Sun.–Thu. 10–8, Fri.–Sat. 10–10.

Meyer's Elgin Smokehouse (512-281-3331; www.meyerselginsausage.com; 188 US 290 East, Elgin, TX 78621) Tried and true Elgin sausage from an old family recipe since 1949. Wrap a Meyer's plain, sage, or hot sausage in a piece of bread and taste the love. Open Sun.–Thu. 10–7, Fri.–Sat. 10–8.

Southside Market (512-285-3407, 877-285-3407; www.southsidemarket.com. 1212 US 290, Elgin, TX 78621) Made of fresh beef and spiced to an agreeable heat, though if you ate here in the '70s, you'll notice they've lightened up on the pepper since then. Open: Mon.–Thu. 8–8, Fri.–Sat. 8 AM–10 PM, Sun. 9–7.

If you're in Austin in October, the Central Texas BBQ Association (www.ctbbqa.org) hosts an annual BBQ Festival and charity event, benefiting Meals on Wheels, at the Travis County Farmers' Market (6701 Burnet Rd., Austin, TX 78757), a great way to sample hot, succulent 'cue smoked up by local BBQ joints and pit masters. Everyone has a favorite; this could be the chance to taste around and find yours.

ATTRACTIONS, PARKS, AND RECREATION

The spring-fed San Marcos River flows through town, joining the Blanco River and merging with the Guadalupe River farther along in South Texas before spilling into the Gulf of Mexico. The river guarantees water recreation in even the driest summer months; generally speaking, there is just enough current to keep tubing and boating interesting, but not enough to make it dangerous. The newly reopened Rio Vista Dam in the **San Marcos City Park** is a good place to get your feet wet; when cracks were discovered recently in the hundred-year-old low-water dam containing the San Marcos River, the city of San Marcos opted for a full-scale redesign of its urban park. Included in the project were provisions for saving wildlife, environmental enhancements to favor the endangered Texas wild rice, and the creation of three artificial rapids to provide for better water flow and more public recreation. The result is a great place for picnicking and swimming, with a brand-new family-friendly river chute for tubing at Rio Vista Dam. A charitable project of the local Lions Club, **Tube San Marcos** (512-396-5466; www.tubesanmarcos.com; City Park, San Marcos, TX 78666) rents tubes for $6–$14. Open: Daily 10-7. The more adventurous can rent canoes and kayaks at **Austin Canoe and Kayak** (512-396-2386 or 1-888-828-3828; www.austinkayak.com; 4554 I-35 South, San Marcos, TX 78666. Open: Mon.–Fri. 10–6, Sat.–Sun. 10–5) located across from the Tanger Outlet Mall (see below).

Aquarena Center

512-245-7570
www.aquarena.txstate.edu
921 Aquarena Springs Dr., San Marcos, TX 78666
Open: Daily 10–6
Admission: Adults $7, seniors $6, children $5, under age 4 free; discount coupon available
    on the Web site

In 1994, Texas State University–San Marcos acquired the dilapidated Aquarena Springs Resort and re-created it as a nonprofit nature center whose focus is education, conservation, and preservation of the spring. Aquarena Center runs a relaxing glass-bottom boat ride that offers underwater views of the Balcones Fault, the springs, and aquatic life. Additionally, you can stroll through the surrounding wetlands on the Floating Wetlands Boardwalk, or watch the 2 PM fish-feeding at the modest aquarium, which is home to several San Marcos salamanders, fountain darters, and Texas blind salamanders, all federally protected species. Ecotourists, the naturally curious, and children will find Aquarena to be especially fascinating and informative. For the adventurous, Aquarena also runs diving training and certification programs and has volunteer opportunities for underwater gardeners. For more information call 512-245-7541.

Wonder World

www.wonderworldpark.com
512-392-6711
1000 Prospect St., San Marcos, TX 78666
Open: June–Aug. daily 8–8; Sep.–May Mon.–Fri. 9–5, Sat.–Sun. 9–6
Admission: Cave only, adults $12.95, children $9.95; combination ticket, adults $17.95,
    seniors $14.95, children $12.95; discount coupon available on the Web site

Wonder World gives visitors a rare view of the geological effects of earthquakes, one of which formed the Balcones Fault and the Balcones Fault Line Cave, the most-visited cave in Texas and Wonder World's main attraction. The cave is small, slippery, and wet, and since it was formed by an earthquake and not from the effects of millions of years of dripping water, it lacks the typical cave formations found in other area caves. The short tour concludes with a ride up the elevator to the top of the 110-foot Tejas Observation tower for a view of the land aboveground. A train ride takes visitors through a petting zoo, where children can feed deer and other tame animals. The antigravity room is fun, and the gift shop is filled with rock candy and other amusements. Wonder World is well suited to families with elementary-age children.

Shopping

Outlet Malls

Popular attractions in San Marcos are the **Prime Outlets** (512-396-2200 or 1-800-628-9465; www.primeoutlets.com; 3939 I-35 South, San Marcos, TX 78666) and **Tanger Outlets** (512-396-7446 or 1-800-408-8424; www.tangeroutlet.com; 4015 I-35 South, San Marcos, TX 78666), which straddle I-35 at exit 200, approximately 30 minutes south of Austin and 45 minutes north of San Antonio. This is a mecca for discount shoppers, and things can get hectic here on the weekends.

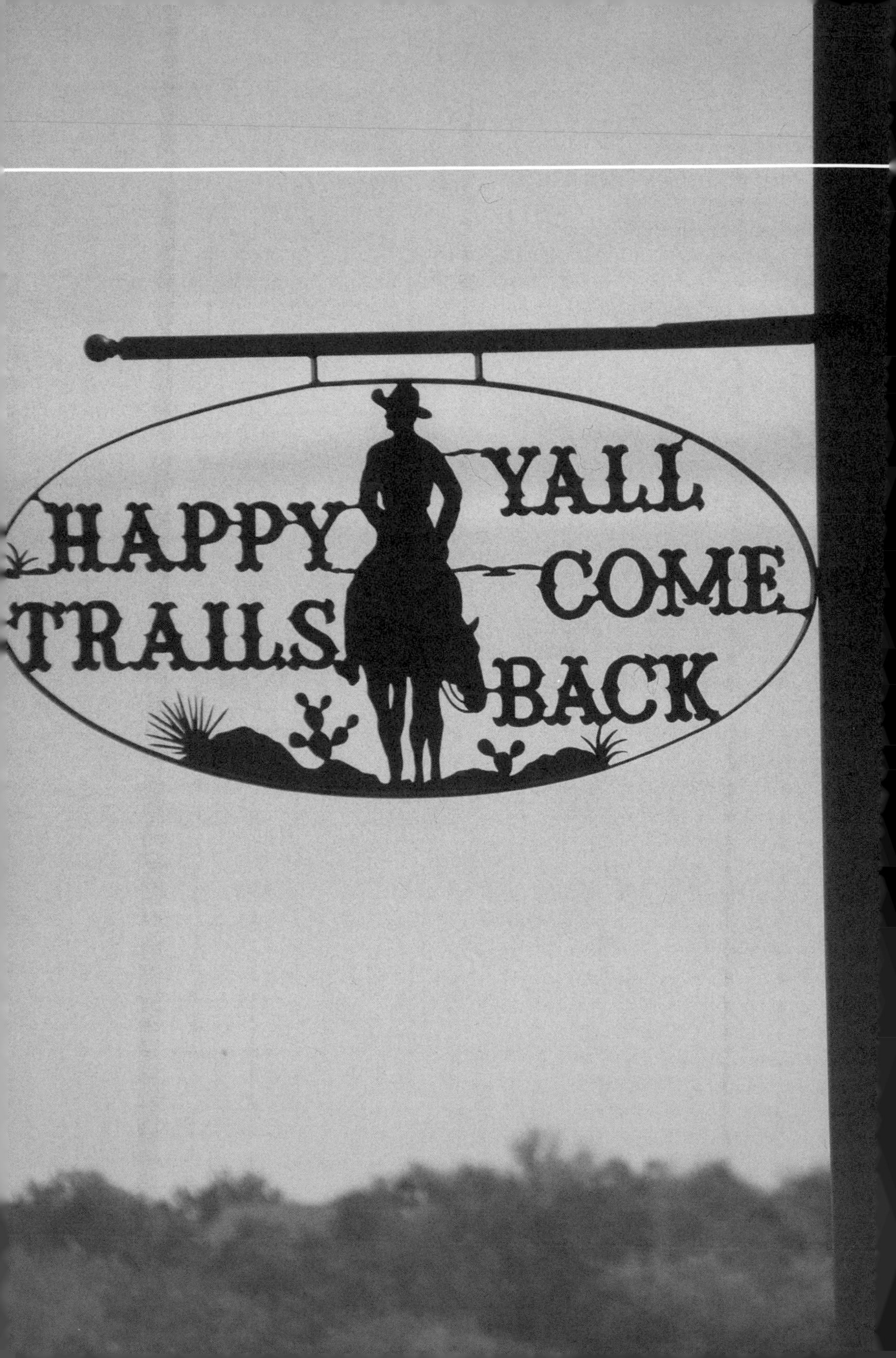
HAPPY
TRAILS
YALL
COME
BACK

7

INFORMATION

Essential Details

Traveling the area covered in this book means crossing several counties, traversing varied terrain, and moving in and out of area codes. The information in this chapter covers the practicalities pertinent to daily life as well as the sorts of details you might need in an emergency:

Emergency Numbers
Area Codes and Zip Codes
Banks and Money
Bibliography
Climate and Weather Reports
Grocery Stores
Handicapped Services
Hospitals
Late-Night Food, Fuel, and Groceries
Licenses
Media: Magazines and Newspapers, Radio Stations
Pests
Religious Services
Shopping
Suggested References
Tourist Information

EMERGENCY NUMBERS

In an emergency, dial 911 and tell the operator your location and the nature of your emergency and your call will be directed to the appropriate responder.
Poison Control is 1-800-222-1222.
For further assistance, see "Hospitals," below.

AREA CODES AND ZIP CODES

Area Codes
Austin 512
San Antonio 210 (Bexar County, including downtown), 830 (Comal County)

THE HILL COUNTRY
Bandera, 830
Blanco 830
Boerne 830, 210
Comfort 830
Fredericksburg 830
Johnson City 830
Kerrville 830
Marble Falls 830
Stonewall 830
Wimberley 512

NEARBY AND IN BETWEEN
Georgetown 512
New Braunfels/Gruene 830
San Marcos 512

Zip Codes
Austin 73344, 73301, 78701–78799

San Antonio 78201–78299

THE HILL COUNTRY
Bandera 78003

Blanco 78606

Boerne 78006, 78015

Comfort 78013

Fredericksburg 78624

Johnson City 78636

Kerrville 78028–78029

Stonewall 78671

Wimberley 78676

NEARBY AND IN BETWEEN
Georgetown 78626–78628

New Braunfels/Gruene 78130–78135

San Marcos 78666, 78667

BANKS AND MONEY

A good many national banks, or banks that participate in national networks, are represented in Austin and San Antonio. However, depending on the bank, you could incur several dollars in fees per ATM withdrawal. Alternatively, many national stores, such as Target
or WalMart, grocery stores, and the post office will allow you "cash back" if you use your
debit card to make a purchase. Though there is frequently a maximum withdrawal of $100,
there is generally no additional fee. In the Hill Country, ATM machines are fewer and farther between, so plan accordingly and be sure to check in advance that a shop or restaurant
accepts credit cards.

CLIMATE AND WEATHER REPORTS

The weather in Austin, San Antonio, and the Hill Country is generally favorable, with about
300 sunny days a year, warm nights, and gentle breezes. Mid-July to mid-September is the
hottest time of year, with temperatures easily reaching the high 90s. Austin and San
Antonio can become stiflingly humid, the Hill Country somewhat less so; the farther west
you travel, the more arid it becomes. Winters tend to be cool but not often freezing, with
snow an aberration. The region gets most of its rainfall in the spring, when steady showers
soak the ground and fill lakes and streams.

The Heat

When it gets hot in Texas, it gets really, really hot. When it gets humid in Texas, it gets
really, really humid. In fact, the best way to describe the summertime in San Antonio, in
particular, is tropical. Since dehydration and heatstroke are not uncommon conditions,
it's important to be aware and prepared. Sunglasses, sunscreen, a light cotton long-
sleeved shirt, a wide-brimmed hat, an umbrella, or even a small spray bottle filled with
water for misting can help provide protection and relief. Staying hydrated is essential;
steering clear of sodas and alcoholic beverages in favor of water, sports drinks, and juice
is considered wise.

Storms

Arriving sometimes without warning, summertime thunderstorms can bring torrential
rain and flash floods. When flash flood warnings are issued, it is best to exercise caution
and avoid creeks, drainage ditches, and low-water road crossings, as signs in these areas
will indicate. Tornadoes frequently accompany thunderstorms, so it is best to listen to or
watch the news for any words of caution. A tornado or severe thunderstorm "watch" serves
as an alert that conditions are favorable for either event, while a tornado or severe thunderstorm "warning" means that either event has been detected on radar and danger may
be imminent. In this case, it is best to seek cover in a substantial building, away from windows. In cooler weather ice storms can occur, and since Central Texas does not maintain a
large fleet of sand or salt trucks, the roads can become treacherously slick and hazardous.
Texas drivers are inexperienced with slick or icy roads, and during storms accidents tend
to be frequent.

HANDICAPPED SERVICES

A good site for information and links worldwide is www.access-able.com. In Austin, San Antonio, and San Marcos, Wheelchair Getaways (1-800-723-6028; www.wheelchairget-aways.com) rents accessible vans. In San Antonio, the Riverwalk will present some challenges for anyone with restricted mobility; see p. 122 for a list of elevators and a Web site address detailing other access points, ramps, and walkways. The Texas Parks and Wildlife Department lists all wheelchair-accessible fishing spots, trails, and wildlife viewing areas on its Web site, www.tpwd.state.tx.us/landwater/land/programs/tourism/wheelchair access.

HOSPITALS

AUSTIN

Brackenridge Hospital (512-324-7000; www.austinsurgicalhospital.com; 601 E. 15th St., Austin, TX 78701)

Children's Hospital of Austin (512-324-8000; www.childrenshospital.com; 1400 I-35 North, Austin, TX 78701)

Seton Medical Center Austin (512-324-1000; www.seton.net; 1201 W. 38th St., Austin, TX 78705)

Seton Shoal Creek (512-324-2000; emergency psychiatric care)

St. David's Medical Center (512-476-7111; www.stdavidsmedicalcenter.com; 919 E. 32nd St., Austin, TX 78705)

SAN ANTONIO

Baptist Medical Center (210-297-7000; www.baptisthealthsystem.com; 111 Dallas St., San Antonio 78205)

Nix Medical Center (210-579-3000; www.nixhealth.com; 414 Navarro St., #600, San Antonio, TX 78205)

Christus Santa Rosa Health Care (210-704-2361; www.christussantarosa.org; 333 N. Santa Rosa Ave., San Antonio, TX 78207)

Hill Country

BANDERA

Closest facility is in Kerrville.

BLANCO

Closest facility is in Fredericksburg.

BOERNE

Closest facility is in San Antonio.

A prickly pear cactus

BURNET
Seton Highland Lakes Hospital (512-715-3000; 3201 S. Water St., Burnet, TX 78611; between Burnet and Marble Falls on US 281)

COMFORT
Closest facility is in Kerrville.

FREDERICKSBURG
Hill Country Memorial Hospital (830-997-4353; www.hillcountrymemorial.com; 211 Medical Dr., Fredericksburg, TX 78624)

JOHNSON CITY
Closest facilities are in Fredericksburg or Marble Falls.

KERRVILLE
Sid Peterson Memorial Hospital (830-896-4200; www.spmh.com; 710 Water St., Kerrville, TX 78028)

MARBLE FALLS
Marble Falls Minor Emergency Center (830-798-1122; www.marblefalls.org; 1701 US 281, Marble Falls, TX 78654)

Seton Highland Lakes Hospital (512-715-3000; 3201 S. Water St., Burnet, TX 78611; between Burnet and Marble Falls on US 281)

STONEWALL
Closest facility is in Fredericksburg.

WIMBERLEY
Central Texas Medical Center (512-847-5512; Wimberley, TX 78676)

Nearby and In Between

GEORGETOWN
St. David's Georgetown Hospital (512-943-3000; www.georgetownhealthcare.org; 2000 Scenic Dr., Georgetown, TX 78626)

NEW BRAUNFELS/GRUENE
McKenna Memorial Hospital (830-606-2180; www.mckenna.org; 600 N. Union Ave., New Braunfels, TX 78130)

SAN MARCOS
Central Texas Medical Center (512-753-3511; www.ctmc.org; 1305 Wonder World Dr. # 100, San Marcos, TX 78666)

LATE-NIGHT FOOD, FUEL, AND GROCERIES

When it comes to food, the pickings late at night are slim, but beggars really can't be choosers in this case. If you find yourself fighting the midnight munchies or starving from a missed mealtime, head to I-35 for your pick of IHOP, Denny's, or any other fluorescently-lit national chain. If you are looking for more local flavor, consider some of the options below.

AUSTIN
Catering to students' insomnia and club-goers late-night tendencies, there are a few spots to eat all day and night in Austin. Conveniently located Katz's Deli on Sixth Street and the many outposts of the friendly Kerbey Lane Café and Magnolia Café top the list (see individual listings under "Dining" in the Austin chapter).

SAN ANTONIO
Las Brazas and Mi Tierra both serve Mexican, and Pig Stand has burgers (see individual listings under "Dining" in the San Antonio chapter).

Grocery Stores / Drug Stores

HEB is a grocery-store chain based in San Antonio with many locations throughout Austin, San Antonio, and the Hill Country. HEB also owns Central Market.

AUSTIN
HEB (512-459-6513; www.heb.com; 1000 E. 41st. St., Austin, TX 78751). There are many HEBs in Austin, but this one is open 24 hours a day with a 24-hour pharmacy (512-459-8308).

SAN ANTONIO
HEB (210-829-7373; www.heb.com; 300 Olmos Dr., San Antonio, TX 78212). The store is open until 1 AM and the pharmacy is open Monday through Friday 9–9, Saturday 9–8, and Sunday 10–5. Pharmacy phone is 210-829-1705.

LICENSES

Hunting and fishing, popular recreational activities in Texas, require state-issued licenses, which are available at numerous locations, including some grocery and sports stores, online through the Texas Parks and Wildlife Department's Web site, www.tpwd.state.tx.us, or by phone at 1-800-895-4248. However, fishing from shore or pier within a Texas State Park does not require a license; check at the park's headquarters for details. For a full overview of state hunting and fishing regulations, go to www.tpwd.state.tx.us/regulations. Texas game wardens are especially strict, and any violation of state hunting and fishing regulations will be taken very seriously.

MEDIA

Magazines and Newspapers
Both Austin and San Antonio have dailies as well as free weekly papers, all of which are likely to include information regarding events in the towns nearby and in between and in the Hill Country.

AUSTIN
Austin American-Statesman (www.statesman.com; 305 S. Congress Ave., Austin, TX 78704; daily) The Austin daily. The *Statesman*'s Entertainment, Calendar, and Life sections and archived reviews can also be viewed online at www.austin360.com.

Austin Chronicle (www.austinchronicle.com ; P.O. Box 49066, Austin, TX 78765; Thursday) Excellent weekly guide to entertainment, with politics and news thrown in. Free.

SAN ANTONIO
San Antonio Express-News (www.mysanantonio.com; 400 Third St., San Antonio, TX 78287; daily) The San Antonio daily news; in print or online.

San Antonio Current (www.sacurrent; 1500 N. St. Mary's St., San Antonio, TX 78215; Thursday) News, culture, free.

HILL COUNTRY
Many of these tiny papers are regional, serving the city mentioned and, oftentimes, the entire county.

Bandera Bulletin, www.banderabulletin.com

Blanco County News, www.blancocountynews.com

Boerne Star, www.boernestar.com

Burnet Bulletin, www.burnetbulletin.com

Comfort News, www.comfortnews.com

Fredericksburg Standard, www.fredericksburgstandard.com

Johnson City Record Courier

Junction Eagle, www.junctioneagle.com

Kerrville Times, www.dailytimes.com

Wimberley View/Hill Country Sun

NEARBY AND IN BETWEEN
Herald-Zeitung (New Braunfels/Gruene), www.heraldzeitung.com

San Marcos Daily Record, www.sanmarcosrecord.com

Williamson Sun (Georgetown)

Radio Stations

AUSTIN
KBPA 103.5 "BOB" FM. Their tagline, "Bob plays anything," says it all.

KMFA 89.5 FM. Outstanding classical since 1967.

KUT 90.5 AM. National Public Radio and outstanding music.

KVET 98.1 FM. Country music and Longhorns sports.

SAN ANTONIO
KLEY 94.1 FM. Tejano music.

KPAC 88.3 FM. National Public Radio and classical music.

KROM 92.2 FM. Mexican pop.

KRTU 91.7 FM. Trinity University station.

KSTX 89.1 FM. National Public Radio.

HILL COUNTRY
KTXI 90.1 FM. National Public Radio.

PESTS

For whatever reason, pests love Texas and tend to thrive in its temperate climate despite efforts to control them. The truth is that many serve an important ecological function and most are harmless, but there are a few pests that should have you watching where you sit, step, or stand.

Fire Ants

The biggest pests in Central Texas are the fire ants, for which you will frequently see warning signs posted. Fire ants tend to make mounds in sunny, open fields and parks, by the side of the road, and at the base of trees and other objects, such as picnic tables. When their nest is disturbed, they swarm and deliver many simultaneous stings, which are similar to bee stings in look and feel. Usually no medical intervention is required, but as with bees, a small percentage of the population may have a severe allergic reaction, in which case emergency medical care is essential. The only prevention is avoidance, so watch where you sit and stand and be especially aware of small children.

Snakes

Snakes are common in Texas, but of the 72 native species and subspecies, only 15 pose any threat to humans. In Central Texas, snakes keep to themselves and do not tend to initiate interactions. Since both poisonous and nonpoisonous snakes bite, if you have the unfortunate experience of being bitten, a precautionary trip to the emergency room would be wise.

Spiders

Of the 900 species of spiders present in Texas, only two groups pose any threat to humans, the recluse and widow spiders. In many cases, if you are bitten by one of these, you may not notice until the appearance of a suspicious wound coupled with fever, chills, nausea, pain, vomiting, or weakness, among other symptoms. In all cases, swab the wound with alcohol, relieve swelling and pain with ice, and call your doctor or, depending on the severity, visit the emergency room.

RELIGIOUS SERVICES

Texas is known for its religious enthusiasm, and there are plenty of places of worship in Central Texas. The *Austin American-Statesman*, the *San Antonio Express-News*, and the newspapers in the larger towns of the Hill Country list upcoming services in their Saturday editions. Alternatively, check the yellow pages of the phone book. While many religious organizations in the region identify themselves as Christian, they are widely varied in focus, practice, and beliefs. You will find the most religious diversity in Austin and San Antonio, where Jewish, Islamic, and other religious communities are active.

SHOPPING

AUSTIN
The Arboretum at Great Hills (512-338-4437; www.shopsimon.com; 9607 Research Blvd., Austin, TX 78759) Mon.–Wed. 10–6, Thu.–Sat. 10–8, Sun. noon–6.

Barton Creek Square (512-327-7040; www.shopsimon.com; 2901 S. Capital of Texas Hwy., Austin, TX 78746) Open: Mon.–Sat. 10–9, Sun. noon–6.

The Highland Mall (512-454-9656; www.highlandmall.com; 6001 Airport Blvd., Suite 1199, Austin, TX 78752) Open: Mon.–Sat. 10–9, Sun. noon–6.

SAN ANTONIO

Alamo Quarry Market (210-824-8885; www.quarrymarket.com; 255 E. Basse Rd., San Antonio, TX 78209) Open: Mon.–Sat.10–9, Sun. noon–6.

Crossroads of San Antonio (210-735-37; 4522 Fredericksburg Rd., San Antonio, TX 78201) Open: Mon.–Sat.10–9, Sun. noon–6.

Ingram Park Mall (210-523-1228; www.ingramparkmall.com; 6301 NW Loop 410, San Antonio, TX 78238) Open: Mon.–Sat.10–9, Sun. noon–6.

North Star Mall (210-342-2325; www.northstarmall.com; 7400 San Pedro Ave., San Antonio, TX 78216) Open: Mon.–Sat.10–9, Sun. noon–6.

River Center Mall (210-225-0000; www.shoprivercenter.com; 846 E. Commerce St., San Antonio, TX 78205) Open: Mon.–Sat. 10–9, Sun. noon–6.

The Shops at La Cantera (210-582-6255; www.theshopsatlacantera.com; 15900 La Cantera Pkwy., Suite 6698, San Antonio, TX 78256) Open: Mon.–Sat.10–9, Sun. noon–6.

SAN MARCOS

Prime Outlets (512-396-2200 or 1-800-628-9465; www.primeoutlets.com; 3939 I-35 South, San Marcos, TX 78666)

Tanger Outlets (512-396-7446 or 1-800-408-8424; www.tangeroutlet.com; 4015 I-35 South, San Marcos, TX 78666)

SUGGESTED REFERENCES

Whether you like to read up on your destination before you go or find that your curiosity is piqued by the trip, below are books recommended to enrich your experience, arranged here alphabetically by author.

Ajilvsgi, Geyata. *Wildflowers of Texas*. Fredericksburg, TX: Shearer Publishing, 2003.

Alsop, Fred J. III. *Birds of Texas*. New York: DK Publishing, 2002.

Awbrey, Betty Dooley. *Why Stop? Texas Roadside Markers: A Guide to Texas Historical Roadside Markers*. Lanham, MD: Taylor Trade Publishing, 2005.

Barkley, Roy, ed. *The Handbook of Texas Music*. Austin, TX: Texas State Historical Association, 2003.

Bryant, Helen. *Fixin' to Be Texan*. Plano, TX: Republic of Texas, 1998.

Bull, David. *The Driskill Hotel: Stories of Austin's Legendary Hotel/A Cookbook for Special Occasions*. Austin, TX: The Driskill Hotel. Packed with tidbits of juicy local lore and history.

Caro, Robert. *The Path to Power (The Years of Lyndon Johnson, Volume 1)*. New York: Vintage Books, 1981.

———. *Means of Ascent (The Years of Lyndon Johnson, Volume 2)*. New York: Vintage Books, 1990.

———. *Master of the Senate: The Years of Lyndon Johnson*. New York: Knopf, 2002.

Cerf, Bennett and Van H. Cartmell, eds. *The Best Short Stories of O. Henry*. New York: Modern Library, 1994. Though O. Henry's muse was New York City, he spent part of his formative years in Austin.

Cornell, Kari A. *Our Texas*. Osceola, WI: Voyageur Press, 2004. Coffee-table book.

Dallek, Robert. *Lyndon B. Johnson: Portrait of a President*. New York: Oxford University Press, 2004.

Fisher, Lewis F. *Saving San Antonio: The Precarious Preservation of a Heritage*. Lubbock, TX: Texas Tech University Press, 1996.

——. *The Spanish Missions of San Antonio*. San Antonio, TX: Maverick Publishing, 1998.

Ford, Norman D. *25 Bicycle Tours in the Texas Hill Country and West Texas*. Woodstock, VT: Countryman Press, 1995.

Friedman, Kinky. *Kinky Friedman's Guide to Texas Etiquette: Or How to Get to Heaven or Hell without Going Through Dallas—Fort Worth*. New York: HaperCollins, 2001. Kinky is a Texas original whose personality, politics, and antics are threaded through the contemporary social history of Central Texas.

Gilliland, Tom, and Miguel Ravago and Virginia B. Wood. *Fonda San Miguel: Thirty Years of Food and Art*. Fredericksburg, TX: Shearer Publishing, 2005. A feast for the eyes as well as the palate.

Goodwin, Doris Kearns. *Lyndon Johnson and the American Dream*. New York: St. Martin's, 1991.

Ivins, Molly. *Molly Ivins Can't Say That, Can She?*. New York: Vintage, 1992. Witty commentary on Texas politics.

Loughmiller, Campbell, and Lynn Loughmiller and Damon Waitt. *Texas Wildflowers: A Field Guide*, revised edition. Austin, TX: University of Texas Press, 2006. Updated version of a 1984 classic.

Meinzer, Wyman, and John Graves (introduction). *Texas Sky*. Austin, TX: University of Texas Press, 1998. Photographs of the awesome Texas sky.

Michener, James A. *Texas*. New York; Fawcett, 1987. Packed with drama and stereotypes, Michener's book paints a bold picture of the state.

Moran, Mark, and Mark Sceurman, Wesley Treat, and Heather Shades. *Weird Texas*. New York: Sterling, 2005.

Peterson, Roger Tory. *Field Guide to the Birds of Texas*. Boston: Houghton Mifflin, 1998. Written by an expert.

Rather, Rebecca, and Alison Oresman. *The Pastry Queen: Royally Good Recipes from the Texas Hill Country's Rather Sweet Bakery & Café*. Berkeley, CA: Ten Speed Press, 2004.

Reid, Jan, and Scott Newton. *The Improbable Rise of Redneck Rock: New Edition* (Jack and Doris Smothers Series in Texas History, Life, and Culture). Austin, TX: University of Texas Press, 2004.

Richards, David. *Once Upon a Time in Texas: A Liberal in the Lone Star State*. Austin, TX: University of Texas Press, 2002.

Rucker, Sid, and Clifford E. Shackelford, Madge M. Lindsay, C. Mark Klym, Shirley Rucker, and Clemente Guzman III. *Hummingbirds of Texas*. College Station, TX: Texas A&M Press, 2006.

Rybczyk, Mark Louis. *San Antonio Uncovered*. Plano, TX: Republic of Texas, 2000. A good look at the history of San Antonio.

Taylor, Tom, and Johnny Malloy. *60 Hikes within 60 miles: San Antonio and Austin*. Birmingham, AL: Menasha Ridge Press, 2004.

Tekiela, Stan. *Birds of Texas Field Guide*. Cambridge, MN: Adventure Publications, 2004.

Thompson, Karen R., and Kathy R. Howell. *Austin (Scenes of America)*. Mount Pleasant, SC: Arcadia Publishing, 2006.

Tveten, John L. *The Birds of Texas*. Fredericksburg, TX: Shearer Publishing, 1993.
  Miraculous photos.
Walsh, Robb. *Legends of Texas Barbecue Cookbook: Recipes and Recollections from the Pit Bosses*.
  San Francisco: Chronicle Books, 2002.
Woods, Randall. *LBJ: Architect of American Ambition*. New York: Free Press, 2006.

TOURIST INFORMATION

Local visitors centers and convention bureaus are great sources of information, maps, advice, and even coupons for discounts on tours and admission fees.

AUSTIN

Austin Convention & Visitors Bureau (1-800-926-ACVB; www.austintexas.org; 301 Congress Ave., Suite 200, Austin, TX 78701)

Austin Visitors Center (1-866- GO-AUSTIN; www.austintexas.org; 209 E. Sixth St., Austin, TX 78701) Open Mon.–Fri. 9–5, Sat.–Sun. 9–6.

SAN ANTONIO

San Antonio Convention and Visitors Bureau (210-207-6700 or 1-800-447-3372; www .sanantoniocvb.com; 203 S. St. Mary's St., 2nd floor, San Antonio, TX 78205) San Antonio Chamber of Commerce (210-229-2100; www.sanantonio.com; 602 E. Commerce St., San Antonio, TX 78205)

Hill Country

BANDERA

Bandera Convention and Visitors Bureau (830-796-3045 or 1-800-364-3833; www .banderacowboycapital.com; P.O. Box 171, Bandera, TX 78003)

BLANCO

Blanco Chamber of Commerce (830-833-5101; www.blancochamber.com; 312 Pecan St., Blanco, TX 78606)

BOERNE

The Boerne Convention and Visitors Bureau (830-249-7277 or 1-888-842-8080; www.visitboerne.org; 1407 S. Main St., Boerne, TX 78006)

Greater Boerne Chamber of Commerce (830-249-8000 or 1-888-842-8080; www.boerne.org; 126 Rosewood Ave., Boerne, TX 78006)

BURNET

Burnet Chamber of Commerce (512-756-4297; www.burnetchamber.org; 229 S. Pierce St., Burnet, TX 78611)

COMFORT

www.shopcomfort.com. Information available in Fredericksburg and Kerrville.

FREDERICKSBURG

Fredericksburg Chamber of Commerce and Visitors Bureau (830-997-6523 or 1-888-997-3600; www.fredericksburg-texas.com; 302 E. Austin St., Fredericksburg, TX 78624)

JOHNSON CITY

Johnson City Tourism Bureau (830-868-7684; www.lbjcountry.com) Located inside the Texas Hill Country Visitors Center (830-868-5700; www.hillcountryinfo.com; 803 US 281 South, Johnson City, TX 78636)

KERRVILLE

Kerrville Convention and Visitors Bureau (830-792-3535 or 1-800-221-7958; www.kerrvilletexascvb.com; 2108 Sidney Baker St., Kerrville, TX 78028) Open: Mon.–Fri. 8:30–5, Sat. 9–3, Sun, 10–3.

Kerrville Area Chamber of Commerce (830-896-1155; www.kerrvilletx.com; 1700 Sidney Baker St., Suite 100, Kerrville, TX 78028)

MARBLE FALLS

Marble Falls/Lake LBJ Visitors Center (830-693-4449 or 1-800-759-8178; www.marblefalls.org; 801 US 281, Marble Falls, TX 78654) Open: Mon.–Fri. 8–5.

STONEWALL

Stonewall Chamber of Commerce (830-644-2735; www.stonewalltexas.com; 115 St. Francis St., Stonewall, TX 78671)

Out to pasture in the Hill Country

WIMBERLEY
Wimberley Chamber of Commerce and Visitors Center (www.visitwimberley.org; P.O. Box 12, Wimberley, TX 78676)

Nearby and In Between

GEORGETOWN
Georgetown Visitor Information Center (512-930-3545; www.visitgeorgetown.org; 101 W. Seventh St., Georgetown, TX 78626)

NEW BRAUNFELS
New Braunfels Chamber of Commerce (1-800-572-2626; www.nbjumpin.com; P.O. Box 311417, New Braunfels, TX 78131) Gruene, www.gruenetexas.com.

SAN MARCOS
San Marcos Convention and Visitors Bureau (512-393-5900 or 1-888-200-5620; www.toursanmarcos.com; 202 N. C.M. Allen Pkwy., San Marcos, TX 78667)

Tourist Information Center (512-393-5930; 617 I-35 North, San Marcos, TX 78666)

INDEX

LODGING BY PRICE CODE

Prices

Inexpensive.................Up to $100
Moderate.....................$100 to $150
Expensive....................$150 to $250
Very Expensive............Over $250

Austin

Inexpensive
Austin Motel, 39
Mi Yard, 39–40

Inexpensive-Moderate
Woodburn House Bed and Breakfast, 38

Moderate-Expensive
Austin Folk House Bed and Breakfast, 36
Brava House, 35–36
Carrington's Bluff, 36
Habitat Suites, 40
1110 Carriage House Inn, 36–38
Star of Texas Inn, 36

Moderate-Very Expensive
Hotel San José, 39

Expensive
Staybridge Suites Austin-Northwest, 40

Expensive-Very Expensive
Stephen F. Austin Inter-Continental, 35

Very Expensive
Driskill Hotel, 33–35
Four Seasons, 35
Hilton Austin, 35
Lake Austin Spa and Resort, 40–41

Blanco

Moderate
Green Gables, 181

Burnet

Moderate-Expensive
Canyon of the Eagles Lodge and Nature Park, 216

Comfort

Inexpensive-Moderate
Comfort Common, 189
Meyer Bed and Breakfast, 189

Expensive-Very Expensive
Riven Rock Ranch, 189

Fredericksburg

Inexpensive-Moderate
The Hog Stop Inn, 195
Inn on the Creek, 196

Moderate
Fredericksburg Inn and Suites, 195

Moderate-Expensive
Das Garten Haus, 194
Hangar Hotel, 195
Hoffman Haus, 195
Two Wee Cottages, 196

Expensive
Ab Butler's Dogtrot at Triple Creek, 194
Settlers Crossing, 196

Georgetown

Inexpensive
San Gabriel Motor Court, 231

Moderate
Harper-Chesser Historic Inn, 230–31

Johnson City

Inexpensive-Moderate
Best Western Johnson City Inn, 203

Kerrville

Inexpensive-Expensive
Inn of the Hills Resort & Conference Center, 209
Y.O. Ranch Resort and Conference Center, 210

DINING BY PRICE CODE

Prices

Austin

Bandera

Boerne

Fredericksburg

Georgetown